It seems in this day and age, money has more value than the truth.

The truth never changes. Yesterday, Today, Tomorrow, the truth will always be the truth regardless of your apparent status in society.

I promise to tell the whole truth, nothing but the truth, so I may rest peacefully at night.

Duwayne Brooks. Without me what would you know?

Steve and Me

My Friendship with Stephen Lawrence and the Search for Justice

DUWAYNE BROOKS

For Steve

First published in Great Britain by Abacus in 2003

ISBN:0-349-11656-3

A CIP catalogue record for this book is available from the British Library.

ISBN: 0 9552689-0-7
ISBN-13:978-0-9552689-0-8

Typeset in Stone Serif by M Rules
Printed and bound in Great Britain

BrooksBooks

Contents

Acknowledgements

Richard, Audrey and Nathan Adams; Alex 'The Greater One'; Harcourt Alleyne; Dev Barrah; Melissa Berry; Biggs; Brian and Vanessa; Briggy; Michelle Brown and family; Charmaine and Trevor; Surinder Cheema; Club Copying; Cringe; Dan Man; Jane Deighton; Deighton Guedalla Solicitors; Robin Denselow; Jennifer Douglas; Earl The Barber; Jo Eggleton; Yanique Ellis and family; Ethleen Figaro; First Choice Office Equipment Maintenance; Paul Foot; Dee Francois and family; Mike Franklin; Mahalia French; Nicole Fuller and family; Galaxy Radio; Genesis Radio; Rebekah Glean; Winston Goode and family; Joyce Goodison; Sophie Goodison; the *Guardian*; Vicky Guedalla; Steve Guise; Prof. Stuart Hall; Lee Halliday-Davis; Eleisha Hamilton; Josie Harper; Kass Harris; Sally Hatfield; Carol Hawley; Peter Herbert; Hyde Housing Association; Baroness Howells; the *Independent*; Adel Jones and family; Lewisham College; Karl Kani; Nick Kent; Knights; Julia Krish; Viviene Lesley and family; Gail Lewis; Beverly Lindo; Delroy Lindo and family; Mark Lindo and family; Michelle Lindo; Liz, Josie, Pat, Alex and Mike; Lonsdale; Lorraine; Lylie; Ian Macdonald; the late Sabrina Mcpherson; Hugh Massey; Marcia; Beverley McBean; Keisha McLeod; Rajiv Menon; Sharon Mensah and family; Sheena Michael; Vanetia Morris and family; Movement for Justice; Andrew Nicol; Nicky;

Nicola; Paddy O'Connor; Helen Oldfield; Jenny Oli; Olu; Ijeoma Omambala; Andrea Parker and family; Noel Penstone; Powerjam Radio; *Private Eye*; Shaki Sanussi; Marika Seivright and family; Lorraine Senior and family; Melly Senior and family; Simon and family; Skip; Snoopy and Joanne; Neil Taylor; Anton van Thomas; Lyle Thompson; Pearl Thompson; Dr Stuart Turner; Tricycle Theatre; Vicky and Richard; Darren White; Tim Whiting; Heather Williams; Winston; James Wood.

There are other people who have befriended me and helped me over the years – many thanks to them. And thanks to all the people who have turned up at court to give me support when it was needed. And, finally, many apologies to anyone I might have missed off the list who should be there.

Prologue

We're sneaking in the back entrance of the Home Office to get an advance look at the Macpherson Report. Why? I've waited six years for this and still everything is cloak-and-dagger. Jane Deighton, my solicitor, tells me it's the only chance we'll get of having an early look. It's 2.30 p.m. and the Report is going to be released at 3.30 p.m., so we've got less than one hour to skim read hundreds of pages of Macpherson. Meanwhile, we know Mr and Mrs Lawrence were let in on its findings hours ago. I don't mind that. So they should have been, but so should I. Yes, I know they lost Steve and they'll never be able to replace him, but sometimes I think they and the police believe I was as good as responsible, rather than a victim. I always say, but for the grace of God it could have been me.

I don't know, maybe it would have been better if it had been me. I'll never forget the way Mrs Lawrence described me as a 'ragamuffin'. Ragamuffin! And if they thought that, what did the Metropolitan Police think of me? On the night of the murder, the police called me surly and miserable. Well, what did they expect me to be like?

Anyway, here we are creeping in the back entrance, 24 February 1999, minutes to go. Jane and me make for an unlikely team. She's smallish, middle-aged, very middle class, a very proper white lady. Me, well I'm just Duwayne – a lanky black working-class kid with lots of attitude. But we are a team.

We trust each other, we look out for each other. I feel safe with Jane, with her work. Even though we're complete opposites – Jane and Duwayne, The Odd Couple – we do have something in common. We're both really demanding. Whoever we're working with, whatever we're doing, we want the best result possible.

We speak to security. He gets on his intercom and a woman comes down for us. She takes us up in the lift to an almost bare room – one little table in the middle, six chairs and me and Jane. She directs us to the chairs, and says she'll be back in a minute with the Report. Plonk! There's the Report. Plonk! 'There's the appendix,' she says. Shit, I think, look how thick it is, how on earth are we expected to get beyond the index in the time we've got? Meanwhile, Jane is already ruffling through her copy, marker in hand. She knows what she's looking for. I suppose all I'm looking for is references to Duwayne Brooks.

Jane is skim reading in silence. I decide to go straight to me. I feel famous, important – a whole chapter on me. I begin reading Chapter Five and find a bit that says if I'd been a white boy I would not have been treated by the police the way I was; I would have been put in a police car and looked after.

'What does this mean?' I say to Jane.

She looks over to see, but can't read it properly. 'What page is that?' she says. 'Quick! Quick! What page?' She finds it and shouts out: 'We've won! Oh my God, we've won hands down. They've agreed with us.'

I feel something strange. I'm not sure what it is. Elation? Relief? Vindication? Anger? Maybe a mix of them all. I don't know. But what I do know is that I felt under pressure to win my battle, and having done so I am going to do my best to help other people in situations like mine – people who have been mistreated by the police.

It's now 3.20 p.m., and in less than an hour we're supposed to be giving a press conference. The Lawrences, their lawyers and support groups will have had ages to plan what to say.

'Go on,' I say to Jane. 'Go on then. What does it say they're going to do to the police? What punishment have they recommended?'

We do some more desperate skimming. Nothing. We look for a chapter headed 'Action against Police'. Not there. There seems to be a chapter on every aspect of the nightmare, but nothing on action against the police.

I look at Jane again, almost pleading. But she's too busy searching to notice. 'They are going to discipline them aren't they?' I ask. 'What about the one who said I was calling them "cunts" and "pigs"?' (I'm no angel, but I don't use language like that.) 'What about the officer who said I was uncontrollable, the one who said I'd nicked the Coke can, the one who claimed that I had broken a window at the police station?' Jane holds her hands up. Nothing. Absolutely nothing.

So that's British justice. It takes six years to admit that a couple of young lads had been neglected and mistreated by the police, six years to admit that if they'd responded adequately Steve might not have lost so much blood that he died – followed by a conspiracy of silence. Why have we come this far?

'What's it all been about?' I say to Jane. Elated a minute ago, I am now on the verge of tears.

She says we've come this far because we have to, if we want anything to change.

'But nothing is changing,' I say to her.

She doesn't answer. So I say it again.

'Look, Duwayne, I'm afraid this is just the beginning,' she says.

Four years later, I'll realise she was right.

He was never Stephen to me, he was Steve. When I saw him written about in the papers, when I saw people grieving over their own tragedy, I couldn't recognise my friend. He didn't seem to be a person anymore, he was a case, an abstract. Would I call him Steven? I refused to call him anything.

Actually I couldn't recognise myself in the papers. Couldn't recognise the way what it always had to be Stephen and Dwayne, Stephen and his best friend Dwayne Brook, as if we were umbilically linked—Stephen and his best friend Dwayne Brook. We were close friends, the closest. But it was never just the two of us. We had a big social circle. There was a group of us who were close mates. Me, quiet David and mad Bert, who knew all the words and all the times to all the ads on the telly. Tony Mason, who was nearly as mad as Bert. Kevin, who always seemed to be there when you were about to get your food or open a drink. 'Go on Brooksy, let's have a bit of your tarta', it was insulted with humour soon as he say something, he'd ask for it, even if he didn't particularly want it. And Michael Wheeler, who forced me into a fight once – we got on fine afterwards. Then there were the Marks. Mark Black, who was white, and fat Mark Amis, who

Chapter 1

Mates

He was never Stephen to me, he was Steve. When I saw him written about in the papers, when I saw people grieving over the Lawrence tragedy, I couldn't recognise my friend. He didn't seem to be a person anymore. He was a case, an abstract. We all called him Steve.

Actually, I couldn't recognise myself in the papers. Couldn't recognise the way that it always had to be Stephen and Duwayne, Lawrence and Brooks, as if we were umbilically linked – Stephen and his best friend Duwayne Brooks. We were close friends, the closest. But it was never just the two of us. We had a big social circle. There was a group of us who were close mates. Me, quiet David and mad Bert, who knew all the words and all the tunes to all the ads on the telly; Tony Mason, who was every bit as mad as Bert; Leon, who always seemed to be there when you were about to eat your food or open a drink. 'Go on Brooksy, let's have a bit of your Fanta.' It was instinct with him: as soon as he saw something he'd ask for it, even if he didn't particularly want it. And Michael Wheeler, who forced me into a fight once – we got on fine afterwards. Then there were the Marks. Mark Blacky, who was white, and fat Mark Amis, who

I used to wrestle with. (It would always end up with him sitting on my chest like Giant Haystacks used to do on the telly.)

And there was Steve. I'd been told to look out for Steve at school. His uncle Martin (his mum's brother) was best friends with my mum's partner at the time and he told me we would be starting at the same time in 1986, when we were eleven. As it happened we ended up in the same class: 1FB at Blackheath Bluecoat School.

There were four houses in each year. The school was certainly never very posh when I was there, but you wouldn't have known it from the names of the houses: Flamsteed, Gordon, Vanbrugh and Wolfe. You would have expected it to be a public school rather than your everyday inner-city comprehensive. The houses were all named after local historical dignitaries, and all had special ties to go with them. In Gordon you wore a red tie, in Vanbrugh you wore yellow, in Wolfe you wore green. Steve and I were in Flamsteed, which meant we were the proud owners of burgundy-red ties.

Steve seemed different from the rest of the group when we started. At first, some of us were jealous of him. For the first three years of school, his life seemed so perfect, so easy. He never had busted shoes or a busted bag. He always dressed properly, while some like me had to make do. In the second and third years he always seemed to have money while I scrimped for whatever I could get. Sometimes his mum would pick him up from school, and his parents always turned up at parents' evening. Not just one of them, both of them. He seemed to be the perfect boy from the perfect family.

The teachers also saw him as that. They didn't say it in so many words, but they obviously held him up as a model pupil from a model background. In fact, they exploited it, bullied him with it. They knew that if the rest of us were out of order and they threatened to tell our dads, it wouldn't have much impact. But they knew Steve responded to that. In the first couple of years they could say what they wanted to him, and he wouldn't answer back, but later Steve changed.

The teachers used to tell him, 'You know you shouldn't be hanging around with these boys, your dad won't like it.' I don't know why – yes we had a laugh, messed around and we were a bit loud at times, but we weren't bad. We didn't harm people. None of us were bullies, none of us were criminals. One of the last school incidents I remember is when the glass got broken in one of the classroom doors, and a teacher, Mr Sitch, asked who had done it. Nobody said anything. So he called Steve out. He took him out of the class and told him he believed he'd broken the glass, though obviously he didn't really think that. Mr Sitch told him the only way he could prove that he hadn't broken the glass was to tell him who had done it. When Steve came back in he was fuming. He told me what was said, then refused to speak. He was so upset. He never told Mr Sitch who had broken the glass. I don't think he knew who'd done it – I certainly didn't. For a long time, Steve didn't realise the teachers treated him differently. Whether they expected more from him or just didn't like the rest of us I will never know. But I do know they wanted to use him against us.

I don't think I really used the word 'racism' as a kid, but looking back there certainly was racism at school. Black kids, especially black boys, were treated differently: we were expected to fail, expected to be indifferent or hostile to learning, expected to be good at sport. The normal pack of clichés. And, of course, often those clichés become self-fulfilling. That's why the teachers treated Steve as an exception: because he didn't fit neatly into the accepted categories. He was a funny mix. In the early years, he was a goodie-goodie, but never a boffin, and always popular. We were both popular. We also came from different types of background. Steve was more pampered than the rest of us, living with two parents in a mainly white area around Woolwich Common. Me? I was hanging round with my mates in Deptford.

When new kids started at the school, they would come up to us, a bit shy, and say, 'All right Duwayne, all right Steve', and I used to wonder how they knew our names. I guess most people in school knew who we were. As I say, we were popular. It felt good everyone knowing you and greeting you: it was like respect.

To an extent the black pupils and white pupils segregated themselves. In our group, there were white lads, but somehow when it got to the classroom there was a black–white divide, with the black kids sitting at the back, and the smartest white kids sitting close up to the teacher at the front. We used to have these fights – blacks v whites. They weren't too serious, but it was a sign of how the school system was working (or not working).

I took and passed some GCSEs, but I couldn't understand why I had to do English literature. It was torture, sitting there through a double period reading *Macbeth* aloud. I just couldn't see how *Macbeth* was relevant to me. What bearing was *Macbeth* going to have on my life? Miss O'Donnell had banned us from talking in class. The only thing was, there seemed to be one rule for us and another for her favourites, who of course sat at the front.

I remember once Steve looked round at me. Yes, just looked round. And she peered over her glasses in that special way teachers do. She'd read and then look up to talk over her glasses.

'All right Stephen,' she said. 'Get out!'

'But I haven't done anything,' he said.

Well he had, but it was hardly a crime was it, turning around?

'Just get out,' she screamed at him.

He got up to go out and I said, 'Don't go! Let her speak to you properly.'

She went ballistic when she heard that. 'Right, Duwayne Brooks get out of my class.'

I said I wasn't going anywhere until she spoke to me properly.

'Do I need to repeat myself?' she said.

Silence.

'Right!'

She went to get the head of year, Mr Sitch, who was a decent bloke despite the episode with Steve and the broken glass.

He asked us politely to leave, so we did. He explained that when a teacher asks you to leave the class you should do so, and I said I'd done nothing wrong and all I wanted was for Miss O'Donnell to show us some respect too.

I suppose I was very militant, always standing up for my rights. Not much different from today.

Even my mates regarded me as facety and a bit rude. The thing is I don't think I ever started rows or fights. Whatever, Steve's parents weren't very happy that he was hanging around with me and our crowd. Mrs Lawrence told him I was a bad influence. Mr Lawrence never said anything. He was always the quiet one.

I don't think I was quite as facety as I appeared, though. In a way I was introverted. I had really bad acne and hated it; I felt ugly and had a terrible complex about my skin. People used to tease me: 'All right Spotty', 'Where's Super Ted?' But while the others in our group started to mess around with alcohol and cigarettes and weed, I wouldn't touch them. Alcohol made me feel bad, and I hated the stink of weed. I also thought they were pointless, because they stopped you feeling normal, slowed you down, made you less able. I've always had a puritanical element.

I also worked hard. Admittedly, not at the lessons, which seemed so pointless and boring, except for maths. My maths teacher was called Miss Callin, and she was great. I had the utmost respect for her because she didn't mess about, she told you everything straight. If you didn't know something, or didn't understand something, she'd give you every opportunity to learn, and then she reckoned if you couldn't be bothered after that it was your tough luck. There were a couple of other great teachers. Mr Porter taught science and basketball and was so down to earth. Then there was Miss Howells, our form teacher. In a way, she was like Steve. Everyone got on with her – no one was rude to her: you just couldn't be rude to Miss Howells.

The basic GCSEs I left school with aren't much to boast about, but I also know I could have done better if I'd been interested. The funny thing is I was desperately keen to learn and spent hours every week in the library reading about any number of things, especially space technology. When I was at school I wanted to be a satellite engineer. I first got interested in space when I was at primary school and everybody was talking about Halley's Comet, which was coming round for the first time in over seventy-five years. There were big projects about it at school, and I was going to watch it from the observatory at Greenwich Park. We were impatient with excitement, counting down the weeks and then the days. In the end, my mum wouldn't let me go to the observatory. I still remember how gutted I was.

I think I was eleven when *Challenger* blew up. It's one of those things that stays imprinted on your mind. I was watching the launch live and I could see the fuel leaking out from the bottom, and I remember saying to myself, 'It's going to blow up, it's going to blow up', and as I was mouthing the words to myself it did. From the angle of the TV camera, I could see something flying up, and I thought, Thank God, they're still alive. But of course they weren't – it was just the booster.

It was in the fourth year of Blackheath Bluecoat that everything seemed to change. I still don't know what it was exactly, maybe just us growing up – Steve and me turned fifteen that year. Steve changed more than any of us. I suppose he had more to change from. You know, there are good people and there are bad people, and Steve was always a good person. Simple as that. People liked him because he had a good pure heart. By the time he was fifteen, he hadn't lost his goodness, but he became less willing to do as he was told, less willing to be bossed about by his mother. He wanted to experiment with life. Steve started doing less well at his school work, and the teachers and Mrs Lawrence blamed it on his mates, notably me. But Steve always said it was his home life that made it so difficult for him to study. We'd always thought it was such a model family, but by now Steve had made it very clear that he wasn't so happy at home.

He felt stifled at home – stifled by his parents' rules and stifled by their expectations. Things also seemed to become more difficult, understandably, when Mr Lawrence lost his job. For the first time in Steve's life, the family was feeling the pinch. Mrs Lawrence was at university doing her degree, Mr Lawrence was at home or at the job centre, and everything seemed to go to pieces.

We'd never had much money, and so we never expected much. I'd always been brought up by a single mum. My dad was married with kids when he had a thing with Mum. Shirley Bailey was only eighteen when she became pregnant with me. She always said she'd been enticed by Ray Brooks. Although my parents never lived together, I've always been emotionally quite close to my dad, who lived near to us. When I look at him I see me in him. Like me, he's always wanting things done the best possible way. He went to Lewisham College to study plumbing and was the only black guy attending his class. He told me that the teachers and fellow students made him very aware of his colour. After twenty-five years working for the council, Dad retired to Jamaica in 1998.

My sister, Sian, who is ten years younger than me, was fathered by a guy who used to live with us called Smiley. He was a good friend of Steve's Uncle Martin. Smiley was a nifty footballer, and I used to go to watch him play at the weekends. Ian Wright was on his team in his pre-Crystal Palace and Arsenal days. Smiley ended up having a terrible car accident a while after splitting up with my mum, and he now lives in sheltered accommodation.

So there were always ups and downs in our house, but in a way there was also stability. We got by. Mum sometimes worked. I qualified for free school dinners, as did nearly all of my mates, because we didn't have much money coming in to the house. The one exception was Steve, whose dad had made decent money as a painter and decorator. Steve had always brought in a packed lunch, and it took me a while to realise he'd stopped. You don't look out for that sort of thing. But after some weeks it dawned on me that I never saw Steve eating any more. He'd mentioned that times were hard in the family, there was no work about for his dad, and just left it at that. I thought, Well, however badly you're doing, it doesn't mean you can't put a few sandwiches together; but I didn't pry, didn't say anything, didn't see it as my business.

One day I said to Steve, 'Why don't you come in with us for dinner?' He said he didn't feel like it. I think he was a bit embarrassed. 'Go on,' I said. 'It's a right laugh' – we always used to make the most noise in the second dinner hall: it was a riot, shouting and flicking food at each other, and it never really seemed right that Steve wasn't there. He said he couldn't because he didn't have the money for school dinners. I'd forgotten he didn't qualify for free dinners. Perhaps he would have with his dad out of work, but then maybe they were too proud to say. Anyway, I said to him, 'Look, you can use my pass and I'll come in later' – I knew he was starving. We often pulled that scam. I'd go in after he came out, and they'd look at my pass and say, 'But your number's been ticked off', and I'd look bemused and say, 'It can't be, you've not seen me in here before have you?'

There were two halls, and often we'd go into different ones because there'd be less chance of being spotted. Occasionally, they'd tell me to get on my way, and I'd do without dinner because I always went in second so there was no way they could pull Steve up. It just meant that if they got stroppy, it would be me they'd have to deal with. I suppose I always felt more streetwise than Steve, and it had been my idea in the first place.

Steve started to talk more about home. He said he found it hard to do his homework because there were always tensions in the house; his parents were often arguing. His attitude to life seemed to be changing. He became more laid-back, less ambitious. Occasionally, he would bunk lessons.

One day a teacher came into the class and asked me where Steve was.

'Oh, he's gone to the toilet,' I said.

The answer was a kind of reflex. He asked me if I was sure, and I mumbled yes, of course I was. Ten minutes later the teacher walked back in and hauled me out of the class. He accused me of lying and told me that he'd seen Steve in Blackheath Village just before he'd come in the class. I said I hadn't lied about anything, I had thought he was in the toilet or the locker room, but the teacher wasn't convinced. I suppose he had a point.

It's strange that we were such close friends. In a way we were opposites. I was very impatient. When I wanted things done, I wanted them done yesterday. He was the kind of person who'd wait all week. He was very organised and patient and could lay out a plan of what needed to be done and follow it. He had been like that with his work.

He'd also do anything to keep the peace. Steve would happily allow people to take the piss just for a peaceful life. One time he sold his jacket to a guy at work. Well I say sold, only the guy didn't want to pay him for it. Every time Steve would go and ask him for the money the guy just shrugged his shoulders and said he didn't have it. I was getting really pissed off about it, but Steve was just calm. It drove me mad.

Steve was a natural athlete. We were both good at sport, but it seemed to come more naturally to him. As with so many naturals, he wasted his talent by not putting in the effort. It used to wind me up when we were playing football and he wasn't trying his hardest. I just knew he wasn't, and I've always had this thing that whatever you do you should do it to the best of your ability. Likewise with running. Steve had a great engine, and used to run competitively for Cambridge Harriers – 400 metres and 800 metres, every Tuesday and Thursday. I thought running was boring, and Steve was much more talented than I was. But whenever we did run against each other, I'd never let him beat me, just refused to. That was my mentality. As I say, I've never been the easiest person to be around.

Again, Steve was different. Everybody liked him. It was impossible not to like him. Peaceful, easy, smart, sweet Steve. I still find it hard to cope with the way he died. It was like a lynching from the days of slavery.

Chapter 2
Growing Up

I know I was a difficult kid. Loyal and bright, but definitely stroppy. I don't suppose I'm that different now. My mum found me difficult to cope with. She was strong and stroppy too. It was inevitable that things would come to a head at home, and sure enough they did. It was 1991.

It was over something so trivial, but so typical. My mum was one for laying down the law – a bit like Steve's mum. And one of her top laws was the washing-up law. The dishes were my responsibility. It shouldn't have been such a big deal, but it was. Sometimes, I would come in exhausted from work – well, school or college, but that's work, too – and it would look like Mum had had a party and there'd be a huge pile of dishes blocking up the sink and trailing round the kitchen, and she wouldn't let me go to bed till they were all done. I thought that was unfair, and told her so.

One day when I was sixteen, I was sitting in the house watching Manchester United on the telly, and Mum said would I do the dishes. I said, 'Yeah, I'll do them after the football.' Well, that was it, she exploded – said I could get out of the house right then. So I did.

That was the start of my travels. For more than a year I moved from hostel to hostel. I'd always wanted to have my own property –

was desperate to get away and be my own person. It sounds strange for a sixteen-year-old, but I was independent, quite mature for my age. I knew that if I moved into a hostel it was the first step on the way to getting my own place. There were different types of hostel, and if I could work my way up to a Housing Association hostel within eighteen months I would get my own flat.

I stayed at the first hostel in Sydenham for a month. That was the maximum time you were allowed there. All the kids were between sixteen and nineteen, all had had problems and were just as relieved as me to be away from home, and all were strong people. They had to be strong to cope with hostel life.

But it was so liberating after home. I just remember thinking to myself, Ah, peace and quiet, peace and quiet. This was a special hostel, one that prepared you for hostel life – so you were taught how to budget, how to use your benefit book, how to look after yourself. In one way it wasn't so different from home – there were strict rules. You couldn't go into the girls' rooms and you had to be in for 11 p.m.

From Sydenham I moved to Camberwell. That was a real shithole. Dormitories, six beds to one room, no privacy. The food there was revolting – the cheapest and the nastiest, all processed burgers and vegetables. I couldn't eat there. However bad the place was, though, I never regretted leaving home. I'd not spoken to my mum since I left. I was pissed off with her, she was pissed off with me, and I just wanted to prove to her and myself that I could make it on my own. For eighteen months, we didn't talk. She knew I was OK though, because I'd speak to one of my aunties regularly, and stayed at her house for a few weeks.

I didn't think about anybody but myself during this period. I knew that nobody else could help me, and that I had to work around my situation. I lost contact with my friends, too. Never saw Steve, not anyone. I missed them, but I literally couldn't afford to see them. I didn't have the money to travel across London.

I soon got into the rhythm of hostel life. And that rhythm involved a lot of waiting around by the phone box – mobiles were new, and I certainly couldn't afford one. You're always on the phone to other hostels, seeing what's available and what's the chance of a move. You're always making plans, always on the hoof, bouncing from hostel to hostel, hopefully in the right direction. It was competitive, too. Whenever I moved, I had to go for an interview at the new place, and they'd want to know what your plans were, what you wanted to achieve, what you hoped to do with your life. It was like applying for a job.

From Camberwell I moved to Stockwell. Hostel life was great, really – a brilliant preparation for the rest of the outside world. You're meeting new people all the time, people of all different races, with different problems. It forces you to communicate and get on with people. Unless the people refuse to let you get on with them, and are looking for a fight.

One night in Stockwell, a group of us went over to the pub across the road to play pool. There was me, my friend Lonsdale, his cousin Nicki and his friend Olu. All the pubs in Stockwell were incredibly white, and any time you walked in as a black boy you could feel the tension, the silence, the stares.

Anyway, we ignored it and went over to the pool table, and we were happily playing among ourselves when a gang of white boys came in. They were baiting us from a distance – you know, talking so loudly that we couldn't but hear.

'What are this lot doing in here? We thought they wasn't allowed in here,' one of them said.

Lonsdale said, 'Let's leave.'

'Why?' I said.

He said, 'I've had a fight with them before, and they dragged me down the road – four white boys dragging me down the road.

There were police watching from their car, and when they saw who was involved they just drove off.'

I didn't believe him, and said we should stay.

More white guys came in and joined them. One came up to the table as we were playing, picked up a cue and just took a shot.

'Oi, what the fuck are you doing?' I said. 'Why are you interrupting our game?'

'You shouldn't be in here anyway nigger,' he answered me.

Then the other white boys came over, shouting, 'You fucking niggers.' There was a scuffle. The barlady screamed at us to get out. In the street, the boys were screaming 'Fucking niggers' and 'Fuck off home' at us, and there was more fighting.

As we left the pub, I noticed a police car parked at traffic lights. The police officers saw everything that was happening and drove off. We managed to get away and ran back to the hostel to get something to fight with if we needed it. We had baseball bats back at the hostel – we'd never used them as weapons but would do in self-defence if necessary. If it meant being killed for our colour or slapping some racist with a baseball bat, I would have slapped the racist with the bat, no problem.

By the time we got back to the pub, the boys were driving off.

In 1992, from Stockwell I bounced temporarily out of the hostel system and into my gran's flat in Grove Park back in south-east London. My gran had a house in Lewisham, and was planning to move to Grove Park, but she hadn't managed to sell her home yet so the flat was free for me to move in to. It was at Gran's that I hooked up with Mum again. She came round to see me, and, of course, she was hurt that I'd not been in touch. She told me I didn't have any respect for her, ignoring her all this time. But I told her I just needed to be in charge of myself. When I lived at home she didn't seem that interested in helping me, but now she came round and wanted to know if I needed anything – clothes, food, money. I told her that I was fine. She wondered what I was doing for money. But by then I'd learned to budget around my benefits.

My gran used to work in a hospital. She had come to Britain thirty years earlier from Jamaica with such dreams, and she hadn't realised any of them. The plan had been to make a bit of money here quick and then return to Jamaica and live like a queen. But she was still in London, with nothing to show for her toil. The same was true of Mum. She now worked as a careworker in an old people's home, and still she was trying to make something of Britain.

Eventually I managed to move back closer to home, which had always been my plan. My cousin Lisa helped me. She used to live in a hostel in Charlton and had been 'promoted' through the system, and now had her own Housing Association flat. She had a word with the hostel people for me. I had my interview to see if I was suitable for a place, and was told that I should be able to move in there in a couple of months' time.

I'd not seen any of my friends for well over a year. So much time had passed, and I was going to be eighteen this year. With Steve it was like I'd never been away. 'Ah, you've finally decided to come back to your friends,' he said. But I didn't get back with all the guys from school – I'd grown apart from some, or they'd moved on. Steve was annoyed that I'd not been in touch, said he'd been worried, but we forgot about it soon enough and we picked up just where we'd left off. He was still at school doing his A levels, and I swapped my engineering course from Woolwich to Lewisham College.

We'd both grown up a bit. I'd found my own way to independence, and Steve was looking for his. For years he had been pampered by his parents. He was brought up wrapped up in cotton wool. In a way, all the rules were just another aspect of this – they wanted the best for him, and they were strict with him so he couldn't mess things up. Then when he started doing stuff that they weren't so keen on, they became increasingly hard on him. He was smoking and drinking a bit, as were most boys his age. Like so many of our crowd, he was into the drink called 20/20. It's ironic really that his mum always warned him against me turning him to drink, when I couldn't stand the bloody stuff. He didn't have a problem with drink, he just enjoyed it.

Steve was finding it hard to live at home. He was arguing a lot with his parents, just as I'd been doing with my mum. He couldn't understand why there seemed to be one rule for him and one rule for his younger brother, Stuart. He said to me that it was affecting his work, and that it was hard to concentrate at home because of the atmosphere. He was also seeing a girl, and his mum wasn't too happy about that either – she thought it was putting him off his work.

Steve asked what chance there would be of moving into the hostel. I said I'd look into it for him. But I never felt sure that he wanted to move out of home. He was torn – he was finding it impossible at home, but despite everything he didn't want to hurt his parents by walking out on them.

We saw a lot of each other that year. There was so much to catch up on, so much to talk about. We'd spend hours and hours just talking about nothing in the way that good friends do, arguing about football, arguing about girls, play-fighting, swapping stories, talking about the future, dreaming.

Chapter 3

The Attack

Steve came down to the hostel on Monday evening – 19 April. We spent the evening chilling as usual and playing Nintendo. There was a bit of football chat, a bit of girls talk. Steve said he was hungry so I told to him to go downstairs and see if my friend Nicola was cooking anything.

The hostel had four floors and two wings. When I first moved in I was on the third floor on the left-hand side of the building. Those of us on the left had to share kitchen and bathroom, while those on the right had a sort of bedsit where they had access to a kitchen and bathroom. Nicola lived on the first floor and was on the left side. She shared with two other girls called Marcia and Lorraine. Marcia was lovely looking with beautiful brown skin, nice hair, nice height, nice size. Nicola was nice too, but not my type. Lorraine was slim and brown, just as sexy as Marcia but in a different way. She moved in towards the end of my stay. Marcia was older than all of us, and treated me like a boy. She knew I liked her so she flirted with me like crazy. I think she just loved teasing me. We all got on well, looking out for each other. We were like a little family. Whenever any of us had a problem, we knew there was always an ear and sensible advice.

In a way we felt more like part of a family than we had in our own homes. An old-fashioned family at that. I would give Nicola money from my giro and she would go shopping and buy food and drink. She and Marcia would do the cooking and I would just come in and eat. This suited me down to the ground because before I was always coming in late, too tired to cook, and wasting the little money I had on fast food. It also meant that whenever Steve came round there would always be something for him.

About 9 p.m. Steve and me started the long walk up to Woolwich Common. Well, I say 'walk'. I had this mountain bike which got me to college and back, so I was riding and he was walking. About ten minutes away from Steve's home we stopped at the 'bangout phone box' so Steve could make a call to his dad. We called it the bangout phone box because of the way it worked. You put your pound in, dialled the number, and once connected you'd talk for a minute, give the box one bang and your pound would drop out – you'd then replace it with a ten-pence piece, but still get a quid's worth of talk.

Steve spoke to his dad. He said he'd be back in ten minutes. That was the regular routine. It took us about ten minutes to walk across the Common to his house. I watched him walk up to his door and got on my bike.

When I got home, Nicola said Steve had already phoned.

'Oh no, he's not been locked out again,' I said. 'This is ridiculous.' If his parents weren't going to let him in why didn't they tell him when he phoned? Mrs Lawrence in particular was very strict with him. It seemed crazy to me – here was an eighteen-year-old kid, basically a good boy who hadn't been in trouble with the police, yet had to be in at 10.30 p.m. Like so many kids, he didn't have an easy relationship with his parents, and he'd obviously now have to make it up with his mum. Then again, me and mum had had plenty of run-ins. Perhaps that was one of the reasons Steve and me got on so well.

Steve rang again and said he'd been locked out; could he come and stay? 'Yeah, that's fine,' I said, 'but you don't need to keep phoning to ask – you can come down any time, and if I'm not here you can stay in Nicola's room, she won't mind that.' He sounded edgy and said, 'Oh, I just need to phone, just in case.' 'Look, Steve, mate,' I said, 'how many times have you been here? You know that if I'm not here my key's normally down there with Nicola. You can just go and get the key from her and go up to my room.'

Twenty-five minutes later he was back at the hostel, and we were on the Nintendo. We played Streetfighter for an hour or so. We were both really competitive, hated losing. I wouldn't move near him and he wouldn't move near me when our energy was low because neither of us could bear defeat. Result? The bloody game went on for ever. Steve was a bit upset – he had wanted to see his mum because she was going away on a course the next day.

The room was not much bigger than a prison cell but we liked it. It had a bed, a chest of drawers, my TV and Steve's video player (that he wasn't allowed to use at home) and my Nintendo. Plenty of evenings we'd just stay in watching films – pirate copies – on his video. I had a pocket TV that I gave to Steve to use in his room because he said he was not allowed to watch tv at home. We went to bed late, about midnight. I slept one end of the bed, he slept the other.

On Tuesday 20th April he went to school and I went to college. Tuesday evening he phoned me at the hostel. I asked if he was coming back. He said no, he had to change his clothes. We agreed to meet down at school on Thursday. He asked me if I could buy him lunch because he had no money. 'What's new?' I said. We arranged to meet up at lunchtime. We also had a date with some girls from John Roan School ten minutes down the road.

*

Thursday morning, I was just relaxing. Every Thursday I had the day off. Usually, I'd go to Lewisham library for a couple of hours and read up about electrical engineering. Not today, though, there wasn't time.

Nicola came up to my room. We were chatting about things, and suddenly she said that she liked Steve and could I put a word in for her. I wasn't surprised – I'd seen it all over her face when he'd been around. 'Well, you should tell him yourself,' I told her. She said she'd heard rumours that he was moving in to the hostel, and asked if they were true. I said I didn't know. He'd talked about it a couple of times, and asked what the chances were of getting a room. I'd spoken to one of the guys who ran the place and he told me there was a queue and Steve would have to wait six months. 'Look,' I said, 'he's my good friend, and he's having problems at home. Can't you do something for him?' So he said, 'OK. Get him to come down for an interview.' Twice he was due for an interview, and twice he didn't turn up. He wasn't normally unreliable.

I said to Nicola, 'I don't know what he's doing, don't know what he wants – one minute he wants to move out of home, the next he doesn't.' I think part of him was frightened of leaving home, and another part desperately hoped that he could make things work with his mum and dad. He liked the idea of happy families. Most of us do.

I met Steve at 12.30 at the school gate. At lunchtime, all our friends used to go down to the roundabout by the Royal Standard pub. We were chatting as we walked down about a problem Steve was having with a Chinese boy who was the brother of a girl he liked, and with another boy called Peter who was supposed to be the girl's boyfriend. The girl was flirting with Steve, even though she was supposed to be seeing this Peter, and then running back to Peter and telling him that Steve was harassing her. Peter thought it was a good idea to send Steve threats through her brother, saying he was going to beat Steve up.

I was fuming when he finally told me because it seemed that

this had been going on for a while and I was getting the full story only now. It also got to me because I had told Steve to leave her alone because she was flirting just that little bit too much for my liking. I thought that he should stick to this other girl called Dion who, in my opinion, was better for him. I suggested that we should go and see Peter and ask him what his problem was, but Steve said he didn't want to be fighting anybody over a girl. What he meant was that he didn't want to be fighting. He'd do anything to avoid conflict.

Steve got kebab meat and chips as usual. I didn't eat meat, or at least not red meat, so I normally got a portion of chips with salt and onion vinegar. But I wasn't hungry and didn't get anything that day. The girls we'd arranged to meet didn't turn up. We were disappointed but it was nothing major. We walked back to the school and we arranged to meet up after school to go to his Uncle Martin's.

I went back to the hostel. There were only a couple of hours before school finished and Nicola and me just sat and chatted about everything. Before I knew it, it was time for me to meet Steve again. I got to the school and then a few of us went off for the 89 bus – me, Steve, his cousin Kareena and a girl called Zerin who was his on-off friend, and a boy called Leon Thompson and his cousin.

We gradually split up from each other. Zerin and Leon changed buses at Blackheath Village while we stayed on the 89 to Lewisham. We walked around some jewellery shops and then visited Earl, the barber who usually cut my hair. Soon enough, it was just me and Steve going up to Grove Park on the 261. I met a friend called Ann when we got to Grove Park and Steve went his way on to his uncle's and I went off with Ann. I said I'd meet him later at Martin's.

About an hour later, I got down to Martin's. Steve was there, as were Martin's partner Melly and their kids. We had a great time – playing Nintendo, fighting, watching TV and just doing nothing. Steve had something to eat. He always seemed to be hungry and thirsty. His favourite drink was sarsaparilla. He always had it when we went to Martin's house. He'd never drink it anywhere else, so when he got there that lovely first-time taste was always there to greet him.   One of the reasons he liked to go round to Martin's was that they always fed him up. But his mum didn't like him going to Martin's because her sister, Cheryl, Steve's auntie, was spreading rumours that Martin was giving Steve weed to smoke. Which was certainly news to me. He did occasionally smoke weed, but as far as I know, he never got it from Martin. Mrs Lawrence had actually banned him from going to Martin's, so we always went on the quiet. Steve felt relaxed there – not only was it family, he also knew they'd look after him, see him right food-wise.

I don't know who Mrs Lawrence liked less – me or Martin. She found it hard to trust people, and always thought one of us was corrupting her little boy. But in truth, Steve also liked going to Martin's because he could watch his videos there. We must have spent hours on end, either at the hostel or Martin's, watching classic kung fu films like *Snake in the Monkey's Shadow* and *Snake in the Eagle's Shadow*. After the movies, we practised the moves, not that we could do them.

Martin had gone out after a while but had told us that he wouldn't be gone for long. Usually he gave us a lift home. Eventually, we called him and left a message on his mobile saying we wanted to go home. We always used to call him Long'ting because he was one of those people who always take an age to do anything. We were waiting and waiting, but Martin didn't return. So at about 10 we decided to leave. We walked to the bus stop and jumped on the 126 to Eltham. We got off at the McDonald's by the corner of Eltham High Street and Well Hall Road and waited there a couple of minutes before deciding to walk up to the roundabout at Well Hall Road. We'd been told by someone at the bus stop that the 161s were on strike that night, and we'd have a better chance with the two buses that went along Well Hall Road.

We hated going this way, but it was quicker than our normal route and Steve was desperate to get home. It's a strange area. It doesn't look rough – the houses are quite posh, built up away from the road, and Well Hall Road itself is thick with parked BMWs and Mercs. The road has two police stations: one down by Eltham High Street and one up by Shooter's Hill. Close to the second police station was Brook Hospital. In a way, if something had to go wrong, if you were to be attacked, you'd imagine there could be far worse places to be when it happened.

But it didn't feel like that. It felt anything but safe. Eltham was an infamously racist area. Black people were always getting beaten up around here, and despite the two police stations nothing ever got done about it. One woman who worked in Accident and Emergency at the Brook, which has now shut down, told the police that they often saw black or Asian people who had been attacked with knives. We were scared that night. Actually, we were scared every time we came down this way.

We started walking down the road and halfway between the bus stop at McDonald's and Eltham Station a 286 came, so I started running. I looked back and Steve was running behind me. The bus driver didn't look as if he was going to stop at all, but a French woman at the bus stop put her hand out and we got on. Steve's mum had come back from her college trip and he wanted to make things up with her after being locked out earlier in the week. I said to him it was much safer staying on and going the other way (the 286 to the Royal Standard pub in Blackheath and then a 53 to Woolwich), and I didn't want to be standing around in Eltham. He kept saying he didn't want to be locked out tonight and he was already late.

So we got off. It was the last stop before the roundabout, the second stop up the road. There was me, Steve and the French woman. We walked over the roundabout and I stood on it and looked back down the road towards Eltham. It was freezing. From where I stood I could see the white light of the Co-op funeral parlour and beneath it a group of white boys walking up the road. It was a clear April night and there were no leaves on the trees and not that many cars on the road to block my view. Later the police told me it was impossible to see so far, but I've come back here a number of times to check and I can still clearly see the light from the roundabout.

I walked over to the 122 and 161 bus stop on Well Hall Road on the other side of the roundabout and looked at the timetable. It was just after 10.20 and the bus was supposed to come at 10.28 p.m. Me and Steve were talking about all sorts of stuff. Plans, school, this girl he was trying to sort things out with, and Dion, the girl I thought Steve should go out with. All sorts of stuff. I was complaining that the bus was taking too long and we didn't want to be staying here and we should go and get a 286 to the Royal Standard or run up the hill. We could have run up Shooter's Hill, no problem, then we could have just walked down Academy Road to where he lived. But we didn't. We decided to wait. I was getting more frustrated because I didn't want to be in Eltham. They don't like black people in Eltham, and although you have a high crime rate in Eltham like you do in, say, Brixton, you don't have the same police presence. I always tried to avoid that route at night as often there would be white boys driving past in their cars, winding down their windows and shouting 'nigger' at you.

As I say, I was a bit more streetwise than Steve. It wasn't that he didn't know the score, it was just that he was more trusting, always thought the best of people.

I decided to walk back down to the roundabout to see if there was another bus coming. Steve caught up with me and was in the middle of the road. I walked back because I saw a bus coming. I don't know why, but I decided that if a 286 went past we should get it. But Steve kept saying to me, 'I'm not getting that bus, I'm not getting that bus. I just want to get the 122 or 161 straight up.' Although we were told the 161s were on strike, we didn't know for sure. While we were waiting a 286 went past and it looked like another was coming. We could have easily run to the bus stop and got on one of them.

I noticed the group of boys had got to the other side of Well Hall Road, past the roundabout. There were six of them and they were parallel with us. I didn't think anything of it, but they were still in my eyeshot. I then shouted to Steve, 'Can you see the bus?' I had to shout because he was in the road. He said, 'What?' I said, 'Can you see the bus from the road?'

Then I heard 'What, what nigger?' First of all the boys were strutting around and saying 'What, what nigger?' and then they came for us. As the boy who first said 'What, what nigger?' was running, he began to draw something out from his trousers. He couldn't run properly till he'd pulled it out. I said to Steve, 'Run', and I just turned and ran. As I got past the tree, up past the bus stop, a bad feeling came over me. It just came to me that Steve hadn't run. Everything flashed in my head. Why hasn't he run? What's he still doing there? Maybe he has run. I hope he has run. All these things were flashing in my head in that split second before I turned round to make sure he was behind me. It was like I was arguing with myself. Yes of course he has run, I was thinking, and then, No he hasn't, he's still there. Yes he has run, he's behind me, he's behind me. I was telling myself, Why would he be still standing there? He's not going to be stupid, he doesn't know who they are, I don't know who they are, the only thing to do is run away. I was sure he was running but couldn't bring myself to turn around. I was too scared. I started to cry. I couldn't help myself. I was running and crying and arguing with myself and it was all happening in those few seconds.

I was scared to turn round because of what I was going to see. Then my legs went to jelly, and I did turn round. I saw the boy who had just pulled the thing out of his trousers strike Steve with it in a downward blow. At the time it looked like it was an iron bar. He struck Steve with it. All this time the people at the bus stop were seeing everything. They weren't under any pressure, yet none of them would later be able to pick out the boys in an ID parade.

Steve had his back to me and this boy ran in from his left and I watched the boy raise his hand and strike a downward blow which I thought hit Steve's head. Steve screamed out, and then the others rushed in to him. Then one of the boys came from round the tree on the corner of Dickson Road with a scaffolding pole in his hand and chased me up the road. I don't know how I started to run because my legs were still like jelly. I didn't think I'd be able to move, and it took a second for my legs to get the message. The more effort I was putting into trying to run, the slower I seemed to be going. I could feel he was getting closer and closer and closer. I was panicking. I didn't want to get caught. If both of us got caught, nobody would be able to tell the story, though at this point I had no idea how horrific it would turn out to be. Because we're black, and nearly everybody in the area is white, nobody would believe those boys had done anything wrong.

Then I just thought, Fuck it, I'm going to stop and he's going to have to run into me, and then hopefully it would be just him and me and we'd have a fight. As I decided to turn and fight, the boy stopped and also turned and ran back. All I could see was his curtain-style hair flapping out at the sides as he ran from me. I looked back and saw Steve on the floor and they were kicking him and kicking him and stamping on him. Steve tried to get up and this boy ran back and whacked him on the back of the head. Steve fell back on the floor and all of them ran off.

Somehow, Steve jumped up. I was already running back. 'Steve, Steve, Steve, are you all right?' I was shouting. He started staggering. We ran across the road and I was relieved. He'd just got a kicking. But then things didn't seem right. Steve now could only stagger. He was crying out, 'Duwayne, Duwayne', and I said to run. He said, 'Look at me Duwayne.' He was running lopsided, but I didn't know how bad it was. I knew there was something wrong, but I couldn't see what. I started crying and crying and crying – something bad had happened. I couldn't stop myself from crying. I don't know why. He kept saying, 'Tell me what's wrong, tell me what's wrong, there's something wrong', and I looked at him and his jacket was all puffed up and there was blood around his neck, and it was running down onto the ground. The blood was in his jacket, billowing it up, and I was saying, 'Just run, just run a bit more. We need to get past the other road.'

The boys had run down Dickson Road, and if you go down Dickson Road and turn into Downman Road you can double back onto Well Hall Road, which is where we were. I was scared we were going to get trapped if they came back round. I knew we had to run past Downman Road, and just beyond there was a phone box I could use. We kept on running and I kept telling him to run, and he kept calling my name. And every time he called my name it was getting fainter and fainter. He called my name one last time and when he called it I went all cold. It was like my heart had stopped beating.

I turned around and looked back at him. He let out a sigh and said my name and fell to the ground. When Steve hit the pavement there was a loud bang. I went over to him. He was still breathing, and by fluke he had fallen down in the recovery position. I ran across the road. I didn't even notice the cars weaving around me. Everything was silent. It was as if I was in my own world, my own twilight zone. I went to the phone box and dialled 999. I was terrified that the boys would come back – they knew one of us had got off without a beating and would know that we were just around the corner.

I tried to explain to an operator what had happened, but I

kept having this strange feeling. My mind was telling me, It's too late. Don't worry, it's too late. He's OK, but it's too late. And I kept saying to myself, No, no, no, you need to get an ambulance. As I was talking to the operator, these thoughts were confusing me. I told the operator the address, but the address in the phone box was incorrect. I told the operator the number of the phone, but that was wrong too.

I got so frustrated that the address and telephone number were wrong that I just slammed the receiver against the call box and let it drop so that it was dangling with the operator still on the other end of the line. After I did that I could hear the traffic again, and I saw the cars coming up and down the road. It was hopeless. I tried to stop a small Peugeot. The driver slowed down, but he just drove round me. Then I saw a couple, who it turned out were the Taaffes, coming out of a church. I went up to them and asked them for help but they just walked straight past me, straight on down the road. They later admitted that they thought it was a ploy to rob them.

I looked across the road and a car had pulled up. I ran back over. A man got out and asked if I'd called the emergency services, and I said yes. He went to the phone box to finish off the call. I sat down and started to cry. It turned out he was an off-duty police officer called Geddis. Mr Geddis and his wife were helpful. He asked me what had happened and I said we'd been attacked and told him what I thought had happened – that Steve had been hit with an iron bar. Mrs Geddis was trying to calm me down, and she got a blanket to keep Steve warm. While we were standing there, the 122 eventually came and went past. Everyone at the bus stop got on the bus. At the time, I didn't even remember people being at the bus stop. I ran past them twice, but I couldn't see anything. Steve and me were in our own bubble. This was just happening to us. Nobody else knew what was going on.

We were waiting, and I could see Steve was losing more and

more blood. I knew it was too late. I knew there was no way anybody could save him now. I was pacing up and down, up and down. I was crying. Then the police arrived with their ridiculous attitude. I became hysterical and loud with them because clearly what we needed first of all was an ambulance, not the police, and that is what I'd asked for. What was the point of the police coming if they weren't going to do anything? Every time a new officer came on the scene he'd ask me the same questions. What happened? Was there a fight? Are you OK to speak about what happened? I'd say, 'I've just told the other officers', and the new officer would say, 'Yeah, well you need to tell me now so I can write it down.' So I'd tell them, and then another officer would come along and start asking the same questions. A woman officer, WPC Bethel, obviously didn't believe what I was saying. 'Your friend is lying there, and you say you don't know who the boys are!' She asked me if I had any weapons on me. I had to tell six or seven officers the same thing, and that's one of the reasons I was getting so frustrated. I was saying to them, 'Why can't you move him?' but they were too scared because the blood looked so horrible.

I'd seen blood like this years ago when I lived in Deptford and this guy had jumped out of a tower block and landed on the floor just where we were playing patball. We heard a big boom! and saw this thing on the floor. I thought that someone had thrown a dummy out. We went over and it was a man and he was lying there with all his guts spewed out and green stuff coming out of his mouth. I was nine or ten at the time, and I remember all the parents coming out and telling us not to look because it would give us nightmares.

But what was happening to Steve was even more horrible. He was lying in the recovery position, unconscious, and his blood was seeping out, frothing because he was so hot. I couldn't tell where it was coming from, and I still didn't know that he'd been stabbed. All I could see was blood running out on his left side and down the pavement and onto the road. It was horrible, a pool of thick frothing blood. It was repulsive, and that's why, I believe, they didn't want to touch him.

The police were supposed to stem the flow of blood, but they didn't turn Steve over to see where the blood was coming from, which is basic first aid. They just kept asking me the same dumb questions. Are you sure you didn't start anything? Why would people attack you out of the blue for no reason?

The blue lights of the police cars were flashing, and neighbours were coming out of their houses. Mrs Geddis had knocked on doors to ask for more covers. It was at this point that the Taaffes thought it safe to return.

I realised Steve was dying on the pavement. I kept shouting, 'Where's the ambulance? Where's the fucking ambulance?' No one could give me an answer. Then it came over the radio that the ambulance was at Well Hall Road roundabout, but from where we were standing we could see the roundabout and there was no ambulance there. I shouted, 'No, it's not, it's not there', and I could hear down the radio the controller saying, 'It is there, it is there. Can't you see it?'

Next thing we heard over the radio was that the ambulance was actually coming from Woolwich, a couple of miles away, rather than from the Brook Hospital just up the road. I asked why it was coming from Woolwich and told them it would take too long. The nearest hospital was about thirty seconds away in the car, but the officers refused to drive Steve there. They told me to calm down, and said it was better to wait for the ambulance. Again, I told them there was no point waiting for the ambulance and that he needed to be taken to hospital immediately. Still no ambulance arrived. An officer went to look for it in a police car, but he returned without any sign of it. I couldn't believe how wrong it was all going.

I began pacing about, up and down. Anger was building up inside me at a rate I couldn't control. Steve was dying and yet the police were just standing around. The whole thing was a disaster. I knew it was a disaster, but at the same time my mind was still arguing with me: telling me to calm down because it was too late. And, of course, the longer we waited, the more true that became. I went to look at Steve again and he just looked empty, like there was no life left in him.

All the people just standing around doing nothing were annoying me. Especially the Taaffes who had ignored me when I first asked for help. The covers weren't doing anything for Steve either, kind though it was of Mrs Geddis to get them. The blood was now a stream, mucky and gooey and frothy. Horrible. But it shouldn't have been too horrible for the police; after all, it's part of their job to deal with such emergencies.

My anger was frightening them. They were threatening me with handcuffs, telling me to be quiet or else. I felt empty, useless. There was no point in protesting any more. One officer, PC Gleason, said afterwards that I hadn't given them enough information to make a street identification, which was unfair. I gave them the information they asked for and I would have recognised the boys if they'd taken me around. He also said that I was 'virtually uncontrollable', and other officers said I was hysterical. I was very upset but I was not out of control or hysterical. I was perfectly capable of answering sensible questions.

Eventually the ambulance came from Lee Green. It had got the call late and taken about fourteen minutes to arrive. The ambulance crew went over to Steve and just by their body language I knew he was dead. They didn't rush. They turned him over, and when they turned him over he was soaked. His blood had saturated his clothing completely. It was like he'd put his clothes on and jumped in a swimming pool full of blood and walked up the steps and come out. They just pushed a tube in his mouth and looked at each other. I knew then that there was no reason to cry any more, no reason to be upset any more, no reason to be angry any more. Then they flung Steve's body in the back of the ambulance. As they had picked him up, a ginger-beer can had fallen out of Steve's pocket. He loved ginger beer. I picked it up. I took it home and kept it. One day the can exploded.

I was taken to the hospital in a police car. I was silent. Later on, one of the officers, WPC Smith, said I was swearing at her, calling her a cunt and calling them pigs, and that she was frightened of me. I still don't know why she claimed that. In fact, she drove me to the hospital and I never said anything in the car because there was no point in being angry any more.

When I got to the hospital I walked behind the stretcher. Steve was taken into a room. One of the nurses asked me to go with her, but I said it was OK and walked off to a waiting room. Again, PC Gleason asked whether it was true that the boys had said 'What, what, nigger?' He said he needed to take a statement.

At the hospital I phoned Melly and told her what had happened. I started crying again. I couldn't speak properly. PC Gleason was asking me questions and trying to get a description. By now I couldn't think straight. Everybody in the hospital was just looking at me. I went to sit in a corner because I didn't want all those people looking at me. I wanted to be invisible. At the hospital, nobody asked if I was all right or if I'd been attacked. I was offered no comfort.

The Lawrences walked in. Apparently, a boy at the bus stop had seen us being attacked and had gone round to Steve's house and told his mum and dad what was happening on Well Hall Road. They drove out to look for Steve, but unfortunately they came only as far as the pub up the road. They then decided to go to the hospital. I think that they must have feared the worst. From where they stopped in the road, they wouldn't have been able to see us. But if they had driven a little down the hill they would have seen the flashing blue lights of the police cars. Mr Lawrence looked devastated. Mrs Lawrence had a what-now? look on her face. I hid around the corner. I didn't want her shouting me down in the A&E Department.

A nurse came and took me into a room. The Lawrences were

already there. The nurse said, 'We tried to save him, but he was already dead.' I got all upset and mad, I was climbing the walls. Mrs Lawrence said, 'I knew it would have something to do with him. I knew he'd be involved. What did I tell you Neville?'

They kept me in the room for ages after that. Mrs Lawrence started to cry. And I just felt like telling her, 'It's all your fault, it's all your fault. If we didn't have to go that way this wouldn't have happened.' It's all your fault, I kept saying in my head. If you'd never locked him out we wouldn't have had to go this way and all this might not have happened. You're the one who's been pressuring him. I was thinking all this, but couldn't say it. I wanted to, but it wouldn't come out. The way Mrs Lawrence was crying I felt sorry for her, but, yes, I did feel she was partly to blame. I knew what I was thinking was unfair, that this attack could have happened just about anywhere, but I did feel that things could have turned out different if she hadn't been so strict.

I never understood why Steve had to live with such a strict curfew. Perhaps Mrs Lawrence was especially protective of him because she had such high hopes for him, and this was her way of trying to keep him safe. Call it tough love.

Eventually, they took me out of the room and said I had to go to the police station. They gave me a choice. Either wait in the hospital or in the police car. I decided to sit in the police car. Just before we left, they took me to see Steve. They said they just had to finish cleaning him up. When they took me into the room, he was lying on the table, normal looking, just as if he was sleeping. Steve had gone, but it was still Steve. The atmosphere was strange. I had felt numb up till this moment, but now I felt a rush of warmth to my head. I took a deep breath. 'I love you,' I said to him, then turned and walked out.

I went and sat in the police car. Steve's Uncle Martin turned up. He drove up to the police car so that we were parked window to window. He asked what had happened, and I couldn't speak. I literally couldn't speak. I was stuttering. My chest started hurting me and I began to cry again. Crying and crying and crying and crying. I couldn't stop. He put his hand through the window and placed it on my chest. It was like I was having convulsions. The more I tried to tell him what happened, the harder it was to say anything. Before Martin asked what had happened, I'd been OK. I knew what had happened, I knew that Steve was dead and I was OK with it. But as soon as Martin asked me, all the pain and all the feelings came flooding back. I couldn't control them.

We drove to the police station and the police told me my mum was there. They asked if I wanted to speak to her and I said no, I just wanted to get the statement over and done with. They took me into the investigation room and gave me a little tour to impress me. I wasn't interested because I was so tired and worn down. It felt like I just needed to go to sleep and once I woke up everything would be all right. It was strange, like I was there and I wasn't there.

The first thing they said to me was, 'Are you sure they said "nigger", are you sure they couldn't have said something else?'

'Yes, it was definitely "nigger",' I said. 'Definitely "What, what nigger?"'

They said, 'Are you sure they didn't know Stephen by a different name? Are you sure you'd never met them?'

I kept telling the police that we had never met them, and that they did say 'What, what nigger?' It was like the police were trying to do a Jedi mind trick on me, and that if they repeated their answers often enough I'd eventually repeat them back to them and they'd hear what they wanted to hear. Again, I said, 'No, they said "What, what nigger?" They called us niggers.'

It felt like I was fighting them. Officers kept turning up and talking about me within earshot as if I wasn't there. They were waiting for the Borough Commander to arrive. And when he did, things got serious.

They asked questions like: Are you sure Stephen and you weren't in a gang? Are you sure you didn't provoke the attack? Why were you in Eltham anyway? I completed a statement, and then they said they needed to take my trainers to get a footprint. I was thinking, Why do you want them? Do you think I'm a burglar? The whole process took over five hours to complete.

The police said my mum still wanted to see me, so I went downstairs. Mum and my cousin Charmaine were down there. I said I was OK, but that was the last thing I felt. I was desperately holding myself in because I didn't want anyone to hear me crying. I didn't want my mum and cousin to see me crying. I told Mum what had happened. It upset her. 'It's a racist murder,' she said.

The police gave me a lift back to the hostel, and asked if I would be all right. It was 7 in the morning by now and I'd been at the station since about 11.30 p.m. I went to sleep as soon as I got in. I was so tired. It was a different worn out to anything I've experienced before or since. I've been worn out plenty of times after football training, come home and been completely shattered, but this was the next level of being shattered. My body was shattered, my mind was shattered, I was shattered. Everything was shattered.

There was banging on my door. I knew it was Nicola, and I didn't want to get up and answer it. I didn't at first, and she started shouting, 'Duwayne, are you OK?' She was crying and shouting, 'Duwayne, are you OK? It can't be true, it can't be true.' Then I let her in.

By now it was on the news. People kept coming round and telling me that I needed looking after, but I just wanted to be by myself. I was tired and worn out. Then the police came round and said I needed to get a solicitor. All day it went on, with people constantly phoning and coming round. Eventually, I just didn't bother answering the door.

Alone at last, I turned on the TV and watched the news reports on Steve's murder.

Chapter 4

Breaking Down

After Steve died, it was strange. I felt different from everybody else; I felt shut off. Every day people would ask if I was all right, and tell me that I needed this or I needed that. I kept saying I felt fine. And I did feel sort of fine – till the rumours started. Suddenly, just a few days after Steve's death, everybody seemed to know who the killers were. So many people mentioned the Acourt boys to me, claimed to know that they were responsible. I didn't understand it. Somehow, they all seemed to know who had murdered Steve, yet at the same time no one could describe what they looked like or where exactly they came from or where they hung out. It was like they came out of nowhere.

Then people began to get more inquisitive. They wanted to know what had happened, whether I could have done anything to save Steve, why didn't Steve run, why did we go that way, any number of questions. I kept saying, 'Stop asking me, I don't know. Stop asking me.' 'Steve must have known them, that's why he didn't run,' they'd say. I am sure Steve had never seen the attackers before, but how could I be certain?

I played the scene over and over in my head, from different angles, over and over and over. Just a few seconds running through my head. And the more I tried to slow it down the quicker it raced through my head. It was driving me mad, trying to capture the boys, their faces, so I could describe them to the police, and just as I thought they were coming into focus they'd be gone. I'd go over it again and again, but I couldn't get them.

Melly said the Lawrences had got themselves a solicitor called Imran Khan, and that it would be best if we had the same solicitor so we'd be working together. I had my doubts, though. Firstly, I didn't know why I needed a solicitor. And secondly, I knew by now that the Lawrences were going around saying it was my fault, telling people that they'd told Steve not to speak to me – all because as far as they were concerned I had had a 'bad' upbringing. Mum had told me that, just after the attack, she'd gone up to their house to offer her condolences, but they made it quite clear they didn't want her there.

I felt trapped. Trapped by all the stuff going on in my head, and trapped also by all the madness going on around me in the real world. There were so many people with so much advice. Everyone was rushing around telling me what I had to do and what I mustn't do. People were saying, 'You've got to go to the Lawrences' house. You've got to tell them what happened. They deserve it.' But I didn't want to go. Of course, I didn't want to go when I knew they were cursing me. More than that, I didn't know if I could explain what had happened, if I'd be able to say anything at all without them seeing me crying.

I told my friends and family that I was staying in the hostel by myself, that I wasn't scared. But I was terrified. There were rumours going round that the white boys were coming for me next, because they knew I had seen everything. It was a weird feeling, being scared witless and at the same time not caring. Maybe that's despair.

I suppose I wanted someone to look after me, but there wasn't anyone who could. I didn't trust the police, and everybody else was against me because I'd been painted as this bad person. So I was stuck on my own. My family wanted me to visit, but I didn't want to be around them because I didn't want anyone else to become involved. It was my problem, and I had to deal with it – I was there at the time, and if I was not supposed to be, I wouldn't have been. That's when I decided to do everything myself. There was only one person who could look after me: me.

I had hooked up with Mr and Mrs Lawrence's solicitor, Imran Khan. He'd come to see me soon after the attack, and I'd decided that I did need a lawyer after all. He told me that I had to give him a statement or a breakdown of what had happened. Imran had been practising for a couple of years at most, and I didn't feel confident giving the statement to him. His assistant was making notes, but I didn't think he could keep up. Actually, I don't think he knew how to take notes full stop. He certainly didn't have shorthand. I don't think Imran thought much of the statement either, because he never gave it me to check or sign. The statement they took was to have disastrous consequences three years later at the private prosecution.

As the days passed, I expected to hear of arrests. But there was nothing. I couldn't understand it – if everyone knew who the attackers were, if they were famous locally for carrying knives, using them, and being racist, and they were seen in the area around the time of the attack, which is what everybody was saying, why hadn't they been arrested? Why hadn't the police done anything to show their commitment to catching the killers?

Another name people had started to mention now was 'Norris'. Wherever I turned I seemed to be told, 'It was Norris who done the stabbing.' Not only that, people were describing how he'd stabbed Steve. How did they know? I certainly never told anybody. Was it just hearsay, or rumour, or was he actually boasting about the murder? Whatever, many people seemed to know more than I did. But David Norris, like the Acourts, seemed to be a mythical figure – people knew his history, his hobbies, even the direction in which he stabbed people, but nobody seemed to know what he looked like. All sorts of names were being thrown around. It was confusing.

I was still baffled by Steve's being stabbed because I never saw a knife. I still didn't know the full extent of his injuries. Nobody had ever told me. Maybe if they had I could have tried to piece together the incident in my head a bit better. I didn't see a knife, and that's what I told the police – the truth. But sometimes the truth is used against you. I suppose what I should have said is that I didn't realise it was a knife. But I kept saying, 'I never saw a knife, I never saw a knife.' The police repeatedly asked me how did he get his injuries then, and all I could say was 'Well, I didn't see a knife.' From my position, it looked like Steve had been hit over his head or in his face with a bar, and the others just ran into him with their fists.

So many people told me how worried they were for me – not just friends, sometimes people I barely knew. 'The Norrises are bad people,' they'd say, 'gangsters. They've got people working for them. Norris goes around stabbing people; that's how he stabs people.' They even demonstrated with imaginary knives. 'But don't imagine anything will happen to them,' they would say. 'They have big contacts everywhere.'

I'm sure they meant well, but it wasn't the most comforting thing to hear. Then someone would take me aside and say, 'Ah yeah, the Acourt brothers, I've heard they're always stabbing people, but they never get into trouble. I'm telling you, mate, they won't get in trouble because they've got friends in the police.' I didn't know what was true.

The Lawrences took the names that repeatedly came up and passed them on to the police. The police didn't do anything about them. Soon enough, people started blaming me for failing to provide perfect evidence. 'Why can't you say what happened?' 'Why can't you say who these people were?' 'Don't you want them to get caught?' 'Can't you do a better sketch?' they'd say. And I'd sit there in silence because I couldn't speak. If I'd opened my mouth I'd have started crying or knocked them out. And all the things these friends and acquaintances were saying to me, without realising it, would bring me further down. Then straight after they'd said it, it would be 'Oh, are you OK, Duwayne? Are you OK? You're not thinking about it are you?' I would tell them I was fine. Just fine. That would end the conversation right there.

There was no point in saying anything else. Whenever anybody saw me, the one thing they wanted to discuss was Steve. 'So what happened on the night? Have you recovered yet?' And then they'd answer their own questions, while I sat in silence. 'Ah, no, no, no. You can't recover yet. It hasn't hit you yet. What are you going to do when it hits you? How are you going to manage?' How the fuck was I supposed to know how I'd manage? I'd never been in that situation before. And neither have you, I'd tell them in my mind.

I'd certainly experienced racism before – seen it, felt it, smelled it. And it stank. When I was growing up there were two clubs at either end of our road. One was a British Legion club, the other was a black men's club. The British Legion club members used to chase us down the road, throwing eggs and calling us niggers. While at the black club I just saw arguments. Men used to gamble, and there were knives and guns. But I never once saw anybody stabbed or shot. It was like a respect – they had their guns, but they never used them. And they didn't abuse the white community. The police were always in and out of the club even though no one had assaulted members of the public, unlike at the Legion. Not surprisingly, the police rarely visited the Legion, and then only for a laugh with its members. We rarely saw the police, in spite of regularly getting racist abuse in the street, and racist literature through our doors.

I suppose that after Steve died I was waiting for this big blow. A big wham in my head, like 'There you go: this is what really happened, Duwayne. Have a good look.' Sometimes as I was lying down I could hear Steve's voice – 'Duwayne, Duwayne' – and it was like he was shouting at me: 'Duwayne! Can't you hear me? Duwayne!' It sounded as if he was over in the corner of the room. I'd jump up and there'd be nothing there. A brief feeling of elation was followed by desperate sadness. I was obsessed by the thought of speaking to him. I just wanted to say 'Steve, why didn't you run? Why didn't you run?'

I noticed I was walking around on my toes on the street just in case I needed to run as hard as I could. People would stare at me, and it would make my heart race. They could be anyone. I needed help, but I didn't have anywhere to go. I didn't want to go to other people's houses in case the killers came looking for me there, and I got my friends involved. Even though people were gathering at the Lawrences', I couldn't go there because they were telling everybody that it was my fault. And I couldn't go to the police because I was convinced that somehow the police were involved and that they were not interested in protecting me. I still felt trapped.

I felt like I was going off my head. One day in June I walked up to a police officer in the street and said, 'Come on! You're coming to kill me – come and kill me, then!' I got arrested and taken to a police station. The police phoned Mum to tell her they thought I was mad, and then they cautioned me and let me go.

It was when I turned up for a football match that I realised how traumatised the attack had left me; how my attitude to everything and everyone had changed. My manager had come to pick me up in his car in Lewisham. We had a cup final in Kidbrooke. There were two other boys, white boys, in the car, and I said to the manager that I wasn't getting in there with those white people – the manager was white but somehow that passed me by. The words just tumbled out.

He leaped out of the car and screamed at me. 'Are you going to stop talking to white people for the rest of your life? You were in an incident that was nothing to do with us – you know we are your friends and would never do that to you. You need to buck up your ideas and decide what you're doing. We need you for the team. Are you coming or not coming?'

I stood there on the pavement, thinking about what he had just said. I could hear him shouting at me, 'Duwayne, Duwayne, are you going to get in the fucking car or not?' I continued standing there, thinking, not really hearing him. Before I knew it, I had got in the car, but I don't remember making the decision to get in. It was as if someone or something had made the decision for me.

I was still thinking about it all the way to the match. Some people had already been on my case. 'You're better off not talking to white people, now, not after what happened,' I'd been told – and here I was on the way to the game with my white team-mates and white manager asking myself how the hell could I go through life without talking to white people? What sort of solution would that be? How could it benefit me? Or even worse, how could I have a normal life after everything was over if I never spoke to another white person?

We got to the match and the manager said that he didn't think he should play me, and then stopped. 'On the other hand, it might be the best thing for you,' he said.

So they did play me and I felt so great on that pitch, so free. We were playing a team full of white boys, and we had four black boys on our side. We were battling so hard, chasing everything, and I was getting wound up because it was taking a long time for us to score. At half time, the manager was roaring, telling us all we needed to do better. There was such adrenalin. Positive adrenalin. I went out there and it felt like I was back to normal. I'd forgotten everything else – the attack, the police, for that match I'd forgotten it all.

Halfway through the second half, the manager made a substitution. He wanted to try something out and didn't know whether to take me off or not. I just looked up at him and that look said, Don't you dare take me off. He took off someone else, and that was it. Within two minutes I'd scored the first goal, then I had one disallowed for offside, then I scored again, then we scored again, and I felt happy. Happy! It was like the joy of having something for the first time. I was so happy. I'd forgotten how great life could be. Then it was time to go home, back to the hostel.

Mum was waiting for me. 'Don't you think you should come home? It's not safe staying here,' she said.

But where would it be safe for me to stay? If it was true that the killers belonged to families who were gangsters and that they had friends in the police, I wouldn't be safe anywhere in London. I told her I was fine and that I was staying there.

A couple of weeks after Steve's murder the police came round to the hostel and said I needed to attend an ID parade because they had finally rounded up the suspects. They had arrested five boys, rather than the six I saw. But I didn't feel capable of identifying anyone. My head was twisting around and around.

I told the police that I couldn't remember what they all looked like. But 'remember' was the wrong word to use, and that was to cause problems. What I meant was that the descriptions were trapped in my head. I literally couldn't get them all out of my head. I had seen what had taken place, but some of it was locked away. I have never been great at describing faces, but it felt like something else here – perhaps my mind didn't want to go back to that night. But this didn't mean that I wouldn't be able to identify the suspects, because when I was there on the night I saw their faces all right.

I sat silently in my room, desperately trying to conjure up the faces. Why couldn't I? The only face I could see resembled that of, I would find out later, Gary Dobson, the boy who I believe chased me up the road with the scaffolding pole. He had

a 'curtain' hairstyle – a parting in the middle with the hair drop-
ping down at either side of his face – and as he was running his
hair was flying out at the sides. That was the description I gave
the police.

The police were treating me as a witness. Every time they
referred to me it was as 'the main witness'. And I didn't know
any better. I thought I was just a witness. I felt that I should be
grateful to be alive, that I didn't have the right to be stressed or
confused – after all, Steve was dead, and I'd got away without so
much as a battering. Only later did I realise that I was also a
victim of the attack. Other witnesses came forward and said they
had seen me get hit before running away. But this didn't happen.
I was never hit. What they might have seen was me running
away and the boy with the curtain-hair chasing me. It all happened so quick, it must have been as much a blur for them as
it had been for me – the attack was estimated to have lasted
seventeen seconds.

I'd grown up respecting the police, but gradually I became
aware of how the police treated black people in our community.
We had a community officer in our neighbourhood and we
always looked out for him – happy to say hello to him, but also
duck out of his way if we were messing around. But soon me and
my mates would start to be stopped by police officers who would
take our details and then say things like, 'Are you sure you
haven't been arrested before? Are you sure you haven't done any
robberies? Only your details aren't coming up on our computer
and that's odd.'

I asked Imran to come to the ID parade with me. I'd never
been to anything like this before. Would the people be able to see
me? I told Imran I didn't want anyone to see me, that I was
scared. Imran said it would be fine, and that he'd try to meet me
down there.

The police asked me for my picture and I said I'd have to
speak to Imran about it. That was the first time the police really

frightened me. Why did they need my picture? I'd never heard of that before. But I'd never been in that situation before. I followed my instincts and said no.

The police came round to reassure me about the ID parade. They said they'd pick me up, take me to the parade and bring me back home. And there'd always be an officer with me. I was so scared that I was empty. How did I know I could trust the police? I didn't. So what do you do when you can't trust the police, but you have to talk to them because there is no other solution?

The first parade was held on 7 May. Joey Shepherd went on it with me. Joey had been at the bus stop and had hopped on the bus that came after the attack. He was the boy who lived on the same estate as Steve and had gone to Steve's parents' house to tell them what had happened. They were supposed to parade Jamie and Neil Acourt and Gary Dobson, but they failed to get enough volunteers and in the end only Jamie Acourt was paraded. I failed to identify him, as did Joey Shepherd. Joey would later claim that his name had been 'inadvertently' revealed to those taking part in the parade and he refused to attend any more because, understandably, he was frightened.

The second parade was on 13 May. The police turned up in a minibus. There was a woman in it, a white skinhead and two other white guys. I'd just been in a racist attack and I get in this minibus and see these people. No one was introduced, so my mind went on the rampage. Where are they taking me? What should I do – get off and run? Should I just sit here and see what happens? But once I sat I couldn't move. I was paralysed by fear. I thought, Shit, they've got me, and I was so simple to catch.

The others started talking. That's when I found out that the skinhead scaring the daylights out of me was Stacey Benefield, who said he'd also been stabbed by one of the suspects.

We got to the ID parade suite at Southwark police station and were all put in the same room. As the others chatted away, I called Imran to ask where he was. He was giving me all sorts of excuses for why he couldn't come, and telling me just to be calm, to follow what they said. I told him I was in a room full of witnesses. He told me to ask them their names. I think he wanted their names so he could question them. I thought, Why can't you be here? Why can't you ask them their names? Why should I be doing your leg work for you? I need support. 'You should be here Imran,' was all I said.

I asked the others their names and they weren't too willing to give them. Why did I want their names? Everybody was edgy. No one wanted to give too much information because nobody knew who was who, and who could be trusted.

I decided to get up and look out of the window. As I was looking out, a van pulled up. Some boys got out and casually walked into the station. It was a good job I wasn't paying attention because I didn't realise that I was seeing something I shouldn't have until five minutes later when an officer rushed up to me obviously flustered.

'Get away from that window,' he said. 'You shouldn't be at that window, you should be sitting down. Hasn't anyone told you not to move?' No. 'There should be an officer in here at all times.' I thought something must be up, but I still didn't realise what I'd seen.

We were all sitting in the room waiting to be called. We had to take turns going down to the ID parade. As I walked from one window to the next, I felt as if their eyes were following me. I turned round, and it was as if the officer had read my mind.

'No, they can't see you,' he said.

I kept looking in and looking away, looking in and looking away. I was sure they could see me. They were smirking. I felt so small, so tiny, wrapped up, tight, tight, tight. I couldn't breathe properly.

'Take your time,' the officer kept saying. 'Walk up and down three or four times.'

But I couldn't. I wanted to walk up and down once and

that was it. I forced myself to walk up and down a second and third time. I just wanted to leave. I didn't want to say any number. I felt there was incredible pressure on me to pick someone out.

I started to panic and thought to myself, I'll have to guess. I couldn't concentrate. I just wanted to run away from the parade. I wasn't prepared for it. I hadn't been instructed how to cope with it. That surely had been the police or Imran's job.

I later found out that I could have asked them to turn to the side, I could have asked them to shout, I could have asked them to do plenty of things, but I was never told any of this. Yes, the police should have told me, but they weren't there to support me. Imran was – or at least he should have been. I went down the line one last time and picked out someone who I thought had been there.

Benefield said he picked out a person he thought was Norris because everyone else was dressed normally and the person he picked was dressed as if he'd just come out of a prison cell. It didn't make sense to me. He was about to explain and all of us were ready to listen when an officer came in. Only then were we told not to talk to each other. But, of course, consistent with the whole investigation, it was a bit late for that.

We were taken back into the first room. An officer came in and said there were drinks in the fridge and we should help ourselves. We had been there hours and this was the only refreshment available. Later on I was accused of stealing a Coke from that fridge. This was like the relief room. When I got into that room, I did feel relieved – I've done it, I've picked out somebody. But I knew I hadn't picked out the person with any certainty. I couldn't concentrate on those faces. The fear was holding me back. There were two more parades that day, then we left. I later discovered that I had identified Neil Acourt, who was charged with the murder of Stephen Lawrence after the parade. But I didn't pick out David Norris or Gary Dobson. Benefield and his friend Matthew Farman identified Neil Acourt and Norris, and they were charged with the attempted murder of Benefield.

I was running away from everybody, even my closest friends. I would lock myself in my room and pretend I wasn't there. To get out, I had to sneak past Nicola's room. I'd go past quietly, and if I saw her door was open, I'd creep back upstairs and leave by the fire exit. But the fire exit only went down to the first floor, so I had to jump from the first floor to the ground.

When coming back in I'd have to run past Nicola's door and hope she didn't see me. It never worked. As soon as I thought I'd got past, it would be, 'Duwayne, Duwayne, what's up with you? I'm sure I just saw Duwayne.' She would run out and I'd be hiding on the stairs. 'I'm sure that was Duwayne,' she'd say to whoever was in the room with her, and then ask them if they'd seen me. I'd creep up to my room, open the door quietly and lock the door. Then I'd get under the covers and just go to sleep.

That was the best thing to do, the easiest thing to do. All I had to do was get into bed, wrap up warm and go to sleep. Sleep came as a relief.

I felt I needed more support. I was introduced to an anti-racist campaigner called Ros Howells, who was later awarded an OBE for her work, my first impressions of her was she was no good for me. She was always at the Lawrences', and then on the way home she would stop off just to say hello to me.

Everybody seemed to be congregating at the Lawrences' and people told me that I should go up there. But I didn't feel able to. A couple of weeks after the attack, Mark, Steve's other uncle, came round and said he wanted to take me for a drive. We went for a drive and then he took me to the Lawrences' and said, 'Don't worry.' He put his arm on my shoulder. 'Don't worry, nobody can't do nothing to you, nobody can't do nothing when you're with me. I know it was nothing to do with you, but I want you to know that nobody can't do nothing while you're with me.' Steve had been tutoring Mark's son at his house. I had been there a few times with him. 'I just want you to tell them what happened,' he said. Nothing more, nothing less. I went inside and walked through the kitchen and into the back garden. There were a lot of people there.

Mrs Lawrence was asking me questions. 'I don't blame you,' she said. 'We just want to know what happened to our son.' But I kept thinking about what she had said at the hospital. I realise she might not have been at her most rational then, but still. It was all going through my head, and I just sat there silent as a lamb, head down. I let them speak, and all I was saying in my head was, Get me out, Mark, get me out, get me out.

I didn't want them to see me crying. I didn't want anyone to see me crying. I felt weak, I felt ashamed, I felt like a baby. The best way to stop myself crying was not to speak, just to be silent, and to say what I've got to say in my mind. I felt like an outcast. Even though everyone was being nice, I found it hard to believe in their sincerity. It felt like it was all a show. They asked me if I needed something to eat, something to drink. Before I had been brought there none of those people had come to see me. Mrs Lawrence had already said that she didn't want any of Steve's stuff in my house, and I couldn't understand why she was suddenly being nice to me. She had never wanted me here in the past. She had said before that I was a thief, a bad influence, and that she didn't want my sort in her house, so why did they want me there now? Was it just because Mark was there or for some other reason?

I would have loved to have been able to tell Mr and Mrs Lawrence exactly what had happened, but I couldn't. I wanted nothing more than justice for Steve, a justice that I'm sure would have brought the Lawrences some peace of mind. 'You should stick close to us because we don't want anything to happen to you. You're all on your own. Where's your mum? Why don't you let your mum look after you? Why don't you go and stay with your mum?' they said. But the whole experience had taught me that I had to be a big boy now.

After that, Mrs Lawrence always claimed that she never knew how Steve died because I wouldn't tell her. But that was unfair. After his memorial service, Mum wrote out a letter to Mrs Lawrence that I had dictated. It started: 'Duwayne wants you and Neville to know this is what happened on the night Steve was murdered. I quote from Duwayne's mouth . . .'

I couldn't drop college because of what had happened. It was my life. How would I earn money in the future without higher qualifications? So I had to continue my education. I'd already decided that I would have to compartmentalise life – there was Steve and the murder stuff, and there was life for living. I couldn't put the two of them together because they clashed. Which was fine in theory, but not in reality.

A day after the first ID parade came the famous march on Welling. They said this demonstration against racism had actually been organised before Steve's death. South-east London was becoming infamous for racial attacks and murders. In 1991, Rolan Adams had been killed. Rolan used to hang around the same places Steve and me did. We didn't know him, but we knew of him. We had friends in common. His murder was shocking. Then in July 1992, Rohit Duggal was killed by a white boy on Well Hall Road – the very same road that Steve was to be murdered on – apparently after trouble in a kebab shop between black and white boys. In the end, only one of the white gang, Peter Thompson, was convicted, just before Steve's death. There had also been a horrific number of black people dying inexplicably in police custody. After Steve's death, Marc Wadsworth of the Anti-Racist Alliance described Greenwich as Britain's race-murder capital. The label stuck. It was decided that the venue for the march should be changed from central London to Welling, where the British National Party's head-quarters were.

Nobody wanted to miss the march. Everyone was talking about it, giving it large – this was our chance to get back at the police, to smash up the white fascist headquarters, which posed as a bookshop. The march against the BNP was going to be our revenge for Steve.

Chapter 5

The March

Even I wanted to go on the march. Me, enthusiastic about something – I'd almost forgotten what it felt like. But everybody was talking about it – this was an opportunity to have our say, to vent our anger.

I saw Nicola before we set off. She pleaded with me to stay away. 'No, Duwayne, you shouldn't go,' she said. 'What if they pick you out? What if the BNP spot you, or the gang that killed Steve?'

That really put the shitters up me. Then I thought, Why should I be scared? Everybody else is going to be there, I'm going to have the most protection – I'll be fine.

We all met up at Plumstead Common. There were about thirty of us, talking ourselves up. Some people said they weren't going to leave there till we'd smashed the place up. I'd never been to Welling, even though I'd lived in south-east London all my life. Welling was almost exclusively white, and the locals were well known for their racist attitudes. Like Thamesmead, it was a no-go area for many black kids.

We didn't know what to expect. We weren't used to going on demonstrations (I'd never been on one like this before), we'd never seen the BNP base before, we didn't know who would be there, or how many BNP people there would be, if any at all.

We started marching and picked up banners. We were all talking about what we were going to do. The march was tense and loud, but non-violent, until we got to the BNP base. That's when everything kicked off. It was just a house boarded up with wooden planks painted blue. There were loads of rumours about the place: it was the headquarters; it was a bookshop; it was the headquarters disguised as a bookshop; it was just boarded up for the day but was still active. There was nothing special about the building, but just the sight of it heated everybody up.

The tension grew. The police were worried, and they overreacted. They came in on horses and tried to surround us. We were trapped, hemmed in by mounted police who looked as if they were ready to charge. But there was hardly any space to charge into. It was claustrophobic, scary, exciting.

Wham! A bottle was thrown. Then lots of people started throwing stuff. Everyone was chanting: 'Get the BNP out, get the BNP out, get the BNP out.' It was wicked. I was up at the front, right by the BNP building, where they had a crowd barrier and a line of police behind it. I had a stick in my hand and was whacking it on the barrier to the rhythm of 'Get the BNP out, get the BNP out, get the BNP out.'

The police came forward and pushed us back. But the people behind us were pushing us forward, and all the time bottles were hitting the BNP building, bouncing off it and hitting the police. Everyone was exhilarated, shouting at the police, 'Why are you protecting the BNP? Why are you protecting their place?' The police said, 'If it was your place we'd need to protect it as well.' But I'd never noticed them being keen on protecting black people before. More police waded in on their horses to disperse the crowd, but that crushed us more. Officers started hitting people indiscriminately with their truncheons. That just made everything worse.

Stones and bricks were thrown at the police on horses. It was madness. Most of the bricks and stones missed the police and hit people around me near the front. Paramedics and ambulance men were running through the crowd trying to get through to people who had been hit or who had been run into by the police on horses. Total chaos.

The stewards were also pushing us. We'd had enough. We managed to break free of the crush and started walking down into Welling town centre.

A group of white boys came round the corner and shouted, 'Come on niggers, come on niggers', and ran off down the road. A group of us gave chase. As we got round the corner there were two young kids standing in a garden with their mum. The idiots on the march jumped over the fence into the garden and shouted obscenities at the woman. She ran into the house, terrified, leaving the kids outside. Other people jumped over and were shouting all sorts at her. I climbed over the fence and told everyone to leave them alone. The door was open and the woman was standing there. I took the kids to the door. It was disgusting. What had she and her kids got to do with Steve's death or the BNP?

'No, they're all the same: once they hate niggers they'll always hate niggers,' said one boy. 'They support the BNP. If they didn't want the BNP here, they wouldn't be here.' I didn't know what to say. The few seconds of argument between us allowed the mother and her children to run inside and shut the door.

The racists had jumped in a car and driven off, so we came back onto Wickham Lane. Everybody was pumped up, as if we were on some kind of drug. We just wanted to get into some violence, do some damage, smash up the place. We wanted revenge.

A lot of people knew Steve, a lot of people knew his temperament, and it was impossible for them to comprehend how he had been butchered in such a way. How could they have done this, and why were those responsible still on the streets, even though everybody seemed to know who they were? How many murder cases do you get where the suspects are known to so many people, and the police receive more than a hundred pieces of evidence telling them who the people are, and then they refuse to do anything about it? The suspects weren't arrested for two weeks and that was on everybody's mind. My friends were saying that the gang had probably destroyed all the evidence by the time they were hauled in.

Get the racists back. Everybody associated Steve's killers with the BNP. There had been so many racist incidents in Woolwich, Thamesmead, Bexley and Plumstead and the police hadn't done anything about them. We were fired up. Damage needed to be done. I'd never felt like this before.

We reached Welling town centre and were surprised to see everybody doing their Saturday shopping and going about their business as if nothing unusual was happening. Obviously they didn't care about the march, because if they did they wouldn't have been on the streets.

I stopped at a shop and bought an apple. As I came out, eating it, I looked over to the right. A group of men were running into our group, hitting people, and then running off. I thought, What the fuck's that? I ran over to where these people were, but they had run into a pub. It turned out that they had run out of the pub, hit people, shouted their racist abuse and then run back into the pub. Brave.

The pub was now under siege. Bricks, stones, wood, anything people could find to throw at this pub, they threw. Windows were broken. Despite all the talk, this was the first bit of damage to property that had been done on the day. (However much we wanted to, we couldn't have wrecked the BNP building because it was all boarded up.) And again, it was in response to mindless provocation. What did they expect to happen if they were running out, smacking people and shouting 'niggers' to demonstrators on an anti-racist march? The madness must have lasted fifteen minutes, while the police called in reinforcements.

We were on a high. 'Come on then, come on fuckers, come and get it then if this is what you want,' someone shouted.

It was a big high. Everyone was running around, looking at each other and laughing. We weren't frightened that we were going to get into trouble. All we wanted to do was show our anger. Looking back on it, I suppose a march like that has got to cause trouble to get noticed. If we'd walked those few miles and nothing had happened, it wouldn't have got a mention in the media. There would have been no press coverage, and no one would have got to know how devastated we were by Steve's death.

By now, shops beside the pub were getting smashed and looted. I saw a group of people run behind a car, trying to lift it, bouncing it and bouncing it. I felt compelled to join them. It was strange: I knew it was wrong, but it was like I was compelled to help turn it over. I ran behind it and just as I went to join in they lifted it and threw it over. I didn't even get a chance to put my strength into it. When I saw the car topple over, it felt good, but I didn't know why. Now I realise that to us it felt like a way of getting back at these people. We didn't have any other way of doing it – we couldn't arrest them, we couldn't trust the police to see justice was done, and we couldn't and wouldn't go out and kill them. Our only way of getting them back was doing damage.

That was what we all thought that day in Welling in May 1993. It may seem simplistic and uneducated, but we honestly felt there was no other option at the time. It was our way of giving ourselves a voice, of saying no, we can't put up with this crap: we the people who had been racially attacked and abused in the boroughs of Greenwich and Bexley. We were all saying that we couldn't take any more, we'd had enough.

The police reinforcements arrived. About ten officers in flashy jackets ran into the space between the crowd and the pub. Then people started taking up dustbins and throwing them to break shop windows, just like in Spike Lee's film *Do the Right Thing*. It looked methodical, as if it had been planned.

There was a martial-arts shop that sold weapons. Loads of the demonstrators were in there. As I was watching, wondering whether I should join in, there was a call: 'The police! The police! The police!' And still half of them stood there in the shop. The police ran in with their batons, knocked one guy down and started kicking him on the floor.

Then the crowd went to attack the police, and the riot police waded in on horses. Those of us who weren't fighting had time to have a look around – one, two, three policemen with video cameras, and a couple of press guys taking pictures, waiting for people to walk past them and then pulling out their hidden cameras and snapping them.

We stood around. What should we do next, where should we go? This is it, Welling town centre, there's nowhere else to go. There was a stand-off between us and the police. We couldn't run home from here. I'd never been here before, I didn't know which way to go.

We thought about getting a bus, but what bus driver would let us on – a group of scruffed-up, wild black boys just coming off the march in the heart of Welling? Nobody was going to let us on their bus because they knew it would get damaged.

The police had successfully blocked our path. Surrounded on all sides, helicopters flying over us, we knew there was no point in fighting. We'd just noticed the police cameras, but they must have been there for the whole march. We didn't want to be on camera. A lot of people had been wearing hoods and they decided to take them off now. They'd done all the damage they needed to, and for some reason they reckoned that the police wouldn't be watching them now. That's how a lot of people were caught.

The police kept us there for about twenty-five minutes. Then we started walking back in little groups to Plumstead Common.

Once we got there we all linked up again, and got on buses. I argued with the bus driver over nothing – I was in that kind of mood. Argumentative and exhilarated. Everybody was.

It was like, Yesss! I fuckin' did this, I fuckin' did that, this person threw a stone and it hit this officer, this person threw a brick and it hit that. Everybody felt they'd done their little bit for Steve. Everybody felt they'd done their bit for all the times they'd been chased in that area for being black. But it wasn't enough. There should have been a much bigger march. We should have terrorised the BNP office, destroyed it, but it wasn't done. Many black people stayed away from the march. That's always been our problem – when something terrible happens, something that demands a united front, we don't stick together.

About six friends came back to the hostel, just to make sure I got back safely. Nicola was waiting for me. She'd already heard about the rioting. She was furious. 'I thought I told you not to go down there. What did you go down there for? You know what's going to happen now? The police are going to come right here. They knew you would go on the march, Steve's friend and everything, and they'd be looking for you.' It rushed out in an uncontrollable flow. Nicola was so upset with me. And for me. Then she turned to my friends and started on them: 'You shouldn't have let him go on the march. You call yourselves friends and you let him go there – you're no friends. How many shops did he break?'

I said I hadn't done anything: no smashed windows; I didn't break into any shops; I didn't nick anything; I didn't hit anyone. I was just there walking.

Then it came on the news. Everyone was looking for themselves. They showed everyone in the hoods. We were jubilant. 'Yes, fuckers, come and get us if you can.' A great feeling. But I was also scared. I think a lot of us were scared. But because there were so many of us we ultimately felt safe. Or maybe we just wanted to look big in front of each other.

After the boys left, Nicola started shouting at me again. 'What did I tell you? Not to go on that march. You can't be doing those things Duwayne. Those people can be anywhere. They can be watching you right now, waiting for you to do something, and they can just grab you.' I thought she must have meant the killers, but she was talking about the police. 'They arrest you and then we don't see you again. I don't want you going nowhere.' She started putting it on me. 'I care about you, Duwayne, I don't want nothing to happen to you. See what they done to Steve', and then she started crying.

I couldn't look her in the eyes. I had to look down. I didn't want her to see me crying. I felt so weak. Helpless. I was thinking about the attack, how I couldn't do anything, couldn't even help, didn't know what to do, just panicked. Every time I cried it brought me right back to the spot – helpless, just standing there.

Nicola was holding on to me. 'You're the only one who saw what happened,' she said. 'You need to get away.'

Get away to where? Everybody was making suggestions, but nobody had the real solution. The only escape was sleep because then I didn't think of anything. I went straight upstairs, locked my doors and slept.

Chapter 6
Saying Goodbye to Steve

Hundreds of people turned up at the memorial service held in London on 18 June. Steve's parents had chosen to bury him in Jamaica, so there would be two events. Mrs Lawrence had said that this country was not fit to bury him in, so Steve's body was going to Jamaica to be buried. I found that sad really.

A lot of people were upset, especially his friends. We wanted a place where we could visit and put flowers on his grave. I was offered a flight to go to the funeral in Jamaica, but would have had to pay the money back. I didn't go.

Trinity Methodist Church was packed. Everybody else seemed to have been invited, but I wasn't. I was just the person they wanted to help catch his killers. I felt used.

I went along to the service anyway, for Steve's sake. People were asking me in the crowd, 'Why are you at the back? Why aren't you at the front?' They started drawing their own conclusions: 'Don't the Lawrences speak to you? But if it wasn't for you, nobody would know nothing. I'm going to have a word with them. They need to know.'

'There's no point,' I said. 'I'll just be here. Steve knows I'm here.'

I walked up to the church from Steve's house, which is where everybody started walking from. More and more people told me to go to the front of the procession. 'No,' I said, 'it's their son, let them have their time.'

In the church the coffin was at the front. Next to the main part, there was another hall – an overspill. I was in the overspill where there were no seats. Nobody had allocated a seat for me in the main room. I wasn't even acknowledged. I stood in the corner with two friends, Rowena and Lianne. Speeches were made, but I was never mentioned. Again, people whispered to me, 'Why aren't they saying anything about you? I think you should go round there.' I'd asked not to be named because I was frightened for my safety, but they didn't even mention 'Stephen's friend'. It felt as if I'd already been written out of his history.

Some of the things the vicar said hurt bad. He talked about the Lawrences' lovely family life. I was thinking to myself, How can they sit there knowing this is bullshit? Some people here must know the truth. They spoke about how he was physically attacked and staggered on before he collapsed. They said an ambulance was called, but it was too late and they couldn't save him. There was nothing about his friend, nothing about the fact that I'd had to call the ambulance. Nothing about what I had to go through with the police at the scene. I had been wiped out of Steve's history.

They praised the Taaffes for praying over Steve, and the vicar said that Steve had whispered his last dying words to them. I couldn't believe what I was hearing. I wanted to storm round there and say 'You liars.' But I just kept my calm. The priest was only saying what the Lawrences had told him to say. In fact, the Taaffes hadn't wanted to help. They said they saw Steve running up the hill and that they thought it was a ploy to rob them. But they never saw anything. Steve had already fallen on the floor. I was in the phone box, ran back to the road, and then I saw them. I thought Steve was unconscious by the time they crossed the road, in which case there was no way he could have whispered his dying words to them.

The vicar spoke about how the Lawrences went out looking for Steve because they felt so worried for him. Tragically, had they gone a bit further they would have seen us. The vicar said they had come to the top of the hill but couldn't find us and that they were agitated so they drove round and back up to the hospital.

I really wanted to go down to the front now, but I didn't want to make an exhibition of myself. I felt if I went round there people would start arguing about me – those who supported me, and those who hated me. I felt that Steve's parents hated me like poison. They told other members of the family not to speak to me and to have nothing to do with me. And if these people did have something to do with me, they said they weren't going to have anything to do with them.

I was friendly with a girl called Michelle, whose mum Bev was to become like a mother to me. After Steve's murder, Michelle and Bev were told not to speak to me by Cheryl, Mrs Lawrence's sister, but Michelle felt that this was unfair and wrong. She said she didn't believe all the stuff they were saying and so told me. Some time after, me and Michelle had been round at Melly's house to celebrate her birthday, and Cheryl and Mrs Lawrence turned up. Cheryl started shouting, 'There's a stink in here, we can't stay here with this stinkiness. It's best that we leave.'

Snoopy, a friend of mine, was there at the time and he just told her where to go. 'How would you know what happened to your son if it wasn't for Duwayne?' he started shouting at them. They didn't listen.

They tried to smear my name. The family told people it was my fault that Steve was out there; if I hadn't been with Steve none of this would have happened; if Steve had been with this other kid Elvin, he would have been OK.

Whenever we had been out together I would never let Steve

walk all the way home on his own from my house. I always used to walk him to round the corner from his door and I'd watch him go in to his door. I don't know why I felt so protective over him, but I did. I always felt I had to watch him, protect him, and because most times I rode home on my bike there was less chance of anybody attacking me.

One of our other friends, Leon, was nicknamed 'Cringe' because he was always cringing. If we were playing computer games he would be cringing, if we were playing cards he would be cringing. When Steve was at his house late at night, Cringe would always walk him to the bus stop, make sure he was all right. He used to say that if Mrs Lawrence had phoned his mum and told her to pack him off home immediately, she would have refused to do it. Cringe's mum was called Pearl, and she was lovely. She had to put up with us lot in her house all the time, and she used to get mad because we'd eat all the biscuits and bread. She'd say we couldn't all come round there like we were and eating her out of her home. On plenty of occasions she'd shout at us: tidy up the place, do this, do that. But we all loved Pearl, and we used to do what she said. She might have got mad with us, but she would never kick us out of her house late at night. If it got too late, she'd tell you that you had to sleep in Leon's room and leave in the morning. And if you insisted on leaving late at night, she always wanted to know how you were getting home, and whether you had enough money.

The way the Lawrences talked about me was so painful. After all, I hadn't wanted to be there that night. I have to live with that memory. And if I hadn't been there, who would have spoken about the incident? Who would have gone to the ID parades to pick out people? Who would have given evidence, knowing some of the suspects had contacts in the police? What did they want from me? I couldn't die in Steve's place for them, but I felt that's what they wanted me to do.

I wish I hadn't been there, but I believe I was chosen to be there on the night because of the kind of person I am, because ultimately Steve's case would need someone prepared to take on the fight. After what we went through, there was no way I was prepared to ever give up the struggle to see justice. It riled me that they said that if Steve hadn't been with me, it wouldn't have happened. The fact was that he travelled that way home on a number of occasions when I wasn't with him, and it could have happened on any of those. He said he was locked out on a number of occasions, and so it could have happened any time he was walking 1.8 miles from Woolwich Common down to the hostel in Charlton.

At the service, a cousin of Steve's sang some songs Mrs Lawrence had chosen for him. After the songs, people from school spoke about what Steve was like. I knew I should have been up there speaking, but it wouldn't have worked. I would have got upset and spoken about things that nobody should have had to hear about at that time. I really wanted to say, 'Liars, liars, liars – so many of you made his life miserable.'

A lot of people were crying. I so wanted to cry, but I couldn't. I had to show a strong face. There were so many people there, and if I had started crying they would have said 'He's broken', and I didn't want anyone to say that. Maybe it would have been better if I had cried.

The service was over, and people started to walk past the coffin. I wanted to go and cross myself before Steve, but I knew the Lawrences would still be round there with their crew, and I didn't want there to be an argument. I didn't want them to say I had disrupted the funeral. I knew that if anybody said anything out of place to me, I would just blurt things out.

I asked somebody to check if the Lawrences were there. They came back and said that they had gone. Most people had moved outside by now. I wanted to walk past the coffin like everybody else had. If I didn't do it, people would wonder why. Once the congregation had started moving, I could feel people looking at me, waiting to see what I would do – whether I would go out the back door or walk past Steve. If I'd gone out the back door people would have thought that I had something to hide, something I was ashamed of.

I walked past the coffin and peeked in. I didn't know how I was going to react to seeing the body. I had been told that he had been cut open, and that all sorts of awful things had been done to the body. I was expecting to see cuts and bruises. Melly had gone to the morgue with Mr and Mrs Lawrence, and she had told me that as she was dressing Steve she had bounced his chin and a big piece of dead skin had just torn away like paper, and she'd had to put it back and patch it up. It came into my mind as I peeped. The first thing I looked at was his chin. But there was just a bruise there from where he had fallen when we were running.

Steve looked completely different: weak and withered. It wasn't him. He had a completely different complexion from when I saw him at the hospital, when he was dead but his body still looked warm. I tried to block out my feelings, so I wouldn't collapse or cry.

The way I was treated that day left me so upset and angry. Part of me felt that on the night I should never have turned back to fight, I should have kept on running. Then I wouldn't have had to go through all I went through. But ultimately I knew I'd done what I'd done not for the Lawrences but for Steve, and that I needed to do it.

To this day, I don't know where Steve is buried. Apparently, they built a tomb for him, but I don't know where it is. I've never been told, and I will never ask. I felt like an outcast that day and have felt like one ever since.

I never went to any of the events that were held for Steve. I didn't feel I needed to. I don't have a guilty conscience about how I treated him. I don't have a guilty conscience about how me and him lived. I don't have a guilty conscience about anything between me and Steve. I would never have had a Stephen Lawrence Trust, and I never will have a Duwayne Brooks Trust. I never wanted money. Money can't bring Steve back. Money can't make your life better when your best friend has been killed in front of your eyes. Nor can accolades, publicity or any awards. Nothing can.

The officer who took me to the third ID parade, which took place on 3 June, was a strange one – even by police standards. His name was Crowley and he caused me big problems. Not just me, the whole case. First thing he told me when he arrived was that neither he nor I could talk about the case, no complaints about that. He said he had to study, because he was taking his exams to move up to rank. So it was silence the rest of the way there. I was annoyed. It was only him.

On the way back to the station, though, we started arguing about the case and who he reckon out, even though we weren't supposed to discuss the matter.

The next day two officers came down to the hostel and said serious allegations were being made against me, claiming that I was only picking out people in the ID parades that other people had described to me. What? I didn't have a clue where that alibi pattern had come from. I didn't know how to respond. How could they say that? Yes, people were telling me who they thought was responsible, and I didn't see how I could stop them from doing so, but none of my mates knew what they looked like. There was a rumour that the Accused had black

Chapter 7

Who's on Parade?

The officer who took me to the third ID parade, which took place on 3 June, was a strange one – even by police standards. His name was Crowley, and he caused me big problems. Not just me, the whole case. First thing he told me when he arrived was that neither he nor I could talk about the case. No complaints about that. He said he had to study because he was taking his exams to move up in rank. So it was silence the rest of the way there. I was surprised it was only him.

On the way back to Charlton, though, we started arguing about the case and who I'd picked out, even though we weren't supposed to discuss the matter.

The next day two officers came down to the hostel and said serious allegations were being made against me, claiming that I was only picking out people in the ID parades that other people had described to me. What? I didn't have a clue where that allegation had come from. I didn't know how to respond. How could they say that? Yes, people were telling me who they thought was responsible, and I didn't see how I could stop them from doing so. But none of my mates knew what they looked like. There was a rumour that the Acourts had black hair, but someone else said they didn't, so I didn't pay any attention.

The officers said that I needed to make a statement. I said I couldn't make a statement because Imran was not around. So they said the best thing to do was to make an appointment with Imran and to come to the police station, or else they'd have to arrest me and take me to the station to make the statement. They repeated that the allegations were very serious.

I told Imran immediately, and he said he'd come down. But he didn't. Every time I phoned his office, his secretary told me he was busy or that he'd just popped out, could I call back? So I did, repeatedly, and always got the same answer. Excuses, excuses.

I asked Melly to call the office, to see what response she got. She rang and got through to him, no problem, then put me on the phone. 'Oh, I'll call you back Duwayne, I'll call you back as soon as possible, I'm just in a meeting.' That happened time after time. He just didn't seem interested in me. The press weren't associated with me, and no one else thought I was important, so he seemed to think I wasn't worth bothering about. He brushed me aside.

It seems strange to me that he now has a reputation as the top 'race' lawyer, because he was useless for me. In the end I felt his treatment of me had been so inept that I sued him for negligence and won without going to court.

The police came back again, and I told them I hadn't managed to get through to Imran. They said they really would have to arrest me next time because they needed the statement. I was panicking, thinking I hadn't done anything wrong, yet they still kept threatening to arrest me.

'You can't have other people telling you who to pick out,' they said.

'Nobody's told me who to pick out,' I answered.

But everyone in south-east London seemed to know the names by now, so how was I not going to find out? More importantly, I didn't want them to think people were telling me what they looked like because they weren't. I felt sick and confused. Here I was, just after having been attacked and seen my best mate killed, and trying to help as a witness to the best of my ability, and they made me feel that I had done something terribly wrong, something criminal.

A couple of days later the police came down to the hostel, and of course there was no Imran. I was terrified of having to give the statement by myself, with no adviser, and the only person there who could take Imran's place as the 'appropriate adult' was the hostel worker. I had no choice. I didn't want to be arrested. So I did the interview, and it proved costly. In my view, that interview proved to be a huge factor in losing the private prosecution. I was manipulated big time, and I had no idea how to prevent it.

They told me the allegations had been made by Detective Sergeant Christopher Crowley, the man who took me to the third ID parade. He told his supervising officer that I'd asked him whether I'd picked out the right boys, and that I'd heard Steve's killers were the Acourt brothers, and that I'd picked these boys out because they matched the description given to me by friends and looked like brothers. He even said that a mate of mine told me I should recognise the Acourts because they'd been to our school, which was absolute rubbish. What happened was that he asked me whether I thought I'd picked out the right boys, and I said yes, I thought I had. It turned out I hadn't picked out one of the Acourts at this parade, I'd picked out Luke Knight. It didn't matter – I'd still picked out one of the suspects. A few weeks later Knight was charged with Steve's murder along with Neil Acourt, who I had picked out at the 13 May parade.

Crowley said I'd told him that at the second parade I'd picked out a lad because he looked as if he'd just come out of a police cell. But he was wrong. I *had* told him that this is what

Stacey Benefield had said to me after the second ID parade, and how bloody ridiculous I thought it was. After the parade, we had all been put in a room, and we discussed who we had picked out.

For good measure, Crowley told his superiors that I'd said I was anti-police and had wanted to call the ambulance rather than the police after Steve had been attacked. I probably had said that to him. But I didn't know it was an offence to be anti-police, and I think events proved that it would have been better if the ambulance had got to Steve before the police. Finally, he said that I hadn't called the police because I intended to exact my own revenge, which was rubbish. I did want revenge – I wanted it in the form of justice. For me, and all his friends, justice would be a conviction of the gang who killed Steve.

I later discovered something very disturbing about Crowley's involvement in the case of Rolan Adams that put things into context for me. It turned out that he had been accused of trying to destroy the credibility of Rolan Adams's brother, who had been with him when he was killed, during the investigation of Rolan's murder. This was another race murder Jane Deighton, the woman who was to become my lawyer, had been involved in.

Nothing came of the accusation, but it was certainly strange that of all the officers at their disposal, the police should choose one who had already been involved in a race controversy to escort me to and from the ID parade.

Of course, the police were right when they said these allegations were serious. Who would be believed in court – me, or an officer who had served more than ten years in the Met?

The police said Crowley couldn't have made it all up. I said he hadn't, told them which bits were true, and suggested that he was lying about other things he claimed I had said. The police wouldn't let me say 'lie'. They refused to put it down in the statement. They insisted I be more tactful and say that he had 'misunderstood' me.

I felt I was being manipulated. OK, they would say, if you didn't say this, perhaps you said that. And I found myself agreeing to things that hadn't happened. They said that if I hadn't been coached by friends as to what the boys looked like, we must at least have talked about it: 'How else would you have been able to pick them out if you'd not seen their faces?' They said that if Crowley had misunderstood what I was saying, perhaps this was a better way of putting what I had said. In the end the statement said that after the first ID parade I'd described the boy I'd picked out and my mates had told me he sounded very much like one of the Acourts. Nonsense. They didn't know what the Acourts looked like. But I was exhausted, upset and demoralised. I caved in. Since then I've been bound to what I was bullied into putting down in that statement – perhaps if Imran had been there to guide me through it, things would have turned out differently..

Imran called me later and said, 'Is everything OK, did it go well?'

'No,' I told him, 'it went anything but well, it was a bloody disaster, because you weren't there, and I was pressured into saying things that weren't true.' The trouble with Imran was that he got a kick from being with the Lawrences – being seen with them, making statements for them. And because they didn't like me I assume he didn't like me either. But it should never have been a question of liking or not liking for him. If he wanted to get a conviction for Steve's murder, he had to look out for the main witness, encourage him, direct him, or advise him to seek a different lawyer and he could then stick with the Lawrences. In fact, he did nothing. He failed me miserably, and in doing so failed Steve and his family too.

A meeting with the police at my mum's house was arranged. They wanted me to run through the events of what took place on 22 April yet again.

'Why?' I asked. 'I've already told you what happened.'

They said they wanted to see if they could remind me of any little details I might have forgotten about – like who Steve and me had spoken to on the night, or who he might have been speaking to during the day. Was I sure that he hadn't had an argument with somebody the week before? That I hadn't had an argument with anybody the week before? Was there any tiny little thing I might have forgotten? It was as if they still couldn't quite believe that we could have been waiting at the bus stop by ourselves and a group of white boys had attacked us without reason. It was beyond their comprehension.

They asked me about the clothes Steve was wearing. They said they had found gloves in his bag and asked me, straight out, if he'd committed any burglaries recently. 'Could he have committed a burglary on the night?' 'Were you with him all night?' 'Did he leave your sight at all?' They were looking for anything to hang on him, to discredit him. I expect that they were asking Mr and Mrs Lawrence similar questions about me – was I this kind of person or that kind of person – just to find any tiny thing to switch it around. They couldn't cope with the fact that we were innocent.

Then the police decided on a new tack.

'Are you sure you didn't go into the kebab shop and have an argument? Because there was a half-eaten kebab found.'

'How could we go into the kebab shop when we were on the bus and the shop is between stops?'

'But the kebab-shop man remembers two black kids coming in, buying a kebab and having an argument with some white boys.'

'And?'

'Well, that might have been you and Stephen. Are you sure Stephen didn't walk in there?'

'How could we if we were on the bus?' I said again.

'Well, we just need to ask in case you've forgotten.'

'How can I have forgotten? We were on the bus. It was impossible to have stopped at the kebab shop. So why are you asking me this? Haven't other witnesses on the bus told you this?'

'Well, we need to ask you in case that's what happened.'

I felt the police were harassing me, and harassing Steve posthumously.

The worst thing they asked was, 'Did you and Stephen have an argument at McDonald's with any white girls and maybe their friends or brothers came after you?'

'No.'

'Are you sure?'

'Yes.'

They gave up on that line.

'Did you or Stephen talk to anybody when you got off the bus at Eltham?'

'Yes, we did. We spoke to the guy who said the 161 may be on strike, and that was it. Nothing else was said.'

'Are you sure?'

'Yes.'

'Are you sure Stephen didn't say anything?'

'Well, what would he have said?'

'We need to ask these questions, Duwayne. We need to find out where these people came from.'

But the police knew where these people came from. I'd told them that they'd come through Eltham station. I told them again that the first time I saw them was from the roundabout on Well Hall Road.

The police said to me that they didn't know where the boys had left from, but there was no way I could have seen them down the road from the roundabout; and they advised me not to put it in my statement and not to say it in court because I would look silly.

The meeting lasted about an hour – me, my mum, my dad,

and the police. At the end, they said: 'Well, Duwayne, have you got any pictures of yourself that we could use?'

Pictures for what? 'Why do you need a picture of me?' I asked.

'We just need to show it to other witnesses who were at the bus stop.'

'Why do you need to show it to them? They know what I look like, they were there.'

'Yes, but we need to show it to other witnesses in the area who might have seen you two.'

'But there are pictures of Steve everywhere. You don't need a picture of me.'

'We need to get as much evidence as possible. You might be hindering the investigation.'

'Hang on,' I said. 'Not having a picture of me does not hinder the investigation.'

Was this normal – to demand a photo of a witness who the police were supposed to be protecting? There were so many things that seemed a long way from what I thought must be standard procedure.

And now they wanted a photograph of me. I didn't trust them. As far as I was concerned, that picture could have been used to show the murderers and their families what I looked like. I had already heard that Clifford Norris was thought to bribe people, and he was said to have bribed Stacey Benefield to stop him pressing charges against his son, David. I didn't give the police a picture. I felt safer in my anonymity. At the time, there had been no pictures of me in the papers, and the families of the killers had no idea who I was. It had all been Stephen, or Stephen and his friend.

Where was Imran all this time? Nowhere to be found. Imran was a voice on the other end of the phone – if I was lucky. Imran was a face I saw on the TV: the Lawrences' solicitor. For me, he was non-existent.

Whenever I mentioned Imran, the police would have a dig at

me. 'Why do you need a lawyer?' they'd ask. 'You're only a witness. Witnesses don't normally have lawyers. They must think you're special for you to have a lawyer.' And it was going through my head, Why do I need a lawyer – Imran isn't doing anything for me, and I am supposed to be just a witness who had seen this terrible incident. None of the other witnesses had lawyers. Why did I need one?

Then I met Noel Penstone and Harcourt Alleyne. Harcourt was head of racial equality for Greenwich Borough, and Noel was one of his assistants. The first impression I got of Noel was that he was concerned about my safety. And that he was genuine.

He asked me what the police were doing about my safety.

I stumbled for an answer. 'I don't know . . . nothing,' I said.

'Where are you living now? Are you still at the hostel?'

'Yes.'

'We've got to get you moved from there,' he said. He was very direct. Next question: 'What have the police done about counselling?'

'Um . . . nothing.' I didn't know what counselling was, or that I was due any. I knew there were some people who were supposed to advise me and make sure I was OK. I didn't know it was called counselling.

'What? The police haven't done anything about counselling?' I could tell he was appalled, whatever this counselling was.

Noel was very concerned about the attackers, but his approach was totally different to the police's. He asked me if I knew them, if I'd seen them before. Unlike police questioning, his questions didn't seem designed to threaten me.

So, had I seen them before? I said no, and that concerned him. He told me that the suspects were tyrants in their area. Noel was convinced that the Acourts were involved. He told me that they used to go to Kidbrooke School, which was just up the road from Blackheath Bluecoat where Steve had still been going and I used to go. I was surprised I'd never heard of them if they were such trouble-makers, because we'd been to meet girls out-side Kidbrooke lots of times. Noel knew about the Acourts' history because of his job as a race officer in Greenwich.

Noel accompanied me to meetings with the police, as the 'responsible adult'. He was difficult, in the best sense, sticking up for me and asking why they hadn't made more progress in their investigations. Detective Sergeant Bevan, who was liaison officer for both me and the Lawrences, got riled with him, and asked him why he was asking all these questions when he was only meant to be present to observe.

'Why can't he ask you a question?' I would say. 'He's here to help me. I don't know what questions to ask because I don't know these people.'

'Yes, Duwayne,' Bevan would reply, 'but this is nothing to do with Noel, it's to do with you.'

'Well, if it's to do with me, and you want me to help you catch these people that did it, then you should be going out there look-ing for them. You must know who's done it because all the world seems to know who's done it.' By now there were so many rumours about the suspects. There were even rumours that Clifford Norris, David Norris's father, who was supposed to be on the run from the police, was actually in league with bent coppers.

Noel helped me move away from the hostel in Charlton. I wanted to move to Peckham or Brixton where there were big black communities, but they didn't have any places available there. So I was found a nice flat in Brockley. It was a converted house, and downstairs lived an old Indian man who was often getting drunk, and then upstairs there was me.

There were two rooms, but I used to live just in the back room. When you climbed the stairs to my flat, there was the main door, then my front door, and then a flight of stairs up to the flat itself. As soon as I got in I'd bolt both doors. When I went to bed I would put a speaker box by the bottom of the stairs and jam the door so you couldn't kick it in. In my bedroom, I'd sleep behind the door in my clothes, just in case. That went on for months and months because nothing was happening. The more nothing happened, the more vulnerable I felt.

The suspects had been arrested two weeks after Steve's murder. It was the day after Nelson Mandela, then leader of the ANC in South Africa, met Mr and Mrs Lawrence. I had seen him on the television saying, 'The Lawrence tragedy is our tragedy. I am deeply touched by the brutality of the murder – brutality that we are all used to in South Africa where black lives are cheap.'

It was incredible to hear Nelson Mandela talk about Steve. But it only reminded me of how much I'd lost and how much of an outcast I was. It felt horrible. At first I thought, How can they be meeting Nelson Mandela, and I'm not meeting him? I was there, I could have been dead. And what if it had been me who had died? Would the police have turned round and made a suspect of Steve? Would the media have made a national hero of my mum? Or would me and Mum not have fitted the profile of the perfect mother and son?

But I soon changed my mind. If I'd been on TV with Nelson Mandela, my face would have been better known and I would have been more vulnerable.

I needed a new solicitor – one who would look after me, direct me, rather than not be available when I phoned for advice. Somebody told me about Jane. 'There's a solicitor called Jane Deighton. She's very good, but she's white. Would you mind if she was white?'

'No,' I said. 'I haven't got anything against white people.'

I'd never had anything against white people. Then I remembered what I had said to my football manager just after Steve died: how I'd told him that I couldn't get in the car with white people; and how people had told me that I'd have to spend the rest of my life only with black people. But that thought had passed as quickly as it had arisen.

I was given Jane's number and made an appointment to see her. But just before the appointment came up, I heard terrible news that made a meeting with Jane unnecessary. It was 28 July 1993, three months after Steve's murder, and Neil Acourt and Luke Knight had just been released and the charges dropped. I left a message with Jane saying there was no point in meeting up.

I was devastated. I didn't know what more I could have done to help the police and to get justice for Steve. I'd done all that they asked: I'd been to all their meetings, listened to all the pathetic unfounded allegations that had been thrown at Steve and me, gone through the attack with them time and time again, been to all the ID parades, picked out who I believed took part, a couple of whom proved to be two of the chief suspects, and now it was all for nothing.

I felt even worse when I found out the suspects had been released partly because of the statement that Crowley made, which undermined my evidence completely. It was such a blow. I felt as if I'd been knocked out but was still conscious – incapable of action, but still feeling all the pain.

I sat down and watched the story of the suspects' release on the news. My friends went ballistic. 'Why don't we just go and take them out ourselves?' some asked. 'Duwayne, can't you point one of them out? Let's go and look for them.'

'No, I don't want to be involved,' I said. 'I know what will happen. Everyone's all hyped up now, but what about when the madness dies down and I'm just left on my own?'

For days afterwards I stayed in my room. I ran to the shop and ran back, and that was it. People used to give me weird looks. I didn't know what it was. Maybe it was because I was dressed in the same clothes all the time. Or maybe they just knew who I was. But what I did know is that it freaked me out. I became ultra-paranoid. If I was walking down the street and you looked at me more than twice, I would scan you up and down – shoes, trousers, top, hair colour – and make a note of the time, just in case.

I'd go home and note it all down. This person looked at me, time and place, and what they were wearing. I couldn't take any chances. I didn't know anybody around Brockley. If I saw the same person more than twice in a day, I thought I was being followed.

I barely saw my family or friends during this time. I kept away from them deliberately. Whenever I saw them they would all too often want to tell me what they thought about the case, who they thought had done it. I just wanted to keep away. The only safe place to me was my house.

Once I got in I followed the normal routine: speaker box behind the door, up to my room and lock the door. I sat facing the window just in case. The only other way to get into the house was through the window, which looked over the back garden. I knew that if anyone went in the back garden I'd hear the Indian man ranting and raving, because even the birds and the cat in the back garden upset him. But I still had to face the window, looking out every minute or so, constantly on guard.

I sat there watching TV day and night. I only slept when I had to sleep, and I always left the light on so nobody would know I was sleeping. I couldn't trust anybody. I'd heard that the Norris family had all sorts of contacts, and I knew that they wouldn't want their son going to jail as 'the Lawrence killer'. There were all sorts of rumours going around that they'd do anything to save him. Stacey Benefield had now admitted to being bribed not to give evidence about being stabbed by David Norris, and by a man he could only assume was Clifford Norris. I was waiting for the dreaded knock on the door. Clifford Norris could offer me money to keep me quiet, or perhaps he'd just have me permanently silenced.

My house was my fortress. I only felt safe behind my two locked doors. Occasionally, my friends would come round.

'You've got to come out,' they'd say. 'You can't just stay in the house. Have you become a hermit or something?'

But they didn't understand because they weren't in it. To really understand the fear, the paranoia, you had to be in it. I never thought the paranoia would leave me. Sometimes it's still there now – if I'm confronted and I think I'm going to have to defend myself. In those situations, I prefer to walk off, or run away if necessary. It saves me getting into any trouble because I know if I had a fight with someone and they got injured it would be all over the press. I'd be arrested and the police would try to discredit me and, by association, Steve. Back then I knew I couldn't have a fight with anybody because with the feelings inside me, the anger, the madness inside me, I'd go completely crazy, and that was just what the police wanted – then they would have been able to turn round and say, 'See, told you so: these boys must have been in a gang, they must have been fighting on the streets, and it must have been a revenge killing.'

Chapter 8

Jane and Me

I met Jane Deighton for the first time at Bexley Heath police station. It was October 1993, and, five months after the march against the BNP, I'd been arrested for criminal damage. I phoned Jane's office and told her what had happened. She said she'd be straight down, and I mustn't say anything to anybody until she got there. 'If they ask any questions, just say, "I'm not saying anything till my solicitor gets here."'

It took a couple of hours for Jane to arrive. I'd never been in a police cell before, and I didn't much like the experience. While I was waiting in the cell I thought back to the only time before Steve's murder I'd been arrested and taken to a police station – when I was nine years old. My friend Leon Brown and me were out on the street. We had nothing to do, just two kids loitering. And at the end of our block there was a cupboard where all the electrics for the estate were controlled from, and it was always open. We thought we'd go in and mess around with the lights – on, off, on, off, just mess about. So we opened the cupboard, and we saw a motorbike in there.

We thought we'd take it for a ride, so we both jumped on. I was the driver. I just thought I could do it, so I did. I had a BMX bike at the time, and I just felt I'd be able to work the motorbike. So I was on the front, Leon on the back, the engine roaring, racing around the estate. Some of the big boys saw us: 'Oi, Duwayne, come back, come back, give us a ride.' They chased us off the estate. So I had to go round on the main road to come back, and it was wicked. Me and Leon Brown on this little motorbike racing around Deptford.

Then on the last stretch to get home we passed a police car. The police car started turning round so we jumped off the bike and ran down the road. 'Shit, shit, shit, follow me,' I said to Leon. 'Follow me back to the estate.' But I ran off in one direction and he ran off in the other.

I looked back and saw the police officers stop. They were searching for Leon, who looked as if he was hiding behind a car. I ran straight back to my house, changed my clothes, came back out and sat back on the wall with everybody else. They were all asking, 'Where's Leon? Where's Leon?' I said I didn't know.

Ten minutes later the police came round looking for the other kid on the bike. So they walked past all of us and I sat there as if nothing was going on. But I was shit scared because I knew what would happen. So I just sat there until five minutes later another set of policemen came and knocked on our door, and said, 'We're looking for Duwayne Brooks.' My mum said, 'He's over there.' They came over to me, looked me over and didn't recognise me because I'd changed my clothes and come back out all smart.

So they went back to my mum and said, 'Is that him?'

'Yes.'

'Has he just been inside the house?'

'Yes.'

They came back over to me. 'Were you just riding a motorbike?'

I said I had been. Then they told me we were going down the police station.

We sat there for ages. So many things were going through my

mind. What was going to happen to me? Why did Leon grass me up? Why didn't he just follow me? If he had followed me straightaway he probably wouldn't have got caught. In a strange way, it's like what happened with Steve and me all those years later. Except, in this case we were in the wrong, and thankfully it didn't have a tragic ending.

I didn't know what to be more scared of: what the police were going to say, or the beating I would get back home if they didn't lock me up. Total fear. They called Leon and his mum, and they went into a room. He was in there for about fifteen minutes. He and his mum came out and went straight home. They didn't even look at me.

Then it was our turn. I went in, and this officer laid into me. 'Don't you ever do that again. This time we're going to let you off with a caution, but do this again and you'll get into serious trouble with the police, and get yourself a criminal record.'

It was going-home time, and I was dreading it. I didn't know what to do. My dad was supposed to be waiting outside in the car, and I thought, Should I try to run off or just take all the beating I can take when I get home?

Even worse than the beating was the teasing I would get the next day from the other kids on the estate. I could get over the beating – it was nothing compared to the teasing.

I got in the car and was dropped home. My dad never said anything to me. I couldn't understand it. He just dropped me off then I went inside. Nothing was said, and I went straight upstairs to my bed.

The next day, Mum started with the screaming. 'Why didn't you tell me they were coming after you? You think you're so smart, the way you came in and changed your clothes. Didn't you think Leon would have to say he was with you?'

I knew I'd never forget that day.

So here I was in a police station again, nine years on, and this time it was for a real crime. This time I could go to jail, a proper criminal, my life ruined. When I say proper criminal, I don't consider somebody who steals nappies for their child because they haven't got any money a proper criminal, or someone who's dying of hunger and steals some food. But there I was about to be charged for rioting.

My mind was running wild in that cell – how long would I be here for, had they got people to identify me? Then I heard somebody coming down, and a woman's voice. 'What's he doing in a cell? Can someone please explain to me what is he doing in a cell? Duwayne Brooks is the surviving victim of a racist crime . . .' That was the first time I'd heard anyone use the word 'victim' about me. '. . . And you've got him stuck in a police cell. Get him out of there.'

I couldn't believe what I was hearing. Was this how solicitors talked to the police? Are you allowed to shout them down when you're a lawyer? And do they always do as you tell them? Because that's what happened. I'd never seen the police act so quickly and with less argument.

As soon as Jane came along and said all that, they opened the cell doors. She walked in. 'How are you? Are you OK? You're sure? You haven't said anything to anybody have you?'

'No.'

'You haven't signed anything?'

'No.'

'OK then.' She looked around, back at the officers. 'Excuse me, I'd like to speak to my client. Is there a place we can go?'

They took us to an interview room and we talked. 'I just want you to say "no comment",' she said. 'Any questions they ask, it's just "no comment". They're going to interview you, and they'll ask you all sorts of questions, and all the answers you give will be "no comment".'

The interview began.

No comment.

'Don't you think it would be a good idea to cooperate for

your sake?' the police said. They were beginning to get frustrated.

No comment, no comment, no comment. The interview finished and I had to wait.

They told Jane that they wanted to search my house. Jane demanded that they get proper authorisation, so they gave up on that one and agreed to search Mum's house, which was the official address they had for where I lived. They were looking for a bobble hat that I had on at the march. They must have had pictures of me wearing it.

Jane told me that they would take me to my mum's house and ask for the hat and that I mustn't say anything in the car no matter what was said to me. She said she'd meet us at my mum's. Jane went ahead of us because the police wouldn't allow her in the car.

We headed off from the police station to Grove Park. On the way the officers kept talking about Jane. 'Who does she think she is, coming into the station and bossing people about? She's only a bloody solicitor. I know what her problem is – she hasn't had it for ages. Dumb cow. That's her problem. She needs someone to give her one, that'll calm her down a bit.' They were saying all sorts of stuff. 'We know it was you, Duwayne, whatever you or your solicitor wants to say, we know it was you, and we're going to get you. Why should you get away with it when everybody else would get done for it? What's so special about you? Who do you think you are?'

I was silent.

'If I was you I'd get that smirk off your face, if you know what's good for you.'

On and on and on they went with their abuse. I never said a word. The journey took about twenty-five minutes.

We parked up outside my mum's house and I stepped out, handcuffed, and walked up to the security door. The police pressed her number and we were buzzed in. Mum was just about to open her mouth when Jane butted in with a line that was becoming familiar. 'No, you don't have to say anything, Mrs Brooks. Don't say anything.'

It was obvious what Mum was about to say. The police knew what it was, but because she hadn't said it there was nothing they could do about it: they had to take this as my real address and search the premises as they had planned.

They started looking around. 'So where's Duwayne's room then?'

Again, Mum, who didn't have a clue what was going on, just said that I didn't live there, but occasionally stayed the night in my brother's room.

'Now which one is it?' Jane said. 'Show them which one it is, Mrs Brooks.'

Mum pointed to the middle room, but none of my clothes were in there. The police were forced to search for my hat, even though they knew this wasn't my room. They began to quiz Mum.

'When was the last time he stayed here then, Mrs Brooks?'

'You don't need to answer anything,' Jane said.

'Well, you're only making it worse for your son, you might as well answer,' said one of the officers. Then they started on Jane. They'd had enough of her. 'Get out of our business. Who do you think you are? There's no reason for you to be here. Please leave.'

'Do you want me to stay?' Jane asked my mum. 'Because I think I should stay.' Mum said yes.

The police argued. 'But you don't need her to stay, you're not under arrest. It's Mr Brooks that's under arrest, she doesn't need to stay.' They tried to build a brick wall between Jane and my mum, but Mum was having none of it. She was great.

I said I needed to go to the toilet because I was busting.

'Where is the toilet?' asked one of the officers. 'How far away is it?'

I said it was right there. There was a discussion about whether I could use the toilet or not. They checked to make sure there wasn't a window that I could escape from. Then they led me to the toilet handcuffed. They were doing all they could to humiliate me. They knew who I was, knew there was no escape, yet they insisted on me pissing in handcuffs. Perhaps they considered it revenge for me taking them to Mum's house.

I had stayed there once or twice recently, but I certainly didn't live there. They were fuming. They took me back down to the car. Jane said she'd meet me back at the station. All the way back in the car, it was the same old shit. 'You think you're going to get away with this, we know you don't live there. You think you're so smart, but we're going to get that hat and when we get that hat, I feel sorry for you.' These officers were so angry that I wondered whether I'd done something to them that I didn't know about.

If I remembered right, all I had done was go on the march. I was there supporting everybody else, and everybody else was there supporting me. Our message was simple – no more race attacks. What had I done that the officers could take it so personally, and could behave so vindictively? It was as if I had attacked them and they were getting me back. Did police officers behave like this with everyone, or just black people? Or just with me?

Back at the police station, they wanted to take me back to the cells.

'There's no reason to put him back in the cells; he can sit here,' Jane said. 'He's no danger to anybody, and why's he got those handcuffs on? There's no need to handcuff him. Please remove them.'

They did as she said.

Jane and the police were arguing about the law and the right they had to search another place, namely my place. Jane was fighting hard for them not to. In the end they had to back down.

It was all very well talking about her behind her back, but they seemed cowed by her when they were in her presence.

The police made sure they took their time doing the paperwork before letting me go. I hadn't actually been charged, but they told me I'd have to come back another time when they would present me with their evidence.

Jane dropped me off at home. I locked the doors and sat down on my bed. Fuck me, what had I really done? I kept going over it, and I couldn't remember doing anything really bad during the riot. I never smashed up any shops, I never beat anybody up, I didn't throw stones. What had I done? Was Nicola right that I shouldn't have gone there because I would be targeted and arrested for nothing? It was like a mantra running through my head: Nicola was right, Nicola was right, Nicola was right. When I tried to think of anything else I couldn't, because my head was blocked up with the mantra.

Perhaps the police were just out to get me because I kept saying that these white boys had called us 'nigger' before attacking us, and for some reason they didn't want to hear that? Perhaps they were angry because I had said again and again that we were standing there minding our own business when they'd attacked us, and they didn't want to believe that?

The whole world found out that I'd been arrested. Well, when I say the whole world I mean the whole family. My mum then told everyone she knew. She phoned people up crying, asking what was she going to do. That really pissed me off, because even though I was devastated I didn't cry. Crying is too easy. You can have a major problem, then have a good cry, and suddenly you feel much better. But nothing has changed. I cried a lot immediately after Steve's death and then trained myself not to. After the first couple of times I cried I felt too good, I felt happy and I shouldn't have been happy because nothing was resolved.

My family were on my back – are you OK, what are you going to do, what happened, what is Jane going to do, is she good enough? Other people told me to get myself a black solicitor; white people may be good and that, they said, but when it came down to it they didn't care about you personally. That attitude infuriated me.

'Why do I need someone to care about me personally? I don't want Jane to care about me personally, I want her to get me off,' I said. That's all I cared about. I didn't want to be best buddies with Jane. She was my solicitor and I'd been told she was the best, so I was sticking with the best. Why change to a black solicitor because they're black? How could that possibly benefit me? I reminded my 'advisers' that Imran was black and he hadn't shown up when I needed him most.

I went to Jane's office in north London to make a statement about what had happened at the riots. The police had sent her some of the evidence – pictures of me holding a stick, pictures of me just standing around, pictures of me walking. Apparently they had video footage of me, which they would show me at the station.

We went back on the bail-return date, to see the videos. Jane made it clear that she didn't want anyone taking pictures of me at the police station. She asked me if I had a hood or cap to wear. I said no. Well, I thought, at least they can't accuse me of being one of the rioters in hoods throwing stones and breaking windows at the demo.

When we arrived at the station, Jane told me to keep my head down at all times. What the police like doing is running out and taking snaps; if a policeman's acting funny, watch him just in case he runs over with a camera. She went ahead of me so she could look out for any video cameras inside the station and point them out to me, so I could hide my face when I walked past. Was this the kind of solicitor who didn't care? The kind of solicitor who was only interested in money and making a name for herself? I didn't think so.

I sat down in the police station, head down just in case, Jane standing in front of me, making sure nobody could run up and snap me.

The police took us to a room upstairs, Jane walking ahead of me. They sat me in front of a TV, with Jane next to me. They were on the right, at a 90-degree angle to me, waiting to see my reaction to the footage.

The tape started rolling. Jane had already briefed me – straight face, no smirks, no nothing. 'Do not give them the impression you recognise anybody, especially do not give them the impression you recognise yourself,' she said.

Fuck me! The pictures were so clear. Where were these people standing at the demo? I could see everybody's face clearly, and you could tell this was a copy of another copy of another copy of the tape. The original must have been Hollywood quality. Half my friends were on the tape, fighting, throwing stones, throwing bottles, removing sticks from the banners to use as weapons. It was fun to watch, but I had to keep a straight face. Two officers tried to hit somebody to the ground then a crowd of people converged on them and started whacking them and they had to run away. I didn't remember seeing that at Welling. Good, fucking good, I was saying in my head. But my face was straight.

Then I saw myself. A quick glimpse. But it was definitely me.

'Do you recognise that person there, Mr Brooks?'

They rewound it and pointed out the picture of me.

'No comment,' I said.

'You sure?'

'No comment.'

'OK.' They played some more. I was wearing blue. 'Do you recognise that person in blue, Mr Brooks?'

'No comment.' Four or five more times they pointed me out. No comment, no comment, no comment, no comment.

They paused the tape and pointed out my friends. 'Do you know this person, Mr Brooks? Do you know that person? You sure you don't? Look, look, you're here talking to this person.'

No comment, no comment, on and on. The way they put the questions to me, I wanted to give them an answer. I felt bad saying 'no comment' all the time. I didn't think it was right. But Jane was beside me.

An officer pressed the PLAY button and I saw one of my friends getting hit by a police officer in riot gear. (Of course, no police officers were charged with assault after the riots.) He was getting whacked on the back of his head – he put his hand to his head, took it away, looked back at the hand and saw the blood. I wanted to shout out how out of order I thought it was, but I couldn't.

Then they showed a close-up of my friend who had just been hit. 'Do you recognise this person?'

I was desperate to say yes because I wanted to complain about the officer who had just assaulted my friend on the tape. I went to answer and Jane gave me daggers. 'No comment,' I said. She breathed a sigh of relief.

The police continued to focus on my friends. 'Don't you think you should give us his name? We want to help him. You don't know, it might help your situation, too.'

'No comment.'

They reached the point where the pub was under siege. It's funny, the video footage didn't show when the guys came out of the pub, throwing stuff and hurling abuse, but it did show everyone attacking the pub in a rage. It made it look like an unprovoked attack.

You could see the people in hoods attacking the pub, but the racists were hidden inside.

I came into the picture, couldn't-care-less attitude, bouncing around. Then I ran over to a group of people who were trying to turn over a car.

'Watch this carefully, Mr Brooks. Let us know what you think is going to happen next.'

They paused the tape and pointed out the person they wanted

me to watch. Me. I'd forgotten about the car. But the video brought it back quick enough.

My face remained expressionless. I just watched myself run to the far side of the car and bend down, out of camera shot, to help lift it over. The car then got pushed over, and I'm seen running from that car, jumping on to another car and then running off.

Fucking hell, I thought. The officers were sitting there, watching my face so closely.

'Do you recognise that person? Is that you, Mr Brooks? It looks like you to us, Mr Brooks.' They said 'Mr Brooks' with such relish.

'No comment.'

'Doesn't that look like you, Mr Brooks?'

'No comment.'

They stopped the tape. 'Can you excuse us, Mr Brooks and Miss Deighton?' They always seemed to get Jane's name wrong. 'It's pronounced "Dyeton",' I always wanted to say. I wondered if they did it on purpose because they heard me say 'Dyeton' often enough, yet still they insisted on making her name sound like 'Deyton'.

They stepped outside. Me and Jane were sitting there. 'Don't say a word,' she said, 'they could have the room bugged.' There were some photographs on the side. Obviously, they had planted them there for me to have a look at. But I didn't move and we didn't say anything.

About five minutes later they came back in. 'Mr Brooks, we've got some pictures we'd like to show you, and we would like you to tell us who these people are.'

There were pictures of me standing up with a stick. I'd been carrying a placard and the sign had fallen off and I'd been left with just the stick. There were pictures of a number of other people walking with sticks, pictures of people throwing things, some of my friends, pictures of me talking to people.

They asked me questions about them. No comment. I don't know why they thought I would speak about my friends. Maybe they thought I'd be so scared of going to jail, which I was, that I would inform on my friends to get myself off. If they thought that, they didn't have a clue about me.

I was taken downstairs to the charge room. I stood around waiting for my turn. Jane told me to take a seat but to look out for any officers acting funny. She walked off to find out what was happening. She was away some ten minutes at the desk talking to the sergeant. She came back and stood in front of me again to stop anyone taking pictures. She bent down and said they were going to charge me. I was shocked, but I wasn't surprised.

There was no doubt that the pictures were of me. But being on a march and walking around with a stick was not a criminal offence as far as I knew.

'Mr Brooks, can you come over please?' At the desk I was formally charged with violent disorder and criminal damage. I was asked if I wanted to make any comment about the charges or had anything to say.

'No comment.'

They asked me to sign a statement written by the officers about what had taken place that day.

'No thanks,' I said.

After being formally charged I had to have my fingerprints taken, and a picture.

'No pictures,' said Jane.

'It's up to your client. If he wants to have his picture taken then we can have his picture taken.'

'He doesn't want his picture taken,' Jane said. 'Do you?'

'No, I don't want my picture taken,' I said.

I was brought into the room. Jane followed me in there.

'You're not allowed to be in here, Miss Deighton,' they said. 'Suspects only and police officers.'

'What nonsense,' she said. 'I've always stood in fingerprint rooms with my clients.'

'Well, you're not allowed in this one.'

So she had to stand at the door. The reason she wanted to come in was to stand in front of the camera.

'Oh, just sit here,' one officer said. Right in front of the camera. They already had my name on the name plate, and my date of birth and 'violent disorder'.

'No thanks, I'll stand,' I said.

They did my fingerprints and said they needed to go and get the stuff to wash my hands with, and I should just sit down here. I forgot and went over to the chair.

'Don't you dare sit down there,' Jane said. 'Turn round and keep your back to the camera.'

The officer then came back with nothing. He looked at the cupboard underneath where he had done the fingerprints and they had the cleaning stuff there. Obviously, it was a ploy to get me to sit down, and then they'd snap the camera. Once they had taken the picture, there would be nothing I could do about it. I couldn't take the film out. The police are allowed to take pictures of you against your will, but they are not allowed to physically hold you down in the seat and force you. Nor are they allowed to threaten you or use bail to blackmail you if you don't want to have your picture taken.

But that didn't stop them. 'Well, I don't think he should get bail if we can't have a picture of him,' the officers were saying to each other. Jane was having none of it. Neither was I.

I was bailed to appear at Bexley Magistrates' Court. We went through all the normal procedures, which meant a couple of attendances at court, and then I was committed to crown court trial, which was due to start in December at Croydon Crown Court.

In between times, the inquest into Steve's death was adjourned three times. They claimed that new evidence had turned up every time proceedings had been due to start, which is why we had all the adjournments.

Along the way, Jane had tried to get the Crown Prosecution Service to drop the charges against me. She had enlisted a psychiatrist, Dr Stuart Turner, to examine me. His conclusion was that I was suffering from post-traumatic stress disorder and was not in control of my actions on the march.

Jane sent the report to the CPS, but they wouldn't drop the case. While investigating how I came to be charged, Jane found out that the police knew I was on the march way back in May.

Strangely, the decisions to arrest and then charge me were made after the charges against the suspects were dropped at the end of July. Jane wanted to know why they hadn't charged me from the outset, and why it was only happening now. She couldn't get an answer. Obviously some senior detective had decided that it was time to get me and so went ahead with the arrest. Jane claimed this was an abuse of process, but neither the police nor the CPS would accept this.

They also refused to accept Dr Stuart Turner's report, so they decided to get one done for themselves. I had to visit one of their psychiatrists. I expected him to be independent, but just from meeting him for the first time, in the first five seconds, I could tell from his attitude to me, his body language, that he was hostile to me. He constantly questioned the answers I gave. He made it clear he thought I was lying. It felt like he had been given a rundown of the case, and had been told what to diagnose: the opposite of what Dr Turner had diagnosed.

I left him and went to the train station. I had been there about ten minutes when he turned up. He stood about fifteen yards from me. While standing there, he did not acknowledge me once, nor did we make eye contact. As the train pulled in he walked past me, as if he was going to the carriage with the most convenient exit for his stop. As he walked past me, he turned his head in the opposite direction so he didn't have to look at me.

Typical, I thought, only people who feel guilty or with an ulterior motive behave like this.

When we got the report, he sort of agreed with Dr Turner that I had post-traumatic stress disorder, but he said it wasn't a significant factor in my behaviour at the march. He decided I was in control of my actions and I knew what I was doing. That meant the CPS could argue in court that the case against me should proceed.

The time was getting near to the trial. It seemed to me that everybody else who had been found guilty had been given two years. Many of the people had been convicted on the flimsiest of evidence, in some cases being given a sentence just because they had been there and were seen running with sticks from the banners.

It wasn't a surprise, given that the jury would have been drawn from people who knew nothing about life in south-east London. They might have heard about the march, but I doubt that they knew why it took place and why people felt so passionate about what was going on. The jury would not have considered that kind of thing, and that was what was worrying Jane.

Jane didn't want the case to go ahead at all, and her fear was making me frightened. I had to be at the court for 9.30 a.m. Jane was worried that I wouldn't be there on time or that I may not be able to find it. She didn't want any judgement to be made against me because I had been late and appeared to have skipped bail.

I met Jane outside. She told me she was going to try to get the case thrown out on abuse of process because a decision not to prosecute had been made and then reversed once the suspects for Steve's murder had been released. She also argued that I was not in control of my actions on the day because of the post-traumatic stress disorder.

The trial started. I didn't really understand what was going on.

I just remember sitting there, looking glum. I'd never been in this situation before, and no friends or family were there with me. I didn't want them to be dragged through what I was going through. Also, I didn't feel like talking to anybody about how I felt. With no one being there, no one could ask me any questions.

Both arguments were put to the judge. I could see him listening intently, and every now and again glancing over to look at me. The whole court watched the videos. The judge looked disturbed. I didn't know whether it was because of my behaviour on the march or my demeanour in court.

He was probably thinking about what long-term effect going to jail would have on me and what effect it could have on any future case against the suspects in Steve's case. The judge ruled that even if the jury found me guilty, he was going to give me a conditional discharge. He advised the CPS that there was no point in going any further, and that it would be a waste of court time and public money.

Jane was happy. It was the best possible outcome. The prosecution barrister went to call headquarters and came back. The judge asked if he was going to accept his recommendation, and he said no, he was going to continue with the case. The CPS wanted a conviction.

Why were they so desperate? Did they want to turn me into a useless witness if Steve's killers were prosecuted? What would I look like to a jury, coming out of a prison cell?

I don't know whether the judge saw this. But in the end he 'stayed' the proceedings, which, Jane explained, was even better than the conditional discharge. She also explained to me why I had got off, and why we had won. I didn't really understand. All I understood was that I wasn't going to jail.

This case turned out to be the first of many battles against the police and their buddies in the CPS.

Chapter 9

Collapse in Court

It was August 1995, more than two years since Steve was murdered. Me and Martin, Steve's uncle on his mum's side, were going to visit a friend called Terry who lived in Plumstead. Terry, a jewellery designer, was making some chops (a big gold bracelet) and a special ring for him. We were cruising through Greenwich, on to Woolwich, when Martin got a call from his partner Melly.

'Is Duwayne with you?' she said. He passed over the phone. She sounded stressed. 'You need to be at court today,' she said.

'What court?' I said.

'The committal. You need to be here for the committal.'

'Yeah?' I said. I didn't really know what a committal was or what would be expected of me. Melly explained that the committal was the court case before the court case where the two legal teams lay out their arguments and the judge decides if there is enough evidence to make a go of it.

I remembered that that morning Melly had said to me she was going to Belmarsh Magistrates' Court, the one by Belmarsh prison. I'd asked her why she was going there and she'd said, 'Them boys are there. Don't you know about it?' She obviously hadn't realised that I needed to be there.

'No,' I'd said.

'Everybody's going to be there,' she'd said. 'The Lawrences, Imran Khan, the press.'

'Well, no one ain't told me.'

'So Jane don't know?'

'If Jane knew she would have told me, so she can't know.' The morning's conversation flitted through my head.

I also remembered that Imran had sent a letter, but he'd not said when I would be needed at the committal. That was also when he sent me a statement to sign – there was a blank space where I was supposed to put my address. He was then going to send this witness statement to the suspects. When I discovered that he intended to send them a statement with my address on it, I was petrified. Luckily, Jane made sure it never happened.

Melly said she had to get off the phone because she was in the court, and that I should get Martin to bring me down. I sat in the car thinking, Bring me down there? I hadn't even prepared. I didn't even know what was going on.

My phone rang. It was Jane's office telling me that I was needed at the court and could I make it there this afternoon. I said I'd try.

'Well, if you don't turn up the case might not be able to continue,' I was told.

I said OK. 'If you don't turn up the case might not be able to continue.' I was so important to it that nobody had told me to turn up till now. What was going on? It was just dumped on me with no notice. 'If you don't turn up the case might not be able to continue.' Then the boys would get off, and straightaway the blame would be back on to me. 'Why didn't you attend the committal?' I would be asked. Who would believe me if I'd said I hadn't known about it, and that the Lawrences' solicitors hadn't informed me? They had informed everyone else because all the press were there, yet they hadn't had the decency or common sense to inform my solicitor and given us at least seven days' notice so I could have prepared, at least mentally. I didn't really understand what a private prosecution was, but I knew that the CPS had said that there wasn't enough evidence to prosecute and that the Lawrences weren't happy with this. The Lawrences had then decided to bring the prosecution themselves, which they were allowed to do.

Surely, they must have realised that they would have had a better chance of getting a conviction for Steve's murder if they had given me more time to prepare. The whole situation was crazy. The Lawrences and their lawyers knew that I was their only hope of securing a conviction, but they were so hostile to me that they couldn't even bring themselves to talk to me – to explain what I would be going through and what evidence I was supposed to give two years after Steve's death – to help them win their case. A private prosecution was all well and good, a great story for the press, but it was pointless if it was going to be such a shambles.

This was the second time I would see the suspects, and they would see me. Everybody knew how scared I was. Ages ago, Jane had talked to me vaguely about the committal, and I had asked whether we could apply for a screen. But no date had been set, and it all seemed so far away.

I told Martin that we had to get to the court. We went to buy trousers and a shirt, and I got changed in the car. When we arrived, we were told by security that there was no parking space and that we weren't allowed in. I said, 'I'm Duwayne Brooks, I'm needed at the committal for the private prosecution.'

'OK, Mr Brooks, drive in and park over there.'

I walked into the court and there were two officers there to meet me. They had radio earpieces on. There were a lot of police in the court and around the grounds. I didn't know what high-profile case was going on. I never thought that all those officers were there for this case and for my safety.

I was frightened. I didn't know what kind of arena I was

stepping into. The police took me to a room and told me I could wait there. I said that Martin had to come with me.

'OK,' they said. 'He can't come up to the court with you, but he can wait here.'

'Why not?'

'Because no one's allowed up there. Only families and the victim's witnesses.'

I said, 'But he's my family.' Of course, he was actually Mrs Lawrence's family – her brother – but he felt like family to me.

'Yes, but we've got a number of family members upstairs already, and there's no space.'

I was getting worried, even though the police were there. Whenever I thought about the suspects, the thing that came to mind, the thing I'd been told again and again, was that these people have friends in the police. Even though the police were there I was terrified. I had no idea if they'd protect me, or whether they had something else planned for me.

They took me upstairs. There was a room with some people inside – white people, two women, one man. The police said that I could sit with them if I wanted to. But I didn't know who they were, so I sat outside the entrance to the room. Something was bugging me about them.

I asked the officer which court I would be going in, and he pointed to a door: the only door to the court. So who were those people in the room? An officer went in and said something about a 'Mrs Knight'. Then it hit me. The hair on the back of my neck stood up, my heart started beating fast, my hands started shaking. Mrs Knight? Mrs Knight? Luke Knight? Luke Knight's mum? They had put me with the families of the suspects. What were they trying to do to me?

'You OK, Mr Brooks?'

'Yes, thanks.' I wasn't.

My name sounded louder than normal. It sounded as if he'd shouted it out. Everybody looked around at the same time. I turned away. I didn't want to see anybody looking at me. But I could feel them looking at me.

I was hoping to be called so I could get out. I could feel my chest tightening. My breathing was becoming restricted. I was panicking. I didn't know what to do. Somebody high up had planned this. They must have done. They knew I was coming to court. They knew I was giving evidence, yet they had left me in the one place where the suspects' families were. And why would the families be there? The suspects couldn't come out of court this way. Why were they in this room? Was it for their security? And if it was for their security, why did the police have to put them in the same room as me.

I was called into the courtroom. In front of me to my right were the Lawrences' barristers. Then there was Mr and Mrs Lawrence. They both sat staring at me. I turned and looked at the magistrate. It was Cooper. I had seen Cooper on a number of occasions at Greenwich Magistrates' Court. Friends had been there when they hadn't paid fines and for minor criminal stuff. He was not the kind of person to give second chances. I remember once I had been sitting in the public gallery waiting for a friend's case to come up, and this guy had come in who hadn't paid his £50 fine for cannabis possession. He said he didn't have any money and he would start paying £2 a week next week when he got his giro. But Cooper wasn't having any of it. He instructed the security guards to take him downstairs and search him. They found £20 on him, and Cooper nabbed the £20 off him, took it off his fine and sent him home. Cooper told him that if he didn't pay his fine again and came back up against him, he would make sure he was taken to his home to have his stuff removed to pay the fine. I couldn't believe it.

Everyone in the public gallery was saying, 'Yeah, that's Cooper, don't mess around with him. If ever you come up against Cooper make sure you empty your pockets.'

When I looked up into his face it felt like he had recognised me. He looked at me. 'I know you' his look seemed to be saying.

Down the far right-hand side was the dock. It was below me, but I can't remember clearly because I tried not to look down there. I didn't want to make eye contact with the suspects. (The Acourts, David Norris and Luke Knight were there; Gary Dobson would be committed for trial later.) Even though I was desperate to see exactly what they looked like in detail, I was scared to. I didn't know how the shock of seeing them would affect me – seeing them close up and knowing it was the suspects for real.

There had been a couple of occasions when I believed I had seen them. I once saw a group standing outside Starburger in Greenwich. I was upstairs on the bus on the other side of the road. Another fleeting glimpse. I believed it was them, but I didn't know for sure. That was in September 1993.

Faces are not my good point. That's one of the flaws about me. That's one of the great flaws in this case – my inability to describe faces in detail.

On the other occasion, in December 1993, I'd been in a pub in Lewisham. Me and this guy called Heenan Bhatti, who was making a documentary for Channel 4, were in the pub when one of the suspects walked in. Tall, slim, short black hair, cut on his nose. I didn't see his face at first, only his body, and there was just something about him. It attracted my attention instantly. I was drawn to him. And he was drawn to me. His body language when he saw me – he knew something was wrong, I knew something was wrong.

Then his eyes gave him away. It is him. It *is* him. What do I do? For months I'd been racking my brain to get the clearest picture of these people because I'd seen them on the night, clear, barefaced – I'd tracked them all the way from Eltham Station. (They had all denied being in that area, but on television David Norris admitted leaving his girlfriend's place just up the road from there. So they had walked down the back, come out of Eltham Station and walked up the road.)

I had tracked them from the roundabout across the road up to the point where they ran across. I'd seen them all, but I hadn't paid attention to them all. In fact, before they shouted out I hadn't paid any real attention to what they looked like. Why should I have? I wasn't in fear of attack from them. I was frightened of being in Eltham, but at that point they were just a group of boys walking up the road.

But here was one of them in my face, clear as daylight. He and a friend of his, who was much shorter than him, with blond hair, went over to the bar and bought a drink. He knew I was watching him and he looked over. I said to Heenan, 'I'm sure that's one of the boys who was there.' Everybody had told me the names, and it just came out: 'That's Jamie Acourt.' I didn't think about it: my brain just matched the name to the body. Heenan didn't believe me. 'Where? You're joking!' It was him. I didn't know it was him, but my body knew it was him. My body went into fear mode.

They sat down near the pool table. Me and Heenan were nearly finished. I said to him, 'Let's get him!'

'What?'

'Let's get him!' I said. In the back of my mind I thought they might be carrying knives, but we were in a public place so if an incident took place there would be plenty of witnesses.

'Let's talk to him,' Heenan said. 'Let's get him over here to play pool and we'll talk to him.'

Heenan went over to them and asked them if they wanted to play doubles. He came back.

'I don't want to play pool with him,' I said. 'I want to whack him over the head with a cue.' Suddenly, all the anger and frustration over what had happened welled up inside me.

'No, no, no. They're coming over in a minute. Let's talk to them. Let's get some information out of them.'

Obviously they didn't recognise me, but I was sure they knew something was odd. They might not have known that I was Duwayne Brooks, but I think they realised I had known Steve.

They came over. We were playing pool. Heenan was talking to them, I said 'all right' and stuff, but the conflict was there – two people who hated each other so badly having to play a doubles game. There was so much hatred there on both sides.

The more Heenan spoke to him, the more defensive he became. I was watching him like a hawk. I tried not to, but I couldn't help it. It was like I wanted to strike, and was just picking my moment. Heenan asked him his name, and he didn't say anything straightaway, and looked down at the floor and said, 'Keith.' Fucking liar, I thought. His friend had called him something else earlier on, but I hadn't caught it.

The game was over and I said to Heenan that I needed to make a phone call. We walked outside. I tried to phone Martin, but I couldn't get through. I wanted him to bring some people down. While I was out at the phone box I noticed one of my friends called Stodge. Stodge used to play football with me at my club, the Elms, in Catford Hill. He was a great defender, and his brother played in the 2002 World Cup for Nigeria. Stodge was as good as him but never got the major break.

Heenan wanted to talk to them more. 'Let's go back inside then, but I'll call in my people,' I said.

'No. It's going to look funny if we walk in, walk out, walk in, walk out. They'll wonder what we're up to.'

'OK,' I said. 'We'll follow Stodge in.' So we went in and I sat down with Stodge. It was obvious they'd found out. They became aggressive towards Heenan.

I could see it, feel it. I told Heenan I was leaving. I walked out. I still couldn't get through to Martin's phone. I went home the long way just in case they had called anybody to follow me.

Heenan called the next day and asked if I was all right.

'Yeah, why shouldn't I be?' I said. But I didn't feel all right.

'Oh, just after the incident last night. I wanted to know if you'd recovered because you were really upset.'

'I was mad Heenan, not upset. Mad, livid, fuming. That's what I was. Not upset.'

He told me what happened after I left. They had become aggressive, and he felt that he had better leave. At the side of the pub was an alleyway that brought you up to Lewisham Station. You could walk round the road, but the alleyway was much quicker. Heenan walked up the alley. While he was walking he turned round and saw that both of them were following him. He said they pulled out knives and he ran. They chased him up to Lewisham Station where he jumped into a black cab and shut the door. They were standing at the cab rank pointing at him. He couldn't hear what they were saying, but he said it looked like a threat. He said he was so scared. His body was shaking and he didn't even tell the cab driver where to go, just to get out of there. It was only when he had calmed down a bit and got his thoughts together that he was able to tell the cabby where he was going.

He had never been in a situation like that before. He tried to explain the fear of running up that alleyway and jumping in the cab. He then began to realise how scared I must have been on the night of the attack. He said that if he hadn't seen them in the pub there was no way he would have been able to recognise them again. When someone's chasing you with knives you don't have time to look at their faces and say, yes, they have this mark and that mark, you just run for your life. He had experienced it. For fifteen seconds, it might have been him running up that hill with Steve.

I told him to tell the police. He said he would. He would make a statement as long as I made one. I said of course I would. I never saw Heenan again after that. I spoke to him a couple of times, but that was it. 'Perhaps we should have called the police on the night,' he said.

That night was like an answer to a question, but it put my mind into more turmoil. It made me try to piece bits together, and I shouldn't have done that. I should have let my conscience tell me, my body tell me.

Back in court Michael Mansfield started questioning me. He was the high-profile brief employed by the Lawrence team. He had a reputation for fighting against injustice. He went through the whole night building up to the incident. I didn't know why we had to go through it in such detail. As far as I was concerned we had to go to the start of the incident itself, at the bus stop waiting for the 122 to come round the corner.

He asked me about the attackers. As soon as he said it, the one who came into my head was the one I'd seen in the pub. He was stuck in my mind. I couldn't answer instinctively. I was desperately trying to remember what I had said before and be consistent with that. But it was hard. I couldn't remember exactly what I had said before, and what these people were looking for. It was more than two years since I'd made the statement. And the slightest contradiction was going to get me in trouble. I went out of my mind.

I was asked who was the stabber. Looking back, I can see now that I described the boy we saw in the pub. I don't know why I did. I couldn't stop myself. I knew it was not the person I'd seen running across the road who had stabbed Steve, but this was the only person I could describe in detail. He was the only person I could put it on, so I said it was him. As soon as I said it, I knew what I'd done. I could hear my mind speaking to me: No, no, no, that's wrong, that's wrong. I wanted to take it back, but it was too late.

The moment I said it I felt crushed. I'd let everyone down. It was so obvious.

I kept being asked how far did I run before I looked back? What did I see? Did I really see their faces? I saw all their faces, but I didn't look at all their faces. I wasn't looking at one individual person. I saw them all when they ran across the road, but

I didn't have time to look at all their faces. The people at the bus stop weren't in fear of their lives, like I was, and they had seen everything that had taken place, and even they couldn't pick anyone out.

The defence twisted me here and there on this fleeting-glance evidence. It was obvious that it was a fleeting glance. I'd never claimed anything else. Anybody who had read my statement would have known. The way I described it, the looking back, was a fleeting glance, but I had seen it regardless.

They went on to the fact that I had said I didn't see the knife go into Steve. I didn't see the knife go into Steve because I didn't know it was a knife at the time. But I had described an object coming down in the same manner that he had been stabbed.

They then read the rest of the statement. I had said that Steve screamed. I felt the court go funny. I knew instantly that few people had known that before – only those who had seen my statement. I heard Mr Lawrence make a funny noise, then I could hear rustling. I looked up from the corners of my eyes and saw him rush out of the court. Everybody's attention was drawn to Mr Lawrence for that second or two, and I felt light. As soon as the eyes were back on me, I felt heavy again.

They went on questioning me, and then I heard a scream. Mr Lawrence was crying outside. They halted the court to see what was happening. I wanted to get out of the seat; get out full stop. I felt so vulnerable. I would have loved to have run out of the building and run and run and run and run. But I knew I couldn't leave.

They started again on the statement I had given after Steve's murder. They returned to the description of the stabber in my original statement. The description I had given was wrong: it was not the stabber. I had just suggested to Mansfield that Jamie Acourt was the stabber – that was wrong. But the description I gave first time was also wrong. In my original statement I described the boy who had chased me up the road as the stabber, because he was the last person in striking distance of me.

I had contradicted myself big time. I'd given different descriptions of the stabber – they were all confused together in my head. But that was for the barristers to deal with. Mansfield had to work his way through it. If they had really wanted me to do my best, surely the Lawrence team would have spoken to me a long time before the committal rather than bringing me in at the last second.

They went on to the Crowley stuff. Crowley had already made statements about me, which I had disputed. He'd claimed I'd been told who to look for at an ID parade. They knew I'd spoken about the riots; how I was mad, I was angry, I wanted to go there for revenge and how people had fed me the names. But names don't help, names are not stuck on people's faces. Everyone was talking about what the suspects might have looked like, but no one knew. There wasn't a week that passed without somebody telling me, 'I know somebody who knows what Jamie Acourt looks like', 'I know somebody who knows what Knight looks like', 'I know somebody who knows what Norris looks like.' The more I told people to stop telling me, the more people told me. Even though I wasn't listening to them, subconsciously I was hearing. And that's what made it so hard. Despite all this, no one I knew had a clue what the suspects looked like.

Again, I was asked about the stabber. Again, I found myself describing the person I'd seen most recently – Jamie Acourt. They made the point that I hadn't identified him as the stabber before. I knew I hadn't. I said I didn't know why, but I did know why. He wasn't the stabber, but he was the last person on my mind, and I just froze and said it was him.

The questioning finished and Cooper said I could leave. I got up and walked straight out. I didn't look at any of the people in the gallery. I walked over to the window and looked out.

'Mr Brooks, are you ready to leave, sir?'

'Yes.'

They took me downstairs. Martin was waiting for me. We got

in the car and drove off. The press were waiting at the car-park exit gates. I got down and put my coat over my head. I didn't want any pictures of me. They had classed me as the main witness, and I was in fear. The main fall guy as well as the main witness.

We drove into Plumstead and Martin said I could come up now. I was crying. I had never felt pressure like that before. We drove straight back to New Cross, where Martin lived.

Cheryl, Mrs Lawrence's and Martin's sister, had phoned Melly. Mrs Lawrence had said she didn't want Martin back at the court again. They were implying that Martin wasn't a 'good sort', and that's why they didn't want him there, even though they knew he was there because I was scared and I wanted someone there I believed could protect me. But they didn't want him to be seen around them. I was there to help the case, and he was there to help me, but they didn't seem to care. That was their problem. If you didn't do things their way, they weren't interested. That's how they had always been. And I had never conformed to their expectations, so they didn't want Steve to talk to me.

For days I just sat down and thought about what I had said. I was so confused. Everyone was talking about me. Whenever I went into a room people started talking about me and the rumours that they'd heard.

I was searching my mind for answers but was being blocked all the time. I didn't understand what was happening to me, why I was behaving like this. Dr Turner, the psychiatrist I was seeing, said it was stress.

This post-traumatic stress disorder was killing me. It made me say things that I knew were wrong. It helped to block information that was deep down, buried in my memory.

I had played perfectly into the hands of the defence barristers. They break you down, then show you your contradictions, then they make you seem unreliable, and once you are seen as unreliable the case collapses.

A few days after the committal I found out that another witness, known as Witness B, had given evidence after me. I felt relieved because I had heard that he was at the scene – I didn't know where and I didn't know at what time, but I was told he had been at the scene. If I hadn't seen him, then the suspects might not have seen him. I was hoping that he would be clearer as to who was there and who did what. None of the other witnesses at the bus stop had picked out anybody.

I was told that Witness B had been given a screen. So why was I not given one? After all, surely I was as much at risk as Witness B. I thought it was odd that my name was mentioned everywhere, and yet Witness B, who was not attacked and was probably not seen by the suspects, could remain anonymous and hidden from the defence.

I must be being set up here, I said to myself. Nobody wants to protect me, nobody wants to ensure my safety, everyone is telling me I'm OK, the police are telling me they need a picture of me, but this other witness was being hidden from everybody. What did he know more than me? Did he see them after, or did he see them before? Was he in the house with them, or was he walking with them earlier on? Was he in the attack, or was he there but didn't take part? All these questions stressed me for days.

Witness B also changed his evidence. I never got to see any of his statements, but that was what I was told. It was just the pressure. Everyone was under pressure.

I spoke to Jane about the committal. She asked me how I thought I had done. I said I'd done well, I'd done fine. But I was hiding it from her, and hiding it from myself. She asked if it had been tough, and I said yes.

'Well, what did you expect?' she said. 'You've got a team of top barristers questioning you about this case. Nobody is going to make it easy for you. It's going to be hard.'

Jane had asked Michael Mansfield if I'd done well and he had told her that I had. He hadn't told her that I'd completely changed the attacker again. He hadn't told her that I'd contradicted myself again. He just said to her I'd done well. But Mansfield knew it had been a disaster.

The newspapers all reported how Mr Lawrence had collapsed when he heard me describe how Steve had screamed. This was when people began to realise that the relationship between me and the Lawrences was odd. How can this be the first time the Lawrences have heard the evidence of Duwayne Brooks? Questions were being asked. Why hadn't Duwayne told the Lawrences what had happened? Why hadn't they been prepared to hear what took place? Don't the Lawrences and Duwayne Brooks speak? Those close to us knew that we didn't speak, but this was the first time that the public began to talk about it.

Chapter 10

The Private Prosecution

It was April 1996. I had received the summons for the private prosecution months ago, but I had put it to the back of my mind. I didn't want to think about it, let alone give evidence. What would I say? What could I possibly say that would get the suspects convicted? Everybody knew that I had just glimpsed them: after all, the attack was reckoned to be over in seventeen seconds. Yet everybody was relying on me.

The Lawrences and their legal team had decided on the private prosecution as a last resort. Yes, it was now three years since Steve had been killed, but surely it was a bit premature for last resorts – there was always the chance that new evidence would emerge, and if this trial failed, as the law of double jeopardy stood, that was it – the three defendants, Neil Acourt, Luke Knight and Gary Dobson, could never be charged again for the murder of Steve. Jamie Acourt and David Norris had been discharged at the committal.

The only evidence they were relying on was mine – what I said I'd seen, or what I believed I had seen. None of the others at the bus stop had made a significant contribution to the evidence. I couldn't believe that nobody had picked out anybody else at the time. It was strange. Equally strange was the fact that

Joey Shepherd had decided not to go to any more ID parades and the police couldn't do anything about it. Joey was the lad who'd been at the bus stop, and had taken the bus – he saw the incident from the bus stop and ran straight to the Lawrences' house to tell them Steve had been attacked.

He had agreed to be a witness, but had a bad experience at the ID parade when a police officer addressed him by his name as he was walking up and down. He was convinced that this had been overheard by one of the suspects or one of the suspects' lawyer and he now refused to be a witness.

I got a call on Friday night. The prosecution said they had been trying to call me all week at Melly's house. They could have contacted me via Jane, but that must have been too logical for them. The Lawrences had given out Melly's number, and they were calling me there. Apparently, the court case was starting on Monday, and nobody knew whether I was coming or not. Well, why did they wait till the last week to ask?

'Are you going to be attending court on Monday?'

'No,' I said.

'Why not? Don't you want to see justice for your friend?' Not for 'you and your friend', just for 'your friend'. 'You're the main witness, we're relying on you.'

'But hold on. What happened to police protection? Was I not guaranteed police protection through the case?'

'Oh, that's not a problem, Mr Brooks. If you want protection, we can organise that for you. It may not be done for the first day, but it shouldn't be a problem after that.'

'No,' I said. 'That's not good enough. If I'm giving evidence on Monday, I should have police protection from now. What if something happens to me?' But nobody seemed interested in what could happen to me. They just wanted to hear what I had to say. Nor did anyone seem to care whether I could give evidence – whether I'd survive it. The prosecution arranged a meeting with me for that weekend.

The prosecution needed to speak to me about the notes taken by Imran and his assistant at the hostel back in 1993. Apparently it had caused confusion because Imran's friend had not written down exactly what I had said. In fact, he'd written down something totally different from what I'd said. So here I was having to make a statement about some notes made three years ago! What were they doing all this time? If it was so controversial, why hadn't they done anything about it beforehand?

I met some people working for Imran's office and we drove up to Blackheath where I had to make the statement about the notes. When I saw them I couldn't believe it. The notes written by Imran's assistant-cum-mate dumped the police in it and dumped me in it. They seemed to say that the police had shown me witness statements describing what the suspects looked like. Now that was impossible because at that time I'd not seen any statements – I don't think any had even been taken. Fair enough, the police were right to be worried. If it had been true, it would pretty much invalidate any evidence I gave. So why hadn't Imran's team dealt with it till now? Simple. Because they were incompetent. As Imran made so clear at the public inquiry, when he had to account for the mistakes he made, he had barely two years' experience as a practising lawyer at the time, and his assistant-cum-mate had none. And did it show. In the end, Imran made an out-of-court settlement and apologised to me in 1999.

The notes also spoke about Elvin, whom Steve used to hang about with at school. It claimed that I'd said Elvin always used to go out with white girls. What! Where on earth did they get that from? Only they could answer.

It was becoming clear to me that this ridiculous fiction had to be declared to the defence. I was speechless. It was going to be near impossible to get a conviction anyway, but what chance did we have when Imran's team was discrediting the police and main witness – me – with false statements? The defence had already got Crowley saying I'd been told what these people looked like and who to pick out – not what I'd said at all, but it was a police officer's word against mine. Now I could imagine the defence flourishing a piece of paper on which I say the police had shown me other witnesses' descriptions of the suspects. Nothing could be more devastating.

They said they wanted me to make a counter-statement. That was the last thing I felt like doing. It seemed to me that Imran should clear up his own mess. Anyway, I did make one, explaining that it was impossible for me to have seen any witness statements at the time and the had Elvin muddled up with someone else.

I also had to sort out the police protection – I refused to go to court without a police escort. In hindsight, I should have just stayed wherever I wanted to stay at night and made my own way there. That way I would have been safer, and no one would have known where I was.

It was the night before the trial and I couldn't sleep. I didn't have a clue how to behave in such a situation, and I didn't know anyone who had been in a similar situation who could advise me. I was shit scared. The biggest British court case of the decade was about to take place, and everything was resting on me. All I could hear was 'Duwayne Brooks, the main witness, Duwayne Brooks, the main witness'. No one referred to me as the victim who had been attacked with Steve. Occasionally news reports would refer to me as the main witness who had survived the brutal attack on Stephen Lawrence, but nine out of ten times I was simply the main witness.

I made arrangements to meet the police escorts at the top of the road at 9 a.m. We needed to get to court early just in case anything happened. I met two white guys at the top of the road, and they gave me the password we'd agreed. We had decided we needed a password in case anybody else tried to pick me up.

We got in the car and they asked me if I was OK. I said I was fine.

'All prepared are we?'

'Don't know. Don't know what I've got to be prepared for.'

I sat in the back of the car and we drove to the Old Bailey. I had this dull sick feeling in my stomach. What was I letting myself in for? How could I control what was going to happen now? How could I stop myself from breaking down in court in front of everyone?

Everybody was going to see what I looked like now. Everybody would know who this main witness was. My big fear was that I'd be attacked on the street. At the committal I had said that I wanted to give evidence with blinds, so that nobody in court could see me. But the court wasn't having it: 'Why do you need blinds? Nothing's going to happen to you.'

We arrived at the Old Bailey. I felt so small, like I was a nobody, flanked by these two police officers. They dropped me off at security. I could hear the protection officers telling the court security I was 'Duwayne Brooks, main witness in the Stephen Lawrence case'.

'Oh, you're Duwayne Brooks?' they said. 'Don't worry, everything will be all right.' The more I was told everything was going to be all right, the less confident I felt it would be. I walked through the special barrier – a cylindrical door closed automatically on me, and for a second it was like I was trapped in a vacuum. Then the other cylindrical door opened to let me through – money, keys, anything metal, all came out of my pockets and into a plastic tray as they scanned for nasties. No bleep. I'd passed the first test.

They took me up to the second floor and into a small room. I saw one of the Lawrence barristers, a short, tubby man called Kamlish. He asked if I was OK, told me not to worry, everything would be all right. I worried more.

Fear. The fear of having to sit in the witness box, the fear of being identified. I was terrified. What would happen if I made another mistake? I'd seen it on TV. Make a mistake and the defence barristers destroy you. That's their job, and any self-respecting barrister loves making mincemeat of you. I'd already been warned that these boys had three top barristers defending them, and they would do their best to screw up my head. Again, I was told to sit in the room until I was needed. Eventually I was taken down to the main witness room, outside Court Number 1. The longer I was there, the more uneasy I felt – cold, freezing, shivering, not knowing where to look, what to do with myself.

Reg came along. Reg was a police officer and part of the Lawrence team, but now he was assigned to me to make sure I was OK and that all my needs were catered for. He asked me if I'd been to the Old Bailey before. I said no.

'Have you heard about Court 1?' I'd not heard about Court 1, but I had heard about all the big cases at the Old Bailey. 'You're in Court 1. Court 1 is where all the major murder trials take place.' I think he was trying to make me feel important. It didn't do much for my nerves.

The area we were standing in was like a church but without the benches and statues of Jesus and Mary. The walls were covered in murals and portraits of important people. Famous judges, I assumed. It reminded me of churches I'd been into where the great and good look down on you from the ceiling, making you feel that they're discussing you – 'Ah, now who's this young man coming before me today?'

I felt I was being watched. My head was pounding. Reg gave me a tour of the hall with a breakdown of who the portraits were of and how they'd earned their place there. Then we started this little game. He said the painter had always painted his face somewhere in the paintings. So we picked out the first one, and the second one, and third. Then it started to get hard. The fourth painting was of a bunch of monks, and it turned out the painter had swapped one of the monks' faces for his own – he was a little bald-headed white guy with a smirk.

Reg asked if I wanted him to walk into the court with me.

'Are you allowed to do that?'

'Yes, I can walk you as far as the witness box where you'll have to get in.' He got a piece of paper and mapped out the court for me, describing where the judge would be, the jury, the suspects, and the public.

'Everyone will be able to see me,' I said. I don't know why, but I was shocked.

'No one's allowed to take any pictures of you, though,' said Reg.

That wasn't much comfort. The suspects, their friends and family would all see me.

'What d'you want to do at lunchtime?' Reg said.

'I don't know. What is there to do? I need to get my mind off court, I need to get out of here, I can't stay here. Where can we go? Where's the nearest arcade? I need to concentrate on something else.' That was the only way to get my mind off the court: play arcade games.

'King's Cross,' Reg said. 'We'll get a tube or taxi down to King's Cross, and play some machines down there.'

'OK. But I haven't got any money to pay for a taxi.'

'Don't worry about it. I'm here to look after you, Duwayne, I'll pay for that. I'll even pay for the machines for you.'

'No thanks,' I said. 'I'm only going to be playing a couple of games anyway. I can pay for that.'

Lunchtime came quick. The morning had been taken up with legal argument. Apparently, it was over my ID evidence, and what I was supposed to have said to Crowley. Predictably, the defence argued that the evidence was contaminated and were trying to get it thrown out.

We jumped into a taxi and headed straight for King's Cross. First McDonald's and then the arcade. I played Sega Rally for about fifteen minutes, and then it was time to go back. Reg said we couldn't be back late because we'd get into trouble.

I was pissed off. Part of me didn't give a damn if I was late because no one had had the decency to tell me what I was letting myself in for. Except for Reg. It was only through speaking to Reg that I began to realise how desperate the situation was.

I had heard they didn't have any evidence, but I didn't know if that was true. Perhaps they were playing clever, keeping their cards close to their chest. But Reg made it clear that with no forensics, no camera shots, and no real eyewitness to the event, they really were depending on me. If the defence succeeded in getting my evidence thrown out, they'd be laughing. And my account of events – which had already been rubbished after I got confused at the committal, and had been rubbished before that by Crowley – was the same evidence they were relying on for the murder convictions.

As soon as we got back to court, the police said my auntie wanted to see me. I said OK, to let her up. She'd been stressing me for ages, telling me, 'You can't go to court, it's a trap. They're going to use you, break you down and then blame you.' I didn't know whether to believe her, but it did feel that I was being used.

She burst into the room. 'What is your solicitor doing about this? You need to change your solicitor. What is she doing about it?' she demanded.

I told her that Jane had already made it clear that I was not fit to give evidence, but she didn't have the power to stop the case. And what would have happened if she did have that power? 'Duwayne Brooks, the only witness, didn't give evidence on the advice of his white solicitor, Jane Deighton.' All hell would have broken loose. If Mr and Mrs Lawrence wanted to risk blowing the prosecution by pushing ahead now, knowing I was unfit, who was I to fight them? It was their decision. Steve was their son.

Dr Stuart Turner, the psychiatrist, had already confirmed that I had post-traumatic stress disorder. But as far as I was concerned,

I didn't have any disorder, I was just sad, I just wanted to be by myself at home, chilling, thinking. That was what they called a disorder: when you don't want to get involved in anything, when you're not interested in what goes on around you because you're in your own world. You still have to communicate with other people, but you don't want the long conversations you used to have. You don't want to talk for more than five minutes because people start asking you all sorts of questions and you switch off because you're not interested. They're talking, but you can't hear them; you're answering, but you're not taking it in – that was the disorder.

Dr Turner had written a report saying that I was unfit to give evidence. The Lawrence team had the report, but they weren't interested. They were carried along on this crazy wave of optimism, talking to the press as if they knew they were going to get a conviction because they had me. I was stuck. Which way could I turn? How could I please everybody and get myself through this situation? I couldn't. Refuse to give evidence and walk away, and I'd be the scapegoat. Mess up the evidence, and I'd be the scapegoat.

Yet, they knew all along that I'd only glimpsed the boys – how could it have been any other way? – the attack was over in seconds. And many judges wouldn't have allowed such glimpsed evidence anywhere near this court.

I kind of knew what my aunt was going to say when she came up the stairs, but I had to hear her out. Reg was in there, but she just started. I asked Reg to leave because this was a private matter. She came straight out with it.

'You know what they're doing don't you?' She didn't give me time to answer. 'They're planning for you, that's all they're doing, planning for you. Everybody knows they've got no evidence – it's just your word against theirs, and there is no way those boys are going to get convicted. They're just using you, and at the end of it all they're going to blame you.'

'What can I do?' I said weakly.

'Let the trial collapse,' she said. 'It hasn't started yet so the boys can always be arrested again.'

How could I let the trial collapse and walk out of the court? Although no one could understand what I was going through, I knew that nobody would ever speak to me again. I would lose all my friends and be a laughing stock. 'Duwayne Brooks refused to give evidence against those accused of killing his best friend.' Nobody would have cared that I was terrified, and that I knew it was pointless or, worse, damaging. They would have just said that I'd refused to give evidence. And then the rumours would have started – maybe he was paid, maybe he was bought off, which was something the *Voice* newspaper mistakenly printed.

I just sat there listening as she went on and on and on. I knew she might have been right – I was not part of this private prosecution, I was not privy to any information, they hadn't told Jane anything. As far as the Lawrence team were concerned they were doing it by themselves. The best way to do it would have been through a civil prosecution for which the burden of proof is lower – that's how O. J. Simpson was finally found responsible in the US for the killing of his wife – and then go for a private prosecution.

My auntie, who like many other family members came to court to support me when I needed it, finished by telling me that I needed to be strong. 'Stick to what you said. Don't let them deter you. Don't let them make you change your mind,' she told me. 'Go into this trap with your eyes open. If it was me I wouldn't do it. If I was your solicitor, I would stop you. If there was any way of stopping this trial I would do, and then regroup and do it again.'

But that doesn't help me now; not now I'm at their beck and call, I thought to myself.

Worse was to follow. Elvin came up to me. We'd hardly seen

each other in the years since Steve's murder.

'You're going to get punched in your mouth. I should punch you in your mouth now,' was the first thing he said.

I stood there, stunned. I couldn't believe he was talking to me like this. This idiot who should have been there to support me was saying to me I was going to get punched in my mouth.

He was ranting. 'How could you say that about me? How could you say I was going out with white girls? You're making me look stupid, I wasn't going out with a white girl.'

'What are you talking about, Elvin?' I said.

'Didn't you give Imran a statement saying I used to go out with white girls?'

'No.'

'So why has Imran written it down then?'

'Don't you think you should ask him?'

'I've seen it,' he said. 'As soon as I came into court this morning I had to make a statement.'

Just as with me, Imran had waited three years to get Elvin to make a counter-statement – on the day the case was starting! What kind of operation was he running? I tried to explain to Elvin that Imran had made mistakes, and that I'd also had to give him a new statement over the weekend. But Elvin was too worked-up to listen. I was so mad, but I didn't have the energy to do anything. I just watched him, thinking, What am I doing here, giving evidence that is going to be ripped apart, while best friend Elvin Oduro who knows nothing is threatening to punch me in the mouth about a statement I never made?

'That's why the Lawrences don't like you, because you tell lies. All you do is tell lies.'

Can anybody tell me what lies I have told? I thought. All I said to Elvin was, 'Don't worry about it.'

'When you see me on the street don't talk to me again,' he said finally. 'Just don't talk to me again. I have never been out with a white girl. You're the white-girl lover.'

What could I say? I hadn't said anything in the statement about him going out only with white girls, but what was the problem if I had and he did? I talk to white girls, I fancy white girls – I don't see the problem. I like anybody who looks nice. I'm not one of those who say, I don't like white girls; I don't like white people; I don't talk to white people when I'm drawing their giro and they're paying my rent because I've not got a job. fools.

At court, I didn't want to speak to anyone any more. I told everybody to go. I was stuck. Well and truly stuck.

I kept thinking back to the committal when everything I said had been rubbished. What was the point of going into the Old Bailey to be rubbished again? If I was a suspect, I would have been feeling so smug. They must have been thinking, The only other witness has been dealt with and he ain't gonna speak, and the so-called main witness hasn't got a clue. If I was a suspect, and had studied the evidence, I would have been laughing. How on earth didn't the Lawrences see this?

The day went on, and I was told I wouldn't be giving evidence. I felt like somebody had just got off my chest. I could breathe properly. I could feel myself properly. Blood started tingling back in my fingers and my toes, my arms and my legs.

'Wait around and we'll take you to the hotel where you'll be staying,' a police officer told me.

'OK.'

'We'll be bringing you tomorrow because you're expected to give evidence first thing in the morning.' I forgot to breathe. The fear returned, only more intensely. It was definite now – I had to give evidence. I had been expecting to today, but I had not been sure about it. And now I had to. Tomorrow.

How do I compose myself? How do I do it?

'You'll feel better tomorrow, Mr Brooks,' Reg said.

'Yeah?'

'I don't see there being a problem.'

'No.'

'OK, I'll see you tomorrow then.'

Ros Howells, a race-relations expert, came into the room. While the Lawrences were saying bad things about me, she was with them and she never did anything to stop them. When I put it to her, she said, 'Oh, they never said those kind of things in front of me.' But that wasn't the point. As far as my mind was concerned, she knew they were saying those kinds of things, and wasn't putting the record straight.

It was funny how Steve's death attracted different groups of hangers-on. The Anti-Racist Alliance, the Anti-Nazi League and the Commission for Racial Equality all had their own agendas. They all helped to highlight the case, which was important, but in the process they helped turn Stephen Lawrence into a martyr rather than the real flesh-and-blood Steve. Every time Ros saw me, it was, 'Oh, you're just like my son. I'll do anything for you. I'll look after you.' If she meant it, why had she let people say those awful things about me – that I was to blame, that I was a bad influence, that I led Steve astray? Ros ignored me, she knew I was scared and confused.

She asked me if I'd be OK for tomorrow, and did I need any money. 'If you need anything you can call me.'

'OK.'

That was the way I answered people – one word. I couldn't face anything more. There was no point. I just wanted to get everything over and done with as quickly as possible. If I had to explain something and it took too long, I'd lose interest and not bother. If I wanted to do something that took hard thinking, I would lose interest – more symptoms of post-traumatic stress disorder.

My auntie came back. 'Say you're ill. That's all – say you're ill. Go to the doctors, let them give you some tablets. If you're ill you can't give evidence.'

How could I be ill tomorrow when I wasn't ill today? I was

tempted, though. I could do that, but how would I manage afterwards?

'I don't want any tablets,' I said to her.

'You don't need to take the tablets. Just get the tablets. You're not well, you're sick. That will stop you giving evidence for a long time.'

But the shame of it. Not only Duwayne Brooks ducking out on the trial but also on tranquillisers. I don't want to be in the papers for that. I don't want everyone to think I'm mentally ill, disturbed. How would that affect my life later?

Again, I forced the tears back. I couldn't let everyone see that I was breaking down. I'd said to myself so many times that I mustn't cry. I'd sit in front of the mirror and think of the worst things of that night. Think of the things that made me cry most, and I'd sit in front of the mirror and tell myself, No crying, no crying. I'd sit there for ages just to strengthen myself so when people said certain things to me it wouldn't break me down.

I knew that's what they were going to try to do in court. So I tried to think like the defence barristers, tried to think of all the possible questions they'd ask me, but I couldn't do it. My mind was too jumbled. I tried to think of every detail. But then when I remembered something new, I'd forget something old. I had to try to empty my mind of all the stuff I didn't need to know, but again I couldn't do that. More symptoms of post-traumatic stress disorder.

'I can't do it,' I said to my auntie. 'I can't pretend that I'm ill. It's not in my nature to chicken out of something.' It was the only way out of the trap, but I still couldn't do it.

Of course, she was right. I was just a pawn in this chess game. And I was going to play it just the way they wanted me to play it. I'd do my best in the court, and after that I'd be gone. I just have to do my tiny bit, and that's it, I told myself.

'Where are you staying for the night?' she said.

'I'm staying at a hotel.'

'Are the police looking after you?'

'Yes.'

'Are you sure? Do you think that's safe? D'you know them devils are in it as well?'

They were all in it, but where could I go that was safe? If something happened to me when I was by myself then nobody would know. If something happened to me when I was with the police then people would have to know.

'Well, I'll be praying for you anyway because them devils are surrounding you. They're all just waiting to take you down,' she said. 'Make sure you don't eat no junk food tonight.' She said it was for my protection, because all the people around me meant me no good, and this court was a very powerful place and I needed protection. I couldn't concentrate on what she was saying. The more I tried to focus, the more my mind shut down. The pain in my head took over, and I sat down. Her mouth was moving, but nothing seemed to be coming out of it. She gave me a folded piece of paper and said I must do what's on it. Then she left.

I sat down and opened the piece of paper. It was torn out of a notepad, about seven inches long, four inches wide, and she'd written down this ritual. She said I had to eat certain fruits, drink water, chant certain things.

I read the piece of paper, thinking, Am I going to do this or not, and if so, how do I do it? I needed to get away, I needed to do something.

I had to wait for the officers to get the car. 'We're just waiting for the officers because we don't know which two are going to be on tonight,' I was told. Eventually they arrived. Reg said he'd see me tomorrow and hoped that I'd be OK.

I said to the officers that I needed to get some clothes to wear for tomorrow, and could they drop me at New Cross and come back for me later. They never spoke to me on the journey. I was glad because I didn't want to talk to anyone, except myself.

They dropped me back at New Cross, and said they'd be back

about seven because we needed to get to the hotel to sort everything out. I went down to Melly's and watched TV. She told me she had seen Mrs Lawrence, who had said hello to her for the first time in ages. A while ago she had told Melly that she had heard that Melly was talking to me, and Mrs Lawrence didn't think anybody should be talking to me and wouldn't talk to anybody who did. She had said what had happened was my fault, and I should have been the one who was dead, not Steve. She'd made that quite clear to her. So Melly was as shocked when she said hello as she had been when she stopped speaking to her in the first place.

I got picked up by the officers and taken to the hotel. We checked in and went up to our rooms. Mine was at the end of the corridor. One officer's room was supposed to be next to mine, and I thought the other was at the opposite end of the corridor. But I wasn't sure. They were supposed to be protecting me, and I didn't even know which rooms they were in.

The first thing I noticed on entering my room was the window. I couldn't climb out if anybody attacked me in the room. I opened the wardrobe – there was no one in there. I checked in the shower – no one. I checked under the bed. I then studied the bed. I had to study it because I needed to know if I could move it to the door. If the bed was by the door, no one could come in while I was sleeping.

I knew I couldn't stay awake for the whole night, no matter how scared I was. I'd often tried it before, when I was sleeping up by the door at my flat in Brockley, but I could never stop myself going to sleep. Anyway, if I didn't sleep there was no way I'd be fresh for court tomorrow morning.

The bed's headboard was bolted to the wall, so moving it was out of the question. There was nothing else to put beside the door. Everything seemed to be bolted into position. Not even the TV would move.

I locked the door and sat on the bed. I sat there for ages,

thinking, If someone comes to get me in this room there is nothing I can do. I'm at the end of the corridor, nobody will hear me if I shout for help.

The officers said they'd come back to check if I was all right. But they didn't. I didn't know if anybody else was in any of the other rooms. I never saw anybody. It felt like I was alone in this big hotel. I was lonely, scared, lost.

I needed to eat. I looked at the menu – everything was so expensive. Even though I knew it wasn't me who would be paying, I didn't want to run up the bill. I was told downstairs by the police not to worry, to get anything I wanted on room service. If I needed to make a call just use the phone. They even joked that if I wanted to phone a prostitute there were cards in the phone box and that they wouldn't tell anybody if I didn't. It was funny to them, but it wasn't funny to me. I ignored them.

While I was in my room they were apparently having a little party downstairs. There were quite a few of them, and it sounded as if they were having a good time of it.

I decided to take a look outside my door. Nobody was there. I thought that police protection meant somebody would sit outside my door all night. How naïve. I looked left, to the end of the corridor, and right down to the other end of the corridor. The corridor seemed to go on for ever. That made me more scared. If I needed to run I'd never get to the end of it. It probably wasn't even very long, it was just my state of mind. I shut the door, sat back down on the bed. I had to check myself. Duwayne, Duwayne, what the fuck's going on? Are you going mad? I started to pace the room, back and forth, back and forth. Fuck, man. What is wrong, man? Calm down, calm down, calm down. My head was pounding, my heart was pounding. Every little sound was magnified. The quietest murmurings – of the heating rumbling away, the clock ticking – came back at me screaming.

I put the TV on, switched all the lights off and turned the TV up. I sat on the floor at the bottom of the bed, in front of the TV. I didn't want to sit on the bed because I felt too exposed there.

I crouched, clustered myself up. I felt safer like that. And then the hunger took over. I picked up the phone and ordered tuna and cucumber sandwiches. They said it would be fifteen minutes.

And then it hit me, the thing you see in movies. Someone comes up pretending to be room service, knocks on the door, 'Room service, sir', you open the door and they attack you. I convinced myself that it was going to happen. My head was working overtime. There are no weapons, what am I going to do? Why did I order room service? Should I cancel it? I was shaking, couldn't keep still. I could hear noises in my head. I began to panic. I jumped on the bed and pulled the pillow over my head.

There was a knock on the door. At first I didn't think it was the door. Then I heard it again. And again. My heart stopped. Everything was silent. The TV was on, but I couldn't hear it. I didn't know whether to open the door or not.

It knocked again. This time I went to open it, but just before I reached it there was another knock. I stopped, petrified, paralysed. Everything stopped, except the voice in my head. They must know I'm in here. I've ordered the room service, they know I'm going to be in here. Say something. Say something, please. I was begging for the person to just say 'room service', or 'sandwiches'. Anything. I went to open the door and the same thing happened again – another knock, and I froze. I couldn't help myself. My body wasn't following my instructions; it was fighting me, doing things I'd never known it to do. When you see how fear makes people act in films, you think it's rubbish, that you'd never do that, but it's not until you experience it that you know that often it does happen that way.

I pulled the door open. It was the room service guy. I was so relieved. I'd expected somebody to hit me. He was standing there, white top, black trousers, a tray in his hands. He stood there, and I stood there. He seemed baffled by the way I was acting. 'Your sandwiches,' he said. He put the tray down and left.

When I was eating I became thirsty. What an idiot, I'd not ordered a drink. My mind said to me before I even thought of asking the question, No way, no way are you calling room service again, no way is anybody coming in this room.

I started thinking about the officers – they hadn't even checked on me. Why not? What was going on? I began to think that maybe what my auntie had said to me was true: they were all involved. 'Watch yourself' was the last thing she had said.

How could I watch myself? They're supposed to be watching me. Here I am, in a hotel, away from everything and everyone I know, supposedly under police protection, and there is no sign of the police.

Eating the food made me tired. I stood by the door, leaning on it to watch TV. My legs were weak with exhaustion, so I sat down against the door. There was a draught coming through, so I took the cover off the bed and blocked it. I tried to relax on the bed, but I couldn't. In the end, I sat back by the door, just in case.

I kept falling off to sleep and waking up, falling off and waking up. I knew I needed some proper sleep otherwise I'd fall asleep tomorrow. I got up and lay on the bed. I had a choice: leave all the lights on or off. In the end, I decided to leave them off. I collapsed, semi-conscious. My body was sleeping, but my mind was awake. I was talking to myself, telling myself that I had to go to sleep.

I woke up at 7 a.m., still in my clothes and shoes. I wouldn't have known if anybody had come in the room during the night because I was so tired. My body was worn out, not through any physical energy I'd used but purely because of the mental energy I'd burned up. The mental trauma was tearing up my body.

I had a shower and watched more TV. The officers knocked on my door. 'Duwayne, are you OK? Are you ready?'

'Nearly. Be back in fifteen minutes for me,' I said.

'OK, no problem.'

Things seemed different today. I wasn't so panicked – still tense, but calmer.

I stared in the mirror in the bathroom for the first five minutes, and did the test to make sure I didn't cry. I thought of all the bad things that had happened that would normally make me cry but couldn't make me cry that day. If the floodgates opened that would be it. I couldn't afford to break down in the witness box.

I went downstairs. The police checked to see what I'd run up on room service, then paid the bill. All I'd had was the tuna sandwiches. We got in the car and made our way to the court. We went through the same security procedures as the day before.

'Are you ready?' Reg said.

Reg told me I'd be going on first. The usher called me and we went downstairs. The walk from corridor to court felt so long. The closer we got to the court doors, the harder my heart started beating. They opened the doors. I felt as if I was walking into the Colosseum. The first five or six steps nobody could see me because of the raised sides. The suspects were on my right-hand side, above me. Once I'd walked past them that was it – everybody could see me. As I walked up to the witness box, my back was turned to everybody. It only took a few seconds, but I felt arrows spearing me in my back. But they weren't arrows that I could feel, they were eyes.

I looked straight at the judge. I tried not to look at anybody else. I didn't want anybody to see me, and I felt that if I couldn't see them they wouldn't be able to see me.

I tried to forget that the suspects and their families were there. But I couldn't. The judge began speaking to me. He took me through the procedures. I solemnly swore to tell the truth.

The judge asked me to tell the jury what had happened. I felt that if one of the barristers had asked me any question – Is your name Duwayne Brooks? How old are you? – I would have jumped out of my skin.

I was asked how big the bar was, or what I had believed to be the bar, that Steve was struck with. I showed them. The jury was shocked. I could see on their faces that they were worried about me. They could see how terrified I was. I never once looked up to where the suspects were. If I could have hidden in the witness box I would have done. The eyes of friends and supporters were also bearing down on me, praying for me to look up, but I couldn't.

Then the questioning started. Sometimes I felt that I'd answered clearly, but the judge still asked me to speak up. My ears were buzzing, my palms sweating. Be calm Duwayne, just try to be calm, I told myself hopelessly.

The defence began to tuck into me. It didn't take long before they were attacking me on the fact that I'd said I'd never seen the suspects' faces. That was all they were interested in – the fact that I only glimpsed their faces. If I never saw their faces, then I couldn't identify them, so in order to have identified two of them – Neil Acourt and Luke Knight – at the ID parades obviously I must have been told who to pick out. That was their logic.

I tried to explain to the barristers what I had meant when I'd said that I hadn't seen their faces – I couldn't describe their faces, that's what I'd meant. I said to them I'm not a person who is good at describing facial features. At the time when I was giving my statement at the police station I couldn't even describe all the different coloured hair that white people have – the blond, the brunette, or whatever. It wasn't part of my vocabulary. I'd never had a conversation where I'd talked about white people's hair.

'Come on, somebody must have told you who to look for and what they looked like?' they said again and again. I tried to stress that none of my friends or associates actually knew what they looked like. Yes, they knew the names, but that's all they were – names. And the names didn't help me at all – it's not as if the suspects wore name tags on the ID parade.

The questioning went on and on and on. My answers weren't going anywhere. I was getting caught deeper and deeper in their trap.

They asked me to look through some pictures to describe how the incident took place and where I was. The barrister gave me the picture book, and he told me to go to one of the numbered pictures. I put my hand on the book and looked up at him. I felt he was toying with me. I turned to the picture. It was Steve's blood splattered on the ground.

'Is that the picture of the bus stop?' the barrister asked.

'No,' I said, and I showed it to him.

'Oh, do forgive me, do forgive me.'

Bullshit! He knew what he was trying to do. All the barristers were focused on my reaction when I turned to the picture. They wanted to see if I'd break down or puke up. And I did want to be sick, but I didn't have any expression on my face. I remembered Jane telling me to keep expressionless. 'Don't let anybody know what you are thinking, or what's going on inside, because once you do, they'll stick to that point and attack you on it,' she'd said.

They were hammering me with questions. I kept saying, 'I don't know', 'I can't remember', 'I don't know.'

The judge interrupted to ask if I had seen my statement. I said no. 'You haven't seen your statement since the court proceedings started?' He sounded shocked.

'No,' I said. 'I haven't seen my statement since 1993.' Proceedings were stopped for me to read my statement. I walked out of the court and felt the eyes looking down on me. I didn't understand court protocol and hadn't thought about the statement before, but its significance was quickly becoming clear to me. Apparently, Imran should have made sure I'd seen it. I felt humiliated.

This just convinced me that my auntie had been right – I was in this trap, being set up to go through the motions so that I could be blamed. How on earth could I be put in the witness box without having seen my statement? I hadn't even seen it at the committal.

So I'd gone in there, without even being reminded of exactly what I'd said three years ago. What was I supposed to do – read it all now, memorise it, and walk back into the court? They told me I had twenty minutes to read through my statement and then I had to go back in, prepared.

But that was impossible. If I'd been a speed-reader I don't think I could have managed it. And the trauma of going into the court had put my head beyond concentrating. I started to read the statement, but the words didn't register. They might as well have been written in another language.

A court official came to tell me there was no point in going back now till after lunch. I felt relieved. Maybe I could study the statement over lunch, eat something, relax. No. The statement was taken off me and I was told I could take a quick look at it when I came back. A quick look! These people were supposed to be supporting me, making sure that I was OK. They could see that I was anything but OK, that I was not prepared, yet still I was offered only a quick look before the court resumed.

Were the prosecution prepared for this case? Did they ever consider how the case would be defended? That it might have been worth making sure I was up to speed? That if I wasn't, I'd be ripped apart, closely followed by the whole prosecution? It was a shambles. It was bad enough having to make a statement the weekend before the case to cover up for Imran's incompetence all those years earlier, but being sent out of court to read through my initial statement to the police halfway through giving evidence was total humiliation. Surely, Imran couldn't have 'forgotten' to show me my statement on purpose? It didn't make sense. He couldn't have wanted me to look stupid and unreliable in court. Could he?

I went outside to get a taxi with Reg. I put my coat over my head to stop people taking pictures of me. My auntie came up.

'What are you doing?' she said. 'You're not yourself. We're all looking down at you in the public gallery, can't you look up?'

I said to her there was no point. 'There's nothing I can do.'

'Duwayne, you haven't seen your statement at all?' she said.

'No,' I said.

'You mean to say they didn't even show you your statement before you came to court?'

'No.'

'What kind of something is this?' she said.

She told me she had never heard of a big case, or any case for that matter, where a witness didn't get to look at their statement before the start. My auntie had worked in a Citizen's Advice Bureau and knew quite a bit about the law and how trials worked.

'See? You see?' she said.

'I know . . .' I said. 'But I just have to go through the motions, don't I? If I don't, imagine what the media will do to me.' I had to say my bit, have it dissected, and then be ridiculed in the witness box.

'What has Jane said about this?' she asked.

'I don't think she knows about my statement,' I said. 'And she doesn't know what's going on in the court because I haven't phoned her. There's no point in phoning her. What can she do?' Jane, of course, wasn't present because this wasn't her case.

We couldn't go to King's Cross in case we got back too late, so we went to a café. I couldn't eat or drink. I just wanted to get back in the box, get it over with, spew it out of me, and then maybe I'd feel different again. Maybe I'd feel relieved. But now I felt heavy. It felt as if I was carrying everybody.

I went back to Court 1, but the jury wasn't there. More legal argument – they always ask the jury to leave for the legal argument in case they talk about stuff that could prejudice them.

They were arguing about my statement. My evidence had to be tested in front of the judge before it went in front of the jury. I was battered from pillar to post by the barristers. It's their job to do that, and they did their job well. After demolishing me, they smiled at me. I don't know if they were taking the piss or genuinely apologising for what they'd done. Perhaps the smile was their way of saying that it wasn't personal.

Michael Mansfield stood up, and I thought he'd lead me through it in a much simpler way, but he didn't. It was strange. I'd heard such brilliant things about Michael Mansfield, yet he was addressing me as if he couldn't really be bothered, as if he'd been forced to be here. He seemed to be going through the motions. He wasn't sparking as I've seen him in other cases since then. He was slow and dull. He had no enthusiasm. He questioned me as if it was a waste of time. If he knew it was going to be a waste of time, why did he summons me? They knew exactly what I was going to say from what I'd said at the committal, and they knew what would happen here, so why bother? Why risk the case being thrown out and losing the chance to convict them at another time?

Perhaps ego triumphed over reason. The press made such a great fuss about this unique step, the private prosecution for murder, that perhaps they were carried away by the hype. And it was this hype that blinded them to the fact that they were never going to get a conviction here. I think they realised this belatedly, and the Lawrence legal team seemed determined to make it look like I'd lost them the case rather than they had.

I gave the rest of my evidence and was then asked to leave. 'Thank you very much, Mr Brooks,' the judge said. 'Please remember not to discuss the case with anybody.'

I walked straight out of the witness box and through the doors without looking at anybody.

I went up to the witness room. Tears were welling in my eyes. An explosion was waiting to burst out of my chest. I held everything down. I rushed to the toilet, looked in the mirror and said to myself, No crying, NO CRYING. But the tears came anyway. I wiped them away with a tissue. My chest was paining me with so much hurt. Everything was building up. What was Mansfield doing? He was supposed to save me. While Mansfield was talking, the defence barristers were laughing among themselves because they knew it was over.

One of the last questions they asked me was, 'Did you not say, Mr Brooks, that you did not see their faces?' I had to say yes, because I *had* said that, but I hadn't meant it that way. Once I said that, there were no further questions.

Mansfield was supposed to ask, 'When you said you did not see those faces, what did you mean?' Then I would have been able to explain exactly what I'd meant: that I didn't think I could describe the faces to the police or the court, but for me that was totally different to being able to pick them out at an identity parade. Of course I saw their faces – they all ran across the road at Steve and me.

Instead, he gave a speech in which he said it for me – that because of trauma I couldn't dig the descriptions of the faces out of my head. But because he said it for me, rather than asking me what I had meant, it sounded like an excuse.

Deep breaths, deep breaths, deep breaths in front of the mirror. I walked back into the room and sat down. I spoke to the barrister for the Lawrences. I said to him I didn't know how Imran came to write that stuff about me having seen other witness statements.

'Yes,' he said. 'Imran's already spoken about it in court and he admits that he made a mistake – he doesn't know how his colleague wrote it down.'

We spoke about other stuff. I told him about when the officers used to drive me around, trying to get me to pick people out on the streets, and took me places to try to jog my memory about where I'd seen some of the suspects. The police weren't allowed to do that, but how should I have known? I thought he'd keep it to himself. He didn't, though. He told everybody. I didn't know at the time, but later, after the case collapsed, I was questioned about it.

'You have made serious allegations about officers in this case,' the police said. 'Would you like to elaborate on them and make a statement?'

'No,' I said. 'I don't know what you're talking about.'

They said that when I was at the Old Bailey I made a statement to counsel. I said I'd never made any statement to him – well, I hadn't made a statement. 'Whatever he says I said, let him write it down,' I told them.

They claimed they already had a statement from him. I said I wasn't making a statement, and left it at that. I'd asked him not to say anything, and he told everybody. Why? What difference did it make to the case? It certainly couldn't have helped us, because the officers in question would then turn round and say, 'I drove him past the Acourts and I drove him past Norris and he never picked them out.' That would have looked great.

Ros Howells came up to the room. 'Hello, Duwayne, how are you? Everybody's worried about you. She had a way of talking – so gentle, so caring, so patronising, but then again, I had never experienced anyone from the Lawrence camp showing a genuine interest. She sat down. 'We all thought you did OK.'

Of course I didn't do OK. I knew I'd not done OK. How could I have?

She said we should play a game. She got some paper and drew up a noughts and crosses grid.

'There's no point,' I said to her. 'The person who goes first always wins. The only thing you can do is draw once you've moved second.' I told her that it was a waste of time coming here.

'Oh no, it's not over yet. Other witnesses—'

'What other witnesses?' I said. 'There are no other witnesses in this case, and there's no other evidence. There is no point in you trying to make it sound good to me.' 'You all know, all of you, all of you know what you are doing, so why are you defending everybody?'

'Everybody cares about you. Everybody's worried about you.'

Ros. Nobody cares about me, nobody's worried. If anybody cared they would have contacted me long before Friday.'

I asked Ros again how we could have come this far with no evidence. She repeated that there was more evidence. I told her I didn't want to speak to her any more. She left and said if I wanted her, she'd be downstairs.

I was blaming Ros again, but this was really nothing to do with her. She wasn't the one that should be looking out for me and it definetly wasn't her bringing this ridiculus prosecution.

The usher told me I wouldn't be going in again today, but that I might be called back tomorrow. I couldn't see what I could say different from today.

Me and Reg were chatting. He told me about his friend in immigration who had told him a story about a man who had gone to Jamaica to import crack cocaine and had been followed by British intelligence. Apparently, he went to an obeah man – these men are supposed to work black magic, white magic, protection, or whatever you want to call it. So the drug dealer had gone to see the magic man who cast a spell so that whenever the drug dealer got stopped at the airport, security would see coffee instead of the crack cocaine. But he'd been seen buying the crack by the spies. As he got off the plane he was stopped at security – his bag was searched and then they let him go. The spies contacted the immigration officers and said, 'Well, what was in there? Why have you let him go?' They said there was only coffee in there. As he reached for a taxi, a different set of officers stopped him again because they couldn't believe he had hidden the cocaine. When they opened his bag they didn't find coffee, they found cocaine.

Reg said that had baffled him all his life: how the first officers saw only coffee and then when the second officers stopped him they found cocaine. The drug dealer used it in court to get off – the first officers had to admit they found only coffee when they searched him even though they had been methodical because they had information that he was carrying drugs. But there was no evidence found on him until they searched him a second time. So the drug dealer argued that the cocaine was planted on him.

I said to Reg that it was not like this case. People had been blind to the obvious, but it was different. When they first searched the suspects, there was no evidence found, not because of black magic, but because of incompetence or, at worst, corruption. The police later had to admit to an inquiry by Kent police into the investigation that they had not searched David Norris's house properly because it was too big. And this was the house owned by the notorious criminal Clifford Norris. It sent out a wonderful message about justice. You want to get away with murder? Well, nick enough money to buy yourself a mansion, and there's every chance the police won't search it thoroughly. I thanked Reg for the story. It had got me talking, which was Reg's aim.

While I was waiting for the officers to take me to the hotel, my auntie strode up to me. 'Are you giving evidence tomorrow?' she said.

'I'm not sure. I'm supposed to be.'

She said she couldn't see any point: anything that I said would only contribute to the defence not the prosecution. I said I knew that.

'Who's the barrister for the Lawrences?' she said. I told her. 'That's not the Michael Mansfield I know.' She had done her research on all the barristers and had told me that, yes, the ones for the suspects were good but Michael Mansfield was much better. 'But what is he doing down there? He doesn't seem very interested in his work.'

'I know,' I said. Mansfield never looked at me while I was in the witness box. He looked down and whenever he asked me a question he looked at the judge rather than at me. I'm the main prosecution witness, yet he doesn't even look me in the eye.

I got in the car with the officers. I was exhausted. I just wanted to go back to the hotel and sleep. I'd had enough with fear and worry. I didn't think anything was going to happen now because it had been seen that I wasn't the threat everybody might have thought I was.

We were driving for ages. I wasn't paying attention to where we were going, but when I looked through the window I saw we were going through Eltham. I asked them why we were going this way.

'Oh, we're looking for a hotel.'

'Why are we leaving the one in central London?' I said.

'The Met can't afford to be paying for big hotels in London for witnesses, so we're going to have to look for a cheaper one.'

I was worried. Why were they bringing me through Eltham? Of all places, why were they bringing me this way? I watched every turn they took, and looked back to see who was following us. At the same time, I was saying to myself, What's the point in looking back, they'll know where we're going, they'll just be waiting for us at our destination.

We stopped at a backpackers' hostel. They said that this was where I would be staying for the night. Dirty and smelly, hair all over the bed, no TV, some side street in New Eltham. Did they really expect me to sleep here? I checked all the windows. They were locked. The door could lock, but it looked as if it would fall over if you leant on it. I wondered if I should just go home. But I was so tired I didn't think I could walk far, and I wouldn't know where I was going.

I definitely couldn't go to sleep here. I sat down and thought – must have been for two hours. I took my stuff, went downstairs, pulled the curtains in the front room and turned the TV on. None of the officers were about for the whole night, so I thought that they must have lived nearby and had just dropped me off and gone home.

In the morning a woman came in and asked if I'd been there all night. I said yes. She asked why I hadn't been in my room. I said there was no TV there. I didn't want her to know that I was frightened. She might have known who I was, she might not have, but I wasn't going to tell her. She asked if I was hungry. I said no.

The officers returned. 'Are you ready, Mr Brooks?'

'Yes.' I hadn't slept all night – perhaps I dropped off for twenty minutes in the morning, but that was all. My brain was tired. It couldn't think. They drove me back to court. I was walking slowly because I was drained from the night.

'How are you, Mr Brooks? You look tired. Didn't you sleep?' Reg said.

'No. I was watching TV all night,' I replied. I didn't let on they had taken me to Eltham. I just said I was tired.

The only person I could turn to was Jane. I called her and told her everything that had happened. She was outraged, but said we couldn't complain about it at the moment, although we could afterwards, depending on how I felt. 'You may just be angry now, once it's all over you may not want to do anything. Wait till it's over, see how you feel about it once it's over.'

Back in the witness room I was talking to Reg for an age. No information was coming out about what was happening in the court – what stage the prosecution was up to, whether the jury was back in. About lunchtime I was told I wouldn't be needed for the day so I could go home. I was dropped off at Melly's and that's where I stayed. I needed to rest up, away from the court environment.

I phoned my friend Winston. 'I need to play some snooker. I need to get this court shit off my head,' I said. The police picked me up and took me down to the snooker hall. They came up to see what it was like, to make sure I'd be safe. Typical – they'd not bothered about my safety till now, and this, the first place they bothered to check out, was the first place I did actually feel safe. 'Nobody will attack me in the snooker hall because all my friends are here,' I said. They police said that they'd be back in an hour.

The next day I didn't expect to be at court. I had been told that I had finished giving my evidence. But then I got a phone call at Melly's house. I might be needed in court that afternoon. How was I going to get there? What was I needed for?

It was nearing the end of the first week of a trial that was expected to go on for many more weeks. A police car was sent to get me. It met me at the top of the road. I didn't want the police to pick me up outside Melly's house. A lot of people knew the police car was for me because so many people in the area knew Melly, but I didn't want to make it more obvious than it had to be.

They put the car's blue light on, and we sped off. It gave me the opportunity to experience just how crazy people act when they have a police car up at their bumper. Instead of moving to the side to allow it to pass, some cars stop dead in panic. We almost had two crashes on the way. Incredibly, we got from Melly's place to the Old Bailey – through miles of London traffic – in eight minutes.

Reg was waiting outside the court. There was an air of panic. I didn't know if it was something I'd said earlier on that they wanted me to clarify, or whether something had happened. Everyone was giving me funny looks. Awkward looks. 'There he is, there he is,' they were saying.

They took me straight back into the waiting room. The feeling was different today. There wasn't the pressure-of-giving-evidence feeling, it was the fear of the unknown. I knew what to expect now in the court – the layout, everybody staring at me – but I didn't know what I was going to be asked or told. I sat there for a while, then asked Reg what was happening. He didn't know.

'There is a possibility that they may call you,' he said.

'Call me for what? I've said all I can say, Reg.'

'Well,' he said, 'they don't know yet. They're waiting for the judge to come back.'

Finally, I'd been given some information. Obviously, the judge was going to make a decision today as to whether or not the case was going to continue. And if it was going to continue, I'd have to give more evidence.

The judge returned. It was all over. My evidence was inadmissible. The defence had successfully discredited my evidence in numerous ways. But ultimately what did it for the private prosecution was that the Lawrence team were completely reliant on my fleeting-glance evidence. You can hardly ever convict somebody on the fleeting glance of one witness. Even if the defence hadn't tried to discredit my evidence, the prosecution was done for from the outset because the Lawrence team failed to find any other witnesses and were relying on my flawed evidence.

Everybody knew from my first statement that all I'd had was a fleeting glance. It wasn't as if I'd just revealed it at the Old Bailey. I had made that first statement just after Steve had been killed in April 1993.

I felt blameful. I was relieved it was all over, but I felt blameful. I knew I was going to be the one who would be blamed. I knew they would use me as an excuse for the collapse of the case. Michael Mansfield and Imran Khan and the Lawrences would never come out and say they didn't really have a case – no forensics, no other evidence – because then they would have been asked why they went ahead in the first place.

Later that day my fear was realised. The headline in the news was 'Lawrence Case Collapses as Main Witness Changes Evidence'. There was nothing about the fact that the police had failed to gather any evidence in the first place; nothing about the fact that there was no way they could have convicted beyond reasonable doubt just from my fleeting-glance evidence.

I knew what people were going to say. I knew how they were going to look at me and I just prepared myself for it. It was every bit as bad as I'd feared. Possibly worse. Everybody was on my back.

'Why did you change your story? How could you do that? You're supposed to be Steve's friend.' Nobody asked me what really happened.

I found it so hard. I felt tired. Every new person I met wanted to know the same thing. Sometimes I'd be on the bus and I'd see people pointing at me, saying, 'That's Duwayne Brooks. That's the one that was with Stephen Lawrence. He went and changed his story, you know.'

The Lawrences and their legal team never considered how the prosecution could affect me or my life in the community. I was the scapegoat.

Sometimes I'd sit in front of the mirror and ask myself what else could I have done. I'd ask myself how could I have done it differently. I'd look in that mirror and say, Why don't you let me see exactly what happened, the case is over now, why don't you let me see? But my head didn't want me to see it. It still doesn't want me to see 100 per cent of what took place that night. It doesn't want me to receive the most disturbing parts. I don't know what it would do to me, but my mind has protected me from it ever since.

People didn't realise what they were doing when they whispered and gossiped. It was so distressing. I felt I had to justify myself to them. I hadn't changed my story, I would say, it wasn't like that, I was confused. Then they'd fire all their hostile questions at me. How were you confused? How could you be confused? Weren't you there? Didn't you see it? So you did run off then, you did run off?

That was what people were saying: that I'd just run off and left

Steve, and when I came back he was lying on the ground already dead. Because nobody had heard it from my mouth, the Chinese whispers spread and everybody added to them until you got a totally different story.

Strangers would walk up to me in the street. It was as if I was public property. They felt they had the right to ask me anything, or tell me just what they thought, so they did. 'How d'you feel about what you done?' 'Don't you feel bad about letting them guys get away?' 'If I was in the Lawrence family I would never talk to you again.' 'How could you let them go to court and you knew you were going to change your story? You must have been paid off!'

People asked me if I knew the suspects. They wanted to make a connection between me and them so they could make sense of what had happened. They wanted to say I was being paid off or maybe I was too scared to tell the truth.

After the prosecution various pressure groups offered to help me and protect me. They realised I was vulnerable and distraught. But really they just wanted to hear my story. And in the end, they could do nothing for me. Once I had told them my story, and when they realised how deep it all went, and when they saw the depth of my needs, they backed out and left me. Time after time groups did this. This is why now I would only be involved with Movement for Justice, which has stuck with me since the Inquiry.

Four years had passed since Steve's death, and still there hadn't been an inquest. They had tried to hold one three times before, and three times it had been adjourned. In February 1997, a year after the private prosecution, it finally went ahead.

Again, there was loads of security around the Coroners' Court in Borough.. Everybody was hyped up. The security was getting me worried. I had to go in and tell the coroner what had happened. It all seemed so pointless. Even though I had told my story over and over again, I felt it hadn't ever got us anywhere.

I had been told by people that the jury was bound to reach a verdict of unlawful killing, but it wouldn't mean anything because there would be no remedy to the injustice we had suffered. No one else would be charged for the murder of Steve and the attack on me. I had been told that once a verdict had been recorded at the inquest that was in effect the end as far as justice for Steve was concerned.

The inquest was the last time I saw Noel Penstone. The way the police treated him that day was disgusting. Noel was there to make sure I was all right. He was part of the Greenwich Racial Equality team and he worked under Harcourt Alleyne. Harcourt wanted to make sure that my needs were catered for because he felt the police had neglected me.

The police came into the room we were in. 'Noel, can you leave?' one officer said.

They felt that Noel was getting in their way. Why? Because he was asking the questions I didn't know to ask. Because of his experience of what was going on in the schools of Greenwich, he knew the questions to ask the police. Early on he had asked them why they hadn't looked at the school records of the suspects. The police felt uneasy whenever he was around. They knew that he knew what type of care I should have been getting. He never told me directly that he was unhappy with how the police were looking after me, but it was obvious that he was agitated by their negligence. He knew things weren't right.

When they asked him to leave, I said I wanted him to stay. They asked him to leave again.

'Well, Duwayne doesn't want me to leave,' Noel said. 'So I think I should stay with him.'

The officer went off and returned with some senior officers.

I couldn't believe what was going on. Jane then said that it was best for Noel to leave. She didn't want him to lose his job because of his support for me. It turned out that Noel's bosses had told him he could lose his job if he continued to support me.

The police had to make out that it was in my interest, that Noel wasn't looking after me in the right way. But how did they know how Noel was looking after me? I certainly hadn't made a complaint. In fact, he was one of the very few people I felt comfortable around. He was the only one who was supposed to be looking after me who I knew was really doing so.

I walked into the court. Everybody was sitting down except for some people at the back to the left who were standing up. On the opposite side of me to the right was the jury. To my immediate right were the suspects.

Mr Levine, the coroner, told me to sit down, to make myself comfortable and not to worry. I was still nervous. Mr Levine looked like one of those people you see in pictures from the 1800s: men with moustaches that came out and curled up at both ends. He was very courteous and kind as well as patient with me.

I explained what happened on the night. I got in a muddle about the bus stop and which side of the road it was, and how far down the road. Me and Mr Levine had a discussion and then he corrected me. The court was laid-back. Everybody there looked like normal everyday people, even though my legal team and the Lawrences' legal team were there in the background.

After I finished I went back upstairs to the room. It didn't seem necessary for me to be there. My statement could have been read out. There was a rumour that the jury had been hand-picked and brought in from the outskirts of London – in other words, it would be all-white. But surely they couldn't afford to have another scandal with a verdict of death by misadventure, knowing no further action would be taken.

The suspects were summonsed, appeared and refused to answer questions. They had been advised by their legal team to say 'no comment'. At one point Michael Mansfield asked David Norris, 'Are you called Mr Norris?' He replied, 'I claim privilege.' It would have been funny if it hadn't been so disgusting.

In the end it was a formality. The rumours were just that. They found Steve had been unlawfully killed, and the jury even went as far as to say that he was killed 'in a completely unprovoked racist attack by five white youths'. Everybody thought they knew who the killers were, but nobody had the evidence to convict any of them.

They sat there smirking, cocky in their body language, throughout. They knew that in the end this court couldn't hurt them one bit.

As time passed, I gradually began to recover my Duwayne Brooks life. Now, the Lawrence life kicked in only when things relating to Steve and the police came up – meetings with Jane or speeches at public events. The rest of the time was for me.

My Duwayne Brooks life began to open up more and more for me. I had my old friends who had stuck by me, I had made new friends, and I was enjoying my work as a photocopier engineer – I had found something I excelled at. The public inquiry into Steve's murder and the failed investigation was looming and I didn't really want to take part in it. I didn't want to have to take time off to attend an inquiry I was convinced would just be another slap in the face for black people.

Jane said I only needed to be there for my evidence. She said an inquiry would be good for us because we could make recommendations, and we could also go public on everything that had happened to me since 1993 and stop anyone dumping on me.

But I wanted to get on with my life. I'd already lost so many years, and I was desperate to make something of myself. I had to be successful in life. Not only for me, but also because I felt that that was one of the things the police would have hated. They would have loved me to commit crimes and go to jail, then they could turn round and say that they had been right all along.

Vindicated

Chapter 11

Vindicated

The Lawrences had called for a public inquiry ages ago, when there was still a Tory government. Michael Howard, then Home Secretary, had snubbed them, though. One of the first positive things Tony Blair's Labour government did when they came into power in 1997 was promise to hold a public inquiry. In a way it was political point-scoring – Steve's murder, and the farcical investigation happened under a Conservative government, and now Labour's Home Secretary, Jack Straw, wanted to show he was big enough to put it right. Indeed, it was considered to be of such political importance that they had promised an inquiry while in opposition.

The public inquiry began on 16 March 1998. It said that its aim was 'to inquire into the matters arising from the death of Stephen Lawrence on 22 April 1993 to date, in order particularly to identify the lessons to be learned for the investigation and prosecution of racially motivated crimes'.

When we discovered that the judge chairing the Inquiry was going to be Sir William Macpherson, or Sir William Alan Macpherson of Cluny as he was more formally known, we were not best pleased. He had a reputation as a fierce right-winger who was unsympathetic to race cases. We were even less pleased when we learned that the 'counsel to the Inquiry', Edmund Lawson, had in the past been hired by the Police Federation to defend officers accused of wrongdoing.

Just before the Inquiry started, the *Observer* ran a story saying that Mr Lawrence had asked Macpherson to stand down. The story repeated all our concerns, and showed exactly why we were worried. In 1991, he had ruled that a white woman from Cleveland was within her rights when she transferred her child from a school after the girl had come home singing 'in Pakistani'. The newspaper also looked at the decisions he had made in immigration cases, and found that of fifteen judges he was the least likely to allow asylum seekers to have decisions against them reviewed by the courts.

Macpherson was livid, and said it might be a good idea to allow him to start the Inquiry before the criticism poured in. But that was our point – once the Inquiry started there was no turning back.

Macpherson was allowed to chair despite our misgivings. The Inquiry lasted more than six months. I attended only three days, and did not testify in person – my barrister read out my statement. The police had wanted to question me, but after receiving a psychiatric report, my barrister said that it would be unfair to put me through it again. I sat with Jane and Beverley, a trainee solicitor at Jane's office, as the barrister, Rajiv Menon, read out my statement for me.

I couldn't have read it out myself – I had to describe what Steve looked like as he was dying, how the police refused to believe that the attack was unprovoked, how all in all I had given the police nine statements and had been on three identification parades, and throughout it all they treated me like they didn't believe me and didn't care for my safety. I would have broken down if I'd delivered the statement in person.

It seemed an age before the report came out. Jane and me had spent a long time talking about what we wanted out of the Inquiry. Ultimately, the most important thing was to have the law changed to make it less easy for the police to treat black people as they had treated Steve and me. We argued that their behaviour and attitudes had been racist, yet somehow many, including the commissioner, were exempt from the Race Relations Act. The most obvious thing was to bring the police under the race-relations laws.

Wednesday 24 February 1999: Macpherson's report was finally to be published. We were invited on *GMTV* to discuss it. I had to be there for 6.30 a.m., and they were hassling me to get there the day before. They wanted me to stay in a hotel. I said no, I'd make my own way there. They sent a taxi to my address and we then went to pick up Jane.

I hate the idea of talking on TV because you never get to say exactly what you want to say. They tend to stick you on if you say something really controversial and then chop you off, so you never see it in context. I preferred to talk to newspapers – I thought there was more chance of my story being told how I'd intended it to be told.

After the programme, I went home to relax because I was tired, having got up so early to go on *GMTV* – to sit around and then be on for a couple of minutes. I had to be at the Home Office in the afternoon to get a sneak preview of the Report.

This was typical of the treatment we received – the Lawrences had already had an unhurried viewing of the Report. Now it was our turn, and we were only going to be given an hour to sift through the three hundred pages. We were supposed to be equal parties in this Inquiry yet we couldn't have been treated more differently. On the first day of the hearing for legal aid there were tables laid out for all the legal teams – all the legal teams that is except the Duwayne Brooks team. That's how significant they wanted me to be.

We arrived at the Home Office at 2.30 p.m. and had to go in the back way. I asked Jane why couldn't we walk in the front like everybody else. She explained that the deal was that if we were to get this sneak preview we had to sneak in the back way. They didn't want the press knowing we were there. Why not? The press knew when the Lawrences were here, so why shouldn't they know when we were too? Were we such a danger that nobody could know that we were here? Or was something else going on?

I couldn't help thinking there was a political motive. From the start they'd tried to sweep us under the carpet – the way they couldn't accept my word that it was a racist attack; the way Crowley had helped to discredit my evidence, by saying that I'd identified suspects after being told what they looked like; and the way they kept me out of everything after that. How many times did we hear about the incident, yet there was no mention of me? I was sure people wanted me out of the picture, and had done so for years. Somehow, the police and the government – the establishment – felt I was a danger. I was the survivor, the one who had seen, albeit imperfectly, what had happened; the one who'd experienced the brunt of police racism at first hand. Somehow, the establishment didn't regard the Lawrences as a threat because they themselves had become part of the establishment. But they were so wary about me. They knew I was explosive, that I wouldn't be shut up easily, that I was liable to question anything at any time.

We were brought upstairs to the second floor, and taken into a room where we sat down. An official-looking lady took us in and said she'd be back in a minute. She came back about five minutes later with the Report, and left us to it. Jane was rattling through it, I was just skimming for one section in particular.

Eventually I found it: 'Duwayne Brooks 5.12', ordered like a passage from the Bible.

We are driven to the conclusion that Mr Brooks was
stereotyped as a young black man exhibiting unpleasant
hostility and agitation, who could not be expected to
help, and whose condition and status simply did not
need further examination or understanding. We believe
that Mr Brooks' colour and such stereotyping played their
part in the collective failure of those involved to treat him
properly and according to his needs.

Macpherson went on to say that if I had been white, he didn't
believe I would have been treated the way I was. The Report was
detailed. The team had obviously spent a long time examining
the ways in which the police had screwed up the investigation
and had stereotyped Steve and me.

I showed Jane. She was ecstatic. 'We've won!' she shouted.

I started reading stuff about the Lawrences and the Inquiry,
but as far as I was concerned there was little else in the Report.
Nothing worth the millions of pounds spent on the public
inquiry.

But we were happy. Jane was happier than me because she
understood the significance of the Report better than I did. As far
as Jane was concerned, we had proved our point – that I would
have been treated differently if I was white – so we had won.

At 3.45 p.m. we left the Home Office through the front door.
Ironic, really. We couldn't come in through the front door but
we could leave through the front door. All the reporters had
been at the front with the Lawrences, but by the time we were
ready to leave most of them had gone off with the Lawrences.
There were just a few photographers out there taking my
picture.

We were due to give a press conference in a short time, at the
TGWU building. The chief executive of the union had given us
a room to use. Everybody was waiting to see what I'd say, but I
was told by Jane to be reserved. 'Don't say too much, and don't

say anything controversial or anything you'll regret.' I said what was on the press statement and nothing more.

I'd never been in this situation before – BBC, ITV, Channel 4, the broadsheets, the tabloids, suddenly everyone wanted to speak to me, everyone wanted to be my friend. 'Oh, Duwayne, could you come here a minute.' 'Duwayne, nice smile! That's lovely.' 'Duwayne, what are your thoughts on the Report?' I made it clear that we'd only had an hour to scan it, and we'd not had the time the Lawrences had to look at it, and that we couldn't see why.

The split between the two camps was huge and unhappy, but we couldn't always hide it. And, yes, of course we wanted to point out that one of the most concrete recommendations in the Report had resulted from our arguments: Macpherson had agreed that the full force of the Race Relations Act should apply to all police officers and the chief constables should be responsible for any of their officers who broke the Act. It seemed crazy that this had not been the case until then. The fact that Macpherson said the police were guilty of institutional racism was for most people the Report's most shocking finding.

I felt it was significant that we went into the Home Office the back way. It said it all. But in a way, it was how I wanted it. I was just continuing my battle, silently creeping along the back stairs while the Lawrences were marching up the front stairs with the press, making all the noises and getting nowhere. Jane had made it clear that our battle was going to be a long, tiring one if we were going to get anywhere. She said that being in the press and the public eye, spouting the same old stuff, could actually distract you from the job ahead, and I agreed.

We had to go to Millbank in the evening to do a discussion on Sky TV, which is where I met black officers from the Black Police Federation. They said anything that I was aggrieved about I should talk to them and they'd do anything to help.

'Well,' I said, 'I'm living in a property where I believe my phone is being tapped.'

'Why do you believe that, Mr Brooks?'

'Look at this,' I said. 'I haven't paid my bills for over twelve months and my phone is still working.'

'That doesn't mean it's being tapped, Mr Brooks. It could just be an oversight.'

'Do you know anybody who hasn't paid their phone bill for twelve months and their line is still operating? If you do, I'd like to meet that person.'

Some of the officers from the Black Police Federation had gone out of their way to help to make sure some of the truth about racism in the Met came out. Detective Inspector David Michael made a statement for the Inquiry that gave an insider's view of how black officers in the Met were treated. But I wasn't impressed with some of the other officers from the Federation. They seemed so defensive to me. It's weird how so many black officers are in denial about the Met being racist. How's that going to help if we have white racist officers patrolling our streets and then we have black and Asian officers defending them? How will that help us move forward? The public will end up suffering.

There was no way the police would accept that they were institutionally racist. I waited for their response, and it came soon enough. They complained that if they weren't allowed to go about their job as they wanted – in other words, if they weren't allowed to make a ridiculous number of stop and searches on innocent black kids – the crime rate would soar. And soon enough they provided the figures to 'prove' their point. They also complained that Macpherson's findings had destroyed morale within the police, that they were the real victims of the Stephen Lawrence Inquiry.

They didn't come straight out with it at first. It was more subtle. Stories appeared saying that officers were breaking down because they were being labelled racist. At first I couldn't understand why they would take it so personally if it wasn't true. Then I realised yes, of course if you weren't racist, and people had all these preconceptions about you, you would be upset. But they were just getting some of their own medicine. After all, it was the police who had labelled me, and countless black kids like me, a mugger. I wasn't a mugger and I'd never mugged anybody in my life and I wouldn't do – what is yours is yours, what you worked for. I respect that, and that is how I was brought up. Yet when I used to walk past white women in the street, they'd grab their handbags. I couldn't get the image of the church-going, law-abiding Taaffes out of my head – how they had refused to come to Steve's aid at first because they thought we were out to mug them.

And for so long officers had gone into the community and arrested black people – mainly young black men – on spurious charges and then let them go. They never felt bad about that, so why should we feel bad about accusing officers of being racist when they'd behaved that way?

If police officers saw me and my friends in a nice car we were bound to be stopped, and it would be, 'Where did you get that car from? Where did you get the money to buy that? Get out of the fucking car, we want to search it for drugs. Stand over there and don't move. Don't any of you move. I don't want to see any of you talking either.'

I was brought up with the idea that you respect police officers. But how can you respect officers who talk to you like that? There has always seemed to be a certain kind of person who went into the British police force – and they've not always been people who want to improve society and keep the peace. Often, I look at officers and think they could have so easily been on the other side of the law. So many of them look brutal and cruel in appearance, like the worst kind of criminal. After Macpherson, I don't think they have changed their attitude. If anything, they have become more intolerant, more angry, more prejudiced. Most police officers still speak to black boys in a totally different way to how they would talk to a white man in a suit. Somehow the uniform changes them: it gives them licence to abuse innocent people.

With the Report published, I thought I may be able to get on with my life. But for the media, it had become the issue that wouldn't go away. I was still working as a photocopier engineer (a job I'd got with the help of the Prince's Trust) Monday to Friday and I was determined that the Inquiry stuff would not interfere with my normal life.

The Report confirmed everything I had thought about the way the police had told lies about me. The great thing was that the officers' statements about me were down there in black and white, and they were riddled with inconsistencies. While PC Joanne Smith called me 'irate and aggressive', Detective Superintendent Ian Crampton, the senior investigating officer, said I was 'truthful and helpful' and 'very calm'.

The most amazing thing was how as time went by in the minds of certain police officers the Duwayne Brooks they came into contact with on the night became more and more of a monster. On the night, PC Linda Bethel, who had questioned me at the scene, described me in her written statement as 'very distressed' and 'very excitable and upset'. I can't really argue with that. Why wouldn't I have been excitable and upset?

By 1994, a year later, she reckoned that I had been 'aggressive', 'anti-police' and 'unhelpful'. Quite a difference. After that, she told the Kent police who were examining the conduct of the initial investigation into Steve's murder that I had been 'powerful and physically intimidating', and that my behaviour was 'horrendous'. Powerful and physically intimidating! In other words, the classic black man of popular prejudice. Macpherson accepted that this 'crescendo of criticism' directed at me showed how racist stereotyping develops. As time passed and the police officers' memories of the real me, the human being distraught at the side of the road, faded, it was replaced by their stereotype of young black men.

A lot of work went in to explaining this to Macpherson. He needed a lot of educating about race. It really was a lot of work, and Jane and me could not do it on our own. She told me about Professor Stuart Hall at the Open University. We gave him, and two lecturers there, Eugene McLaughlin and Gail Lewis, all the stuff the police had said about me. They spent hours and hours analysing it and discussing it with Jane and then wrote the report that explained racial stereotyping to the Inquiry. We got a lot of strength from having them on our side, and the three of them did all of that work for free.

The parents of Rolan Adams gave painful statements about how they were treated by the police after he was murdered by racists. His brother Nathan, who was also attacked when Rolan was killed, and had been in a similar situation to me, told Macpherson how he had been brushed off by the police. His friends also told how they were treated after being racially attacked. It all helped to make clear to Macpherson that it wasn't just Steve and me: there was a pattern to the ignorant way police treated black victims.

Soon after Steve's death, the police had set an internal inquiry in motion supervised by Detective Chief Superintendent John Barker. Even the establishment recognised that it had been a whitewash. In the course of compiling the report, Barker simply asked seventeen police officers if their judgement was influenced by the fact that Steve and I were black. In other words, did they think they went about their work in a racist manner? Not surprisingly, they answered no. Even less surprising was the report's conclusion: they found no evidence to support the allegation of racist conduct by Metropolitan Police officers. Barker admitted to Macpherson that he had not wanted to rock the boat. He had the cheek to suggest that if he had named and shamed officers involved in the initial investigation, it might have reduced the prospect of getting a conviction against the murderers.

While the public inquiry did not say officers were overtly racist, it did find that the police as a whole were institutionally racist. That is to say, their racism was unconscious rather than conscious. I think Macpherson was being generous to them, giving them the benefit of the doubt. Anyway, this is how Sir William defined institutional racism:

> The collective failure of an organisation to provide an appropriate and professional service to people because of their colour, culture, or ethnic origin. It can be seen or detected in processes, attitudes and behaviour which amount to discrimination through unwitting prejudice, ignorance, thoughtlessness and racist stereotyping which disadvantage minority ethnic people.

Macpherson produced numerous examples of this institutional racism. During the course of the Inquiry he spoke to officer after officer who saw no problem in describing black people as 'coloured', and who admitted even six years after Steve's murder that they could not quite believe racism was the motive for the attack.

The Inquiry also agreed that I had been totally sidelined on the night. The police seemed to be too busy working out my involvement in the attack to listen to any information I had to give them. They didn't follow my leads, and it turned out they didn't even take proper notes on the night or, as some of the officers later claimed, they had mysteriously 'lost' them. They didn't even chase after the gang down the street I pointed out.

I felt the Report vindicated Jane as much as me. For years, she had been trying to get through to the police that I was as much a victim of the attack as witness to it. Macpherson certainly recognised this. It took him six weeks of listening to evidence to do so, but when he did he hammered the police for not even inquiring if I was OK or giving me any type of help on the night. In fact, he said, they did quite the opposite.

I had complained about the way they tried to pressure me into giving them a photograph. And Macpherson said I was right to kick up a fuss about it. He said it was bound to make me think I was being treated as some kind of suspect. After all, no other witness had been asked for a photograph.

An unsettling discovery made by the Inquiry was that, because of 'an inexcusable misidentification', the police had suspected me of breaking a window at the police station on the night Steve was killed. Somehow, they had managed to keep this from me. Apparently, they soon discovered that it was another black youth who had broken the window. (Hey, we all look alike!) But the very fact that they assumed it was me showed what they thought of me and black people in general.

At the hospital, the police left me alone. Macpherson said I would have been well within my rights to have gone off home such was their indifference or negligence.

Officers were exposed as having told blatant lies – if they weren't lies, they had the kind of memory that should have made them unemployable. Detective Constable Mick Tomlin said I refused to give him the address of my girlfriend's where I was staying. It was rubbish. And as Macpherson said, if I'd not given them the address, how come they managed to find me there when they arrested me after the demonstration at Welling?

I still felt Macpherson was not treating me as an equal with the Lawrences. He talked about the abject apologies offered to Mr and Mrs Lawrence. And of course they deserved them. But I also felt I was equally deserving of the police's abject apologies. Having said that, he did eventually treat me with some respect. One of the most important things for me was the fact that he said, again and again, that I was in no way to blame for the collapse of the case. In my head, when I was being logical, I knew that. But when you read in the papers that 'trial collapses after vital witness changes story', and you know that the Lawrences and their lawyers are blaming you, you can't help but start doubting yourself.

Macpherson said that they should never have had to rely on my 'glimpsed eyewitness' account, and that it was ridiculous, unbelievable in many ways, that the police had found no other witnesses. The Report acknowledged that I had turned up for every ID parade, and had given nine statements. I was the victim of racist stereotyping on the part of the police, and I had not been treated how I should have been despite doing everything that could have been expected to help.

> The fact that the prosecution of three of the suspects failed is certainly not something for which he can in any way be blamed. The circumstances are such that his evidence was not, when tested, of such strength that it could be used to prove the case against the suspects. That is in no way the fault of Mr Brooks. 'Fleeting-glimpse' evidence is always difficult to use. The problems of the evidence in this case were great, and the trial judge's decision established that this was so, quite apart from the complication of the evidence of Detective Sergeant Christopher Crowley.

Macpherson criticised the Lawrence legal team for bringing the private prosecution, but they made such a fuss about it when they saw the draft report that he withdrew the criticism.

The Lawrences' lawyer Imran Khan was criticised for failing to recognise I was a victim and for failure to provide adequate support for me and most of all for the ridiculous note he and his 'assistant' took, which suggested that I had seen statements made by other witnesses. Macpherson made the point that his confused statement helped undermine our evidence at the private prosecution: 'That note and the evidence of Mr Ratip and Mr Khan played its part in the destruction of the validity of the evidence of Mr Brooks at the Old Bailey.'

The way I was treated was so different from the manner of Imran and Michael Mansfield. The Inquiry recognised that I was ill with post-traumatic stress disorder and that it might be bad for me to attend in person. It said I could appear in front of it and give my evidence directly, but it also said it was up to me and that it didn't want to cause me unnecessary hurt when I'd already been through so much. In the end, I turned up at the Inquiry for three days in May 1998, and the statement I made was read out by Rajiv. I heard about the Inquiry every day from Jane.

Even the police accepted that they had treated me badly on the night. Assistant Commissioner Ian Johnston said, 'There is a real lesson for us to learn in how we handled Duwayne Brooks at the scene. I don't think we dealt with Duwayne Brooks very well at all. I think we let him down . . . This is one of the major lessons from this Inquiry: he should have been dealt with better.' It still gets to me that those admissions had to be extracted out of the Assistant Commissioner by Jane when she was cross-examining him, while the police volunteered an apology to the Lawrences.

The Report said:

> The greatest trauma suffered by Mr Brooks was that he
> saw his friend murdered, dying on the pavement, and
> dead as he was carried into the hospital. And he has had
> to endure that night, and the whole course of the failed
> investigation. He was a primary victim of the racist attack.
> He is also the victim of all that has followed, including
> the conduct of the case and the treatment of himself as a
> witness and not as a victim.

It was when I attended the Inquiry that I discovered what Mr and Mrs Lawrence had said about me to Macpherson. I was shocked. Devastated. Soon after Steve's death, we had agreed not to say anything personal about each other. Till then, I had always stood by the agreement. But for years I'd heard second- or third-hand that they were bad-mouthing me. And now here it was, all official in their statement. I don't know whether they said what they did because they believed it or simply because they wanted to hurt me, but it certainly made me feel terrible when I read it.

Mrs Lawrence had suggested Elvin was Steve's real friend and that I had needed Steve much more than Steve had needed me, and that he never really liked me. If that was the case why did she say in her statement to Macpherson that Steve used to complain that it was unfair that he had a curfew when I didn't? Mr Lawrence said that he was surprised that Steve had been out with me that night, and he presumed it must have been because Elvin wasn't available. If he didn't know it at the time, he certainly realised later that what he said was both unfair and wrong. At the Inquiry in 1998 he stopped me in the corridor to apologise, but I walked into my room. Later on, I got a knock on my door from the father of Rolan Adams, who had become a friend of Mr Lawrence, and he asked if he could have a word with me. He told me Mr Lawrence had asked him to talk to me, to apologise for all the things he had said about me, and that he had only gone along with it to keep the peace with Mrs Lawrence. Mr Adams told me I should accept his apology and make up with Steve's dad. But I couldn't. Perhaps they were traumatised, but what the Lawrences said was for the record and will remain on the record.

It was some time after the Report was published that I managed to read it in detail. Although I'd known the police had had a lot of leads to the five main suspects, I had never realised quite how much they had on them. What appalled me was not simply the number of people who named the Acourts and Norris as being responsible, but the amount of history the police had on them. Within forty-eight hours, a witness known as K had told the police that he went to the Acourts' house just after Steve had been killed, and that he'd seen one of them without his top on, with wet hair. Witness K also said that they were already denying their role in the murder – before anyone had accused them.

Witness B said that he had seen David Norris and Neil Acourt acting suspiciously just near the scene of the attack and straight after it, although some of his evidence was shown to be flawed. A man, given the alias James Grant by the police, turned up at Eltham police station saying that the Acourts and David Norris were responsible for Steve's murder, and claiming that they had stabbed at least three people he knew of. He said that Norris had stabbed Stacey Benefield, and that the gang were linked to the racist killing of Rohit Duggal in July 1992 on the very same road Steve had been killed on.

Now most investigating teams who had just received the information James Grant had given them would not believe their luck. The first thing they would do is officially sign him up as an informant, and make sure he got a suitable reward. Amazingly, the investigating officers didn't sign Grant up. They told Macpherson that they had done, or thought they had done, but when it came to finding the forms, well, they just weren't there. The police allowed a vital informant to drift away. Why? Was it incompetence or convenience?

And there was a phone call made by an anonymous woman the evening after the murder. She said that two white boys who thought they were the Krays were responsible – the Acourts called themselves 'the Eltham Krays'. It also came out that two anonymous letters had been left for the police, one in a phone box and one actually on the rear windscreen of a police car. Both claimed that Jamie and Neil Acourt, David Norris and Gary Dobson were 'involved' in the attack on Steve and linked Neil Acourt and Norris to the Benefield stabbing. The police had both letters within forty-eight hours of Steve's murder. By 29 April, a week after Steve's death, the police had received twenty-five anonymous calls naming the Acourts, Norris and Dobson. And there weren't arrests for another week.

When they did bother to take account of what witnesses had to say, the police still managed to piss them off or frighten them to such an extent that they withdrew their cooperation. Joey Shepherd, who had seen the attack from the bus and rushed off to the Lawrences' house to tell them what had happened, was, of course, one of the prime witnesses. He was also, initially, one of the most willing. But somehow the police even managed to scare him off. The public inquiry pointed out that after the first ID parade, when he was named by one of the officers and was convinced this had been heard by the suspects, he refused to turn up for another ID parade.

Surely an important part of the job of policing is to win over the trust of those people who can help you. But the officers involved in this investigation did the opposite. Take the case of Witness K, who told them what he had seen at the Acourts' house just after Steve was killed. By the time the police convinced him to make a statement, almost a month later, Witness K would admit he had been round to the Acourts' house but refused to make any mention of the wet hair or the fact that they were known to have stabbed people.

You would think that as soon as the police had done their research they would have realised that most of the suspects – even though they hadn't been convicted – had the type of history littered with alleged stabbings and racist incidents that made them likely to be responsible for a racist killing.

It turned out that Jamie Acourt, David Norris and Luke Knight had allegedly been involved in assaulting two brothers called Witham in May 1992. Norris was charged with the wounding, and Jamie Acourt with possession of an offensive weapon. The charges were later dropped by the Crown Prosecution Service, which said that it wasn't in the public interest to pursue them 'on the grounds of staleness'. But the team investigating Steve's death somehow managed not to discover information about this stabbing.

Kevin London, a sixteen-year-old black boy, alleged that he had been confronted by a white gang in November 1992, and that Gary Dobson had threatened him with a knife. No charge was brought against Dobson. On 11 March, a month before Steve died, a twenty-two-year-old Asian man called Gurdeep Bhangal was stabbed by a white man after he served him in the Wimpy Bar on Eltham High Street, and the description of the attackers matched the Acourt group. No charges were brought.

If the police had done a little bit of basic research in the first few days, rather than concentrating their energies on trying to find a way to blame Steve and me for having been attacked, they would have discovered even more. In 1990, Jamie Acourt was excluded from his school twice. He was interviewed by police after threatening a black kid with an airgun shaped like a Smith & Wesson. No charge was brought. Neil Acourt, armed with a lump of wood, had pushed another boy, Sean Kalitsi, down concrete stairs and left him unconscious. After another fight with black pupils, a monkey wrench was found in his bag. That was when he was permanently excluded from school. In 1992, Neil Acourt brandished a knife and threatened a black boy at the Samuel Montague Sports Club. Both Acourt brothers were banned from a youth club for daubing 'NF' on the walls. No charges were brought. Detective Constable Dennis Chase admitted to Macpherson that no one on the team had considered investigating the schools or clubs the white gang went to.

As for David Norris, he was also expelled from school for being violent and uncontrollable. Amazingly, his name didn't seem to ring a bell with Detective Superintendent Crampton, despite the fact that Crampton had just been working on the murder of another man also called David Norris who had claimed to be a cousin of Clifford Norris. Clifford Norris, David's father, was on the run from the police and was a well-known and feared local criminal. He had made his money from drugs and had a history of violence.

So why didn't the police act on the information? Detective Superintendent Crampton said that they were waiting to get enough evidence to make the charges stick. Macpherson called it a 'vital and fundamental mistake', and said he would have been much more likely to get the evidence by arresting them and searching their homes thoroughly early on, and looking for forensics while they were still fresh.

The bigger question was did the police actually want to arrest the white gang? The thing that seemed to sum it all up for me was the fact that they had diverted resources from observing them to observing a black lad who was suspected of a minor street crime.

The police had said that they found it difficult to get witnesses to go on the record because it seemed they were all so frightened of Clifford Norris. What they were less willing to talk about was their own relationship with Norris. If local people were terrified of him, who was to say that individual officers were not equally scared? Then again, if Clifford Norris had bribed Stacey Benefield not to give evidence, who was to say that he wouldn't bribe the police to lay off his son's gang?

The more I looked at the evidence presented to Macpherson, the more I couldn't help feeling he'd let them off the hook. If it hadn't been in such tragic circumstances, the police surveillance of the Acourts' family home would have been hilarious. The police admitted, with a straight face, that they saw the suspects removing black bin bags from the house, but admitted the information couldn't be communicated between officers and no one was able to seize them.

When Gary Dobson was interviewed by the police, he told them that he didn't know David Norris. Well, the police actually saw Norris visiting his house – and this time they even managed to take a photograph of it. Only one problem – they failed to confront Dobson with the photo and ask him why he was lying to them. At one point, officers told Macpherson that it was difficult for them to survey Norris's house properly because it was too big.

Not that their surveillance of the Acourts was any better. The police were told that the brothers kept knives under their floor-boards. So you'd assume that one of the first things the police would do would be to lift the floorboards? Think again.

It also emerged – after a fight with the counsel to the Inquiry, who later apologised for 'overlooking' the documents – that one of the protection officers assigned to me, referred to as Sergeant XX, also happened to associate with Clifford Norris. Macpherson ruled that Sergeant XX was not directly involved in the investigation into Steve's murder, but how thin is the line between being directly involved and not being? In fact, he had worked closely with the first senior investigating officer, Crampton, on previous cases. Sergeant XX had earlier been disciplined and demoted for an incident unconnected to his friendship with Clifford Norris. After his demotion, he went to Crampton for a reference, who duly wrote what a first-rate copper Sergeant XX was.

Macpherson ultimately decided that Sergeant XX had not corrupted the Inquiry because the link from Clifford Norris to Sergeant XX to Crampton was too remote. But in another way Sergeant XX was linked very directly to the case. It wasn't until Macpherson that I discovered one of the officers who (supposedly) looked after me at night when I was giving evidence at the private prosecution was none other than Sergeant XX. It's hard to believe that something like that could happen accidentally. After all, everyone in police circles had been talking about the fact that he'd been mixing with Norris. Was it some kind of sick joke? Were they hoping I'd know all about him, and be terrified? All I can say is that I'm glad I didn't find out who he was till way after the trial.

Macpherson examined whether there was any evidence of corruption rather than simple incompetence in the investigation into Steve's death. He said from the outset that this would be much more difficult to prove because the burden of proof he had to apply was that which would stick in a criminal court, whereas they could conclude other things, such as institutional racism, on the strength of evidence you would need for a civil case, the balance of probabilities.

Not surprisingly, the evidence gathered by the Inquiry failed to meet these standards. But Macpherson made it clear that this did not mean he had proved the investigation was not corrupt. He had simply failed to prove that it was corrupt. At times, he himself seemed baffled as to how the police team could have been quite so hopeless without being bent.

In the chapter on me, Macpherson concluded:

> Our hope is that once this part of Mr Brooks' life is over he will be able to cope with his memories and lead a normal life again. He has suffered greatly as a result of the events of 1993, and also because he too is obviously affected by the failure of the investigation into his friend's death. Perhaps acceptance of his case to the extent here set out will help him to come to terms with life for the future.

I hoped so too. I really did think that now I could start to put everything behind me. Little did I, or Macpherson, realise what the police had in store for me.

Chapter 12

They're Out to Get Me

Everybody wanted to interview me about the Macpherson Report. At the Inquiry, everything had been going along quietly until my statement was read out. It rocked the Inquiry because it showed exactly what the police were doing. There would not have been a public inquiry into the murder of Steve if Mr and Mrs Lawrence had not persistently called for one, but they didn't actually have that much to say about the police because they had not really been on the receiving end of their abuse. All they knew was that the police hadn't done their job properly.

In my statements to Macpherson I said a lot of things that the police didn't like – that their racism was ingrained and that the then Commissioner Paul Condon should be sacked. But Jane and me felt sure that a deal had been done to save Condon's dignity. He wouldn't be sacked, but he would resign in his own time – the classic police get-out. You couldn't have the police commissioner sacked because of the untimely death of one black lad, after all. Mind you, I couldn't help thinking that if a white boy had been murdered by a black gang, and the police had shown the same degree of incompetence and corruption, heads would have rolled.

On the day of the Report's publication I went on BBC's *Newsnight*. It was common knowledge that I wanted Condon to resign because his position had become impossible to defend. And I certainly wasn't alone in calling for it – the Lawrences were also after his head. And this was our big chance to put the case to the nation.

We hoped Condon was going to be on the panel. It was supposed to be me, Jane, Mr Lawrence, Mansfield and Condon. But guess what? Condon didn't show up. They sent the Metropolitan Police Federation spokesman, Glen Smythe – the man with the task of defending the police whatever the situation.

Everything was going well and I was waiting for presenter Kirsty Wark to ask me about Condon, so I could say my bit. But they asked me about some petty incident in which Mrs Lawrence had been called racist names in a car park – she felt aggrieved about it because it was just after Steve had been killed, and the police didn't want to prosecute the car-park racists because their dad had just died. Of course, it was wrong, but what did it have to do with me? What could I say about it? I was still waiting for the Condon question.

But then Kirsty Wark just moved on to Mr Lawrence. 'Do you still feel Mr Condon should be sacked?'

Ah well, if I couldn't do it, at least he would give Condon what for. But something strange happened. He bottled it, refusing to give a straight answer.

He stuttered, and he moaned and he groaned. I was going, 'Say it then, say it: he should be sacked, he shouldn't be forced to resign, he should be sacked. Say it.' I wasn't just saying it in my head, I was actually saying it down the mic and obviously the producers could hear me. 'Ask me,' I was saying, and I was staring daggers at Kirsty, begging her with my eyes. Ask me, ask me, ask me, and I'll tell you straight. But she didn't.

The *Newsnight* team were waiting for Mr Lawrence to say yes, of course he should be sacked, but he never did. It was baffling because he'd made all that fuss before over Condon being forced out. And now he said nothing about it.

A number of other people backed down after the Report was released. The Home Office Minister Paul Boateng had also said Condon should resign, but then it seemed that his strings were pulled and he had to toe the line. He turned out to be a useful 'alternative' face for the Establishment: someone who appeared to have clout but seemed ultimately to be nothing more than a black puppet. No surprise then that Boateng went on to be Britain's first black Cabinet Minister.

What was going on? It was one of the few times in a TV interview where I knew the right words would have just flowed out of my mouth. 'Yes, of course he should be sacked' – I knew exactly what I would say. I was already saying it to myself: Condon himself has made it clear that he was taking a personal interest in this case, so therefore he cannot say he is not responsible for his individual officers and their actions; he must have known the ins and outs of the case from top to bottom, therefore he should be sacked.

They never came back to me, and I was fuming. But I was still happy that I was there. At the end we went downstairs and they were having a little party. The show was good – but it could have been so much better.

Mr Lawrence was downstairs and I went and sat a couple of seats away from him. His face was twisted as if he was writhing in agony. It was painful to watch. He looked so full of regret.

How on earth can the head of the police force not be blamed for the behaviour of his officers? In any other job the person responsible for their workers would shoulder the blame when everything collapsed. But here in the police force the commissioner is not responsible for his officers. What a bloody joke. And what made it more of a joke was that the Lawrences supported him being kicked out and then changed their minds. As far as I'm concerned once you're interested in finding justice you stay on the justice road – you don't divert for any reasons whatsoever, not for the offer of money or other favours or to preserve your social standing; you stay on that justice road. And I decided then I was staying on it. What that meant was that I had to tell as many people as possible how the police had treated Steve and me.

Everyone jumped on the big headline that the police were institutionally racist, but they weren't interested that underneath the headline nothing had really changed, and in a way things would be even worse for black people. Because that's what they do – give you a little, and take back a lot, or at least that was to prove true in my experience.

A few days after the Report was published, the Home Office announced that it was to give £300,000 to the Stephen Lawrence Trust. I couldn't believe it. Three hundred grand. And for what? Would the Trust help victims of crime? It didn't have to be just black victims of crime, they could be black or white. But no, the Lawrence Trust was to help budding architects. Of course, that was part of the mythology that had grown up around Steve – he was all set to be Britain's greatest architect because he had done a couple of weeks' work experience at an architect's office.

Now Steve wanting to be an architect is completely different from his being one. Let's face it, we all wanted to be something at that age. The fact is, bright though Steve was, the way things were heading at school, he wasn't on course for being an architect. He wasn't working hard enough, and he didn't seem to want it enough. Actually, I'm not sure that he wanted it at all. He certainly never spoke much about it. The late teens are a funny time, when many of us cut ourselves off from our parents, demand our privacy. I did it, and so did Steve.

I don't think Mr and Mrs Lawrence really knew what he wanted to do at that stage of his life. They didn't know because they didn't speak much to him and he didn't speak much to them. Yet they set up this trust for architects, and now the Home

Office was giving them £300,000. I'm not sure whether Steve would laugh or cry at the idea of the Trust in his name. I certainly don't think he'd be very happy about it. It seems so removed from who he was – the young kid who liked a laugh, played games, watched videos and was a talented athlete in the making.

I was kept out of everything. A steering group was set up to look at ways of remodelling the police into a respectable organisation. Mr and Mrs Lawrence were on it, but I wasn't asked. I was upset. It's not that I wanted to be on TV, or hogging the headlines, but I did want to be involved in trying to transform the police from a racist organisation to one that both black and white communities could trust and respect. And who better to have on the committee than someone who had been so comprehensively shafted by them?

You criticise the police at your peril. I was beginning to find this out. Get too close to them, start saying things they don't want to hear, and funny things start happening in your life. It may begin with your car, move on to your house, and before long you can find yourself at the receiving end of all kinds of weirdness.

In February 1999, Alex Owolade, who headed the pressure group Movement for Justice, which supported people who had been wronged by the criminal justice system, had organised a march to Downing Street to protest against police brutality and deaths in custody. We had decided to hand a petition in at Downing Street because that would ensure publicity.

We went to Downing Street to hand the petition in. Tony Blair wasn't there – I think he was attending King Hussein of Jordan's funeral at the time. There were lots of cameras and reporters. Everything went well.

Later that evening I was staying at my friend Bev's house. She lived in a quiet residential street. You couldn't breathe on the street without someone knowing about it: you couldn't drop money on the floor without someone seeing it and returning it to you. The road was so narrow that only one car could pass at a time. I parked my car and went inside. The same night my car was broken into. This is when the harassment started.

Was it a coincidence that my car was broken into the same day I'd attended the march? The strange thing is that there was nothing in my car to steal, and there were more expensive cars on the road. They stole my football stuff, my aftershave, deodorant, and my tool kit. What was the point of nicking all that? Maybe they could have sold the odd screwdriver or spray-can, but it didn't really make sense.

I phoned the police and said that my car had been broken into.

'Well, it's not an emergency,' said the officer at the other end of the line.

'It is an emergency,' I said, 'because obviously I've been targeted.'

'Why would you be targeted, Mr Brooks?'

'Because I was on the march yesterday, and obviously people high up in the Met didn't like that.' I was fucked off. I knew I had no evidence it was the police, but I just had an instinct.

They came round and put up one of those yellow boards asking for witnesses. It was lip service, to show me they were doing something. But actually they didn't even bother with the basics.

'Is that the best you can do?' I asked.

'We haven't got the manpower to do door-to-door.'

A few days later my car got broken into again.

I used to work for a firm called First Choice Copiers, based at the Leyton industrial estate. There was no lighting outside on the estate, so once it got dark it got proper dark. The lady staff used to complain that when they were locking up they felt unsafe – once you came out of the front door it was pitch black. I'd come back to the office to pick up some stuff about 7 p.m., and it was dark. I was in the office for fifteen minutes maximum. When I returned to my car the door was open. My suit jacket, my radio cassette player and my phone had all been stolen.

Who could it have been – kids, someone else on the estate or the harassers? There was only one way in and one way out of the estate. If you were walking it would take you ten minutes minimum and fifteen minutes for most people to get out of that estate. There was no one working on the estate at that time of night – all the shutters were down and the lights were off. So who could it have been? Kids on bikes could put the stereo and phone in their back pockets, but how were they going to ride away holding my jacket? And they'd look pretty suspicious wearing it. And what is the point of nicking a suit jacket? Not for money, because you couldn't sell it for much.

I reported the break-in to the police. They came round, told me that unfortunately there was little they could do, and they were as good as their word. It seemed that the more I talked publicly about Macpherson's findings and my experience with the police, the more funny stuff happened to me.

Although I knew there were more people who wanted to hear my side of the story, there were still many times I felt I was excluded. The Tricycle Theatre in north-west London had dramatised the Macpherson Inquiry. The *Guardian* journalist Richard Norton-Taylor had edited the transcripts from the interviews and turned them into a play. Everybody seemed to have been invited to the premiere. Well, everyone except me. I was livid.

I phoned up the theatre and was put through to a guy called Nicholas Kent. It turned out that he ran the theatre, and in the near future he'd do me a really good turn. But at the time I wasn't best pleased with him.

'Hello, it's Duwayne Brooks here. Why haven't you invited me to your play?' I didn't bother with niceties.

'Well, I just thought you'd be coming with the Lawrences.' He said he presumed that we were all friends.

'No,' I said. 'Why would we all be friends? Have you ever seen me and the Lawrences together?'

I was aggressive on the phone because he was behaving just like the rest – I was an irrelevance, and so long as he looked after Mr and Mrs Lawrence everything would be OK. This was despite the fact that I was one of the main characters in the play. It was fine to have public debates about me, fine to turn me into a dramatic character, but somehow people found it difficult to consult me about it or treat me with respect.

He was apologetic. He said he'd organise however many tickets I wanted. Nick told me that after the play there would be a discussion and the Channel 4 news presenter Jon Snow, Michael Mansfield, the journalist Brian Cathcart, who had just written a book about Steve and the Inquiry, and Jane would be on the panel. No problem, I said, I was happy with that.

I went to the play with Melly. It was great, because I'd only attended three days of the Inquiry and what had happened throughout the rest of it intrigued me. This was a well-edited summary of everything that had gone on. After the play everybody was asking questions. I waited till just before the end to ask my question. I wanted to ask Michael Mansfield if he knew anything about the corruption surrounding the investigation that everyone was talking about – but I thought that was pushing it. I suppose I just wanted to embarrass him. I could never forgive him for the way he refused to look at me at the trial and treated me as if I was an untrustworthy idiot. I put up my hand, and the chair of the panel spotted me and said my name.

'Mr Mansfield,' I said. He gave me a look that I'll never forget. Actually, I couldn't ever remember him looking at me before. Even when we walked past each other at court, he didn't look at my face – not at the committal, not at the trial. He always turned his head the other way. But this time he looked me straight in the eye.

Mansfield went white. I sat there for a second and then gave him an easy question. Mansfield joked it off. He started laughing, and I started laughing, but he knew I wasn't happy. He knew I felt that for some reason he'd not put in his normal performance for me at court, that the prosecution should not have happened when I was unfit. He knew I'd be savaged by the defence barristers, and I wanted to know why he'd let it go ahead. I promised myself that one day I'd find out.

A few weeks later there was another discussion panel – this time at the Stratford East theatre. The Lawrences were due there, Michael Mansfield, Imran Khan, the police and me. Ros Howells was the chairperson. And it turned out to be complete chaos.

It was so strange – Imran, Michael Mansfield, Jane, me and Mr Lawrence in the one room. Michael Mansfield, Imran and Mr Lawrence predictably ignored me. None of them could look me in the face. The people who were around – the cast and theatre staff – didn't know what to do, didn't know what to say, didn't know where to put themselves as we all ignored each other. And I have to admit I felt good because I didn't have a guilty conscience about anything. The Lawrences and their legal team must have felt bad about something not to be able to look me in the eye.

The panel discussion got under way and I asked Mr Lawrence why didn't he and Mrs Lawrence support Alex Owolade and his Movement for Justice when they were supporting them.

Mr Lawrence got upset. He said he never told anyone what to do, he never told anyone what marches to go on, so why should anyone tell him. But we weren't telling him: we were just asking why they didn't support us. They had so much influence in the black community and with the police, but they weren't prepared to make the most of it. Like so many people, the Lawrences seemed reluctant to get involved in anything not directly to do with them and their family.

Ros Howells interrupted to try to calm things down, and Michael Mansfield tried to change the subject by talking about their film production of the Lawrence story. 'Watch it for the brilliance of Duwayne,' he said. I think he meant the person who played me.

'Why watch it for me?' I said. 'It's nothing to do with me, I'm not involved in it.' A few months before, while the Inquiry was still going on, Mansfield's wife Yvette Vanson, who ran Vanson Productions, had asked me to be involved in a docudrama about the Lawrence case. It seemed weird to me: a conflict of interests. There was her husband representing the Lawrences, and here was Yvette Vanson making a TV movie about it. I felt that they were on the verge of turning Steve into an industry.

They had wanted my support for the film and tried to tie me up in a contract for £50. But I'd been told that the budget for this docudrama was a couple of million pounds. Yet they wanted to tie me up in a contract for £50. And they were supposed to be socialists! I told her I wasn't interested. But she persisted. I wouldn't budge. I didn't trust her. I thought that they would make a film that showed everything from the perspective of the Lawrences. I was convinced that they'd listen to what I had to say and then switch it round to make me look bad, because their sympathy was with the Lawrences.

It was chaos in this room. All the splits, the tensions, of the past few years were coming to the surface. Marc Wadsworth, the leader of the Anti-Racist Alliance, which had thrown its weight behind the Lawrences, then stood up and started shouting at Jane, and saying to me I shouldn't let her represent me. I defended Jane: I didn't know what his problem was, but if it hadn't been for Jane my case would have got nowhere. I later learned that he was angry because Jane had represented Ken Livingstone after Marc had assaulted him.

After the show I was standing with some friends in the corridor reading about the productions that had been on at Stratford East. I saw Yvette Vanson. Her film about Steve was going to be shown on television in a few days' time. I asked her if she had really wanted me involved.

'Of course, Duwayne,' she said. 'We would have loved you to have been involved.'

'So how much was the budget for the film?' I said.

She suddenly looked livid. 'Oh, Duwayne, why don't you fuck off?' she said in front of everybody. It was great. People turned round in amazement. She just walked off, straight through the crowd.

People looked at me, awkwardly, and wanted to know what that had been all about. I just told them. 'We were talking about their film, and I just asked her what the budget was, because I'd heard it was a couple of million pounds, and they'd offered me £50 to take part and I didn't.'

It wasn't the money though: I made it clear that I hadn't taken part because I thought it would be one-sided – just the Lawrences' version of events. I didn't feel I would be able to influence the slant the film was clearly going to be given.

When I eventually saw the film, my worst fears were confirmed. The way they portrayed me, it was like I was some bad boy, some rude kid – or as Mrs Lawrence had called me, a ragamuffin.

Even though more and more of my life seemed to be given over to Steve and the Inquiry – whether it was in my dealings with the police, or talking in public about what we had experienced – I continued working as normal, Monday to Friday. I was determined that the Lawrence Inquiry stuff wouldn't interfere with my normal life. But it was easier said than done. Inevitably, there were overlaps.

Jane received a call from a Mr Carling in Belfast. Somehow he had heard about me and what I was going through. I called him back and he asked if I would go to Belfast to be on a panel to talk about the racism I'd suffered in England. The whole debate was going to be about racism. Now, in Northern Ireland they have a different kind of racism, if you can call it that – Protestants against Catholics. The Protestants were like the white majority;

the Catholics were like the black minority. And as with black people in Britain, it had always been the Catholics who found it hard to get jobs and houses.

The panel was to consist of a lady whose brother, Robert Hamill, had been kicked to death in front of the RUC as they stood by and watched, and there was also going to be a representative of the murdered civil-rights lawyer Rosemary Nelson.

I asked Jane about it. She said she thought I should go. But I was worried. All you ever heard about Northern Ireland on the news was the riots, the bombings, the killings. I was sure that even I could find safer things to be doing with my time.

The plane to Belfast took only forty-five minutes once it was up in the air. I went with Melly and we met up with David Carling and his wife. David was mixed race, and his wife was white. They took me into Belfast and showed me around. It seemed peaceful, but I thought it had to be a lie.

'How come it's so quiet?' I said to David.

'That's how it gets sometimes,' he said, 'and at other times it's deadly to be out on the streets, especially when it's dark, and especially if you've got colour in your skin.'

When I got to the meeting I was panicky. I'd been asked to speak for twenty-five minutes, and I'd written out a statement. I'd never done anything like that in my life. While I was walking around the city centre beforehand, I saw posters announcing that Duwayne Brooks would be here to speak at the meeting. How on earth could so many people know about me in Belfast? It amazed me.

Not many people really knew about me in London, yet here in Belfast posters were up and everybody seemed to know my story. They knew about the Lawrences, but they also knew about me.

They also seemed to recognise that my fight was different from the Lawrences'. That amazed me, too. Mr and Mrs Lawrence had spent years fighting for their son, and it was a very important fight. And their fight for Steve had evolved into a bigger fight for justice for black people. But I don't think they were ever interested in becoming representatives of the black people who were harassed by the police on a daily basis. Theirs was a very particular fight for a very particular boy – that's why they chose to start up a trust for budding architects rather than, say, victims of police brutality.

I got up to speak and realised there were more than two hundred people in the audience. There were a lot of political people at this meeting – Socialist Workers and various political people from the left. And they understood that it was because we were fighting so hard for change that the police and the Lawrences wanted to keep us out of the picture.

The twenty-five minutes went so quickly. I started with the incident, talked about what had happened since, and how the police had behaved throughout. Then they stood up and clapped for what seemed like ages. It felt so good. So, so good. The chairperson thanked me and then everybody talked. It was so strange listening to the plights of other people. The lady whose brother had been killed spoke with so much pain as she described how he had been kicked to death with the police casually looking on, doing nothing about it. I heard all about the good work Rosemary Nelson had done as a lawyer – so good that the Unionist terrorists thought she was best out of the way – and how she had received death threats and feared for her life. Rosemary told the police about the threats, but they ignored her and refused to give her protection. It was a shocking story, but not an unbelievable one.

We heard from other people who had experienced hatred, not because of their colour but because of their religion. Everyone was praying to one God, yet Catholics and Protestants wanted to destroy each other over that belief. So much blind hate, so much stupidity. Yet here in this room there was so much warmth and hope and love.

I spent the Saturday and Sunday just walking around town. I was with Melly and we were staying in the Europa hotel in Belfast city centre. It was pretty expensive considering it was supposed to be the most bombed hotel in Europe, but I suppose they needed the money to glue it back together every so often.

The ladies I came across seemed to be intrigued by me. I think it was because I was black, and most of them had never seen such a dark-skinned person, certainly not in Belfast. Walking around town was fascinating – soldiers on the streets, helicopters in the air, and people living normally through all this. It's amazing how resilient we are.

We got a taxi to Burger King. I was sitting down eating when three girls came up to me. They wouldn't leave me alone. They kept commenting on how nice I was, touching my skin, and giving me a cuddle. They asked Melly if she minded if they kissed me – they didn't ask me, they asked Melly! Then they all tried to kiss me at once. I was like something from a Victorian freak show. They followed us back to the hotel and milled around in the lobby. We were talking and joking and laughing. They asked me to talk all the time, so they could hear my accent.

The most I paid for a cab when I was there was about £1. It wasn't like in England where you had the cab to yourself. Here the driver just picked up more people till the cab was full. That also seemed weird. Here we were in a country where people were in constant fear of attack, yet they were willing to share cabs with strangers. The bombs and the shootings were still in the back of my mind, but everyone seemed to be so friendly.

A couple of times I walked from the games arcade to the hotel and women driving past in their cars would stop and ask if I was OK, if I needed a lift somewhere, if I was lost. I don't think they were propositioning me, I think they were just being kind. You'd never get a white woman stopping to see if you were OK in London. But racism is complicated. Perhaps the strangers were so nice to me because I was such a curiosity, and that there hadn't been an opportunity for racism to rear its head in Northern Ireland simply because there weren't enough black people for it to be considered a problem.

Then again, David had already warned me that it wasn't safe for black people at night. Night-time was completely different from day. You couldn't really be on the road walking. If you were going from one place to another you'd have to take a taxi – straight out of the taxi and through the door, no loitering.

I was taken to a pub in the city centre. I don't normally drink, but there was no way I could refuse here. By the time I left I thought my belly was going to burst. Everybody wanted to buy me a Guinness. When I stepped into the pub I was offered a pint of Guinness, when I was trying to leave I was offered a pint of Guinness. In between times I was offered numerous Guinnesses. 'Oh, you'll have one more just before you leave, well at least a half, go on you'll be having a half,' I was told on my way out. I didn't spend anything in that pub. Even people who obviously had next to no money insisted on buying me a drink.

I had never imagined I would go to Belfast, least of all to talk about racism. But the more I talked to people, the more I realised that our problems were the same – I found hatred and prejudice, just as at home.

I returned to London exhilarated.

One Saturday night, I was staying at a friend's house. Actually, she was more than a friend. She was a special lady friend, who lived in Tufnell Park, north London. Often, when I was driving I would get this feeling I was being followed by the police. Most of the time it didn't really bother me – after all, I knew I wasn't doing anything bad. The only thing I was really worried about was the safety of my friends and my special friend at that time. I knew what the police were like and didn't want anything to happen to them, especially in their jobs, or any damage to happen to their cars or their houses.

So whenever I went to my special friend's house I used to try to make sure I wasn't followed, and I had my own anti-surveillance strategies, which varied. Before setting off, I would always check under the car and look at all the other cars in the near vicinity. I would often drive around the block twice before actually setting off on my real journey. I would occasionally take the long way to somewhere to see if anyone was following. That night, though, I was exhausted and had forgotten to shake the police off my trail.

I woke up the next morning and my car had been broken into. My tool case had been stolen again.

I was beginning to feel more like my old self, more capable of dealing with the situation. The stronger I felt, the more angry I was at the way Imran had treated me just after Steve's death and at the private prosecution. I wanted an apology from him – just like I wanted one from the police – an apology for what he made me go through, and an apology for the fact that he broke client confidentiality by releasing the incorrect note his assistant took of our conversation in 1993 without consulting me. For ages, an apology would have been sufficient.

But the longer he refused to apologise, the more pissed off I got with him. I said to Jane that we had to do something about this. She wasn't keen – she said it would look bad if we took action against him.

A letter was sent to Imran in April to let him know what I was prepared to do if he didn't apologise. I gave him a deadline to apologise – that's all we asked for: an apology. As usual Imran didn't get back to us. We faxed him again. He still didn't get back to us. So we issued a writ, forcing him to respond. I felt good issuing a writ. It was my only way of getting an answer out of him because he wouldn't answer my calls – just like in the bad old days when he was supposedly my lawyer. I wanted to show him that he had to respect people, regardless of who his most important clients were.

It cost me £100 to issue the writ, but it was worth it. I'm not the gloating kind, but I did want to be able to gloat when I saw Imran, I did want to be able to laugh at him, because his lack of care and incompetence could have destroyed me – almost did. I wanted to be able to say to him, 'Look what not apologising has cost you, and that initial apology would have been free and easy!'

I took every opportunity to talk about the police. I just wanted the truth to be known. So I went on pirate radio stations and told listeners how the police had let me down in the first place, and targeted me when I refused to shut up.

Then it happened again. My car was broken into. This time nothing was stolen, it was just ransacked. There were only boring technical documents about photocopiers in the car, but they were still disturbed. Obviously, they were looking for something, perhaps letters between me and my solicitor.

Sometimes my bins were also ransacked. Rubbish would be tipped out on the block. It never bothered me because I didn't put anything in the bin without tearing it up. Most times I would take my rubbish and drive off with it, and dump it in a different bin.

Meanwhile, the police tried to make me feel like I was a some-body – 'the surviving victim of the murderous attack on Stephen Lawrence'. They brought me up to the newly established Racial and Violent Crime Taskforce headquarters at Scotland Yard. I think they were trying to impress me, so I looked suitably impressed, smiled as they wanted, pretended I felt important. But I knew it was a game. Promises were made – I'd be brought to the training centre to see how the training was done; I'd be asked to recommend changes; I'd be consulted on the racial-awareness training.

They had a poster stuck up, proclaiming the Met's dedication to eradicating racism. It had a picture of Steve on it. Some big names had signed up. They asked me to sign, and I said no.

They asked me why not. I said that nobody had been convicted for Steve's murder so why should I sign the poster. The Racial and Violent Crime Taskforce sounded very impressive, but I wanted to see what it achieved before I signed up to any campaign.

The number of reported racist incidents in London had risen: in February 1999 it had been about 1200; in March 2200 racist incidents had been reported. What did the increase mean – that more racist crimes were occurring or that after the Lawrence Inquiry more were being reported? Or simply that officers were now bothering to record the racist assaults? I didn't know. All I did know was that the arrest and conviction rates were dismal.

Probably, the main reason for the increased number of reported racist crimes was that the police now had to log all racist incidents as such if the victim considered it to be a racist attack. The police no longer had the power to turn round and say that they didn't think it was racist – which is just what so many officers were still saying to Macpherson six years after Steve's death. It gave people more confidence to come forward after they'd been attacked.

My car was broken into yet again in May – less than three weeks since the last time. A couple of hundred pounds' worth of copier equipment was stolen, plus manuals and toner, and a few of my papers. This time it happened outside my house. What was the purpose of nicking the stuff? There hadn't even been anything to tempt them with – nothing on display, nothing on the seats. This time the mystery vandal had to go in the boot to find the stuff. Was this just an opportunistic crime? Somebody nicking stuff to satisfy their drug habit? I didn't think so. After all, another vehicle had to have been used to carry the stuff away. And it's not so easy to flog photocopier toner at the best of times. And as for my papers – well, you're not going to get the general public bidding much for them.

The more times my car was broken into, the more convinced

I was that it could only be the police. Their behaviour was so strange – on the surface, they were treating me with a new respect, introducing me to their radical new initiatives, yet at the same time I was sure they were intent on breaking me down by whatever means possible.

Maybe it was the paranoia resurfacing. I discussed it with friends. None of them really believed that it was the police – what would be the point? But who else could it be? Was it because of what I'd said at the Inquiry? Before the Inquiry my car never got broken into.

The police came to my house. Again they said there wasn't much to be done, but they'd see what happened if it got broken into again. Surprise, surprise, it happened again a week later, in June. This time the lock in the car was pulled out of the door. The only thing stolen this time was my tool case.

I phoned the police.

'I'm being victimised big time here,' I said. I told them straight up. 'It's only people in the police or people associated with the police who could be doing this.'

I phoned up work. I was pissed off, but not as pissed off as they were. They said I should have been taking my tool case out of my car every night, and next time my kit was stolen I'd be paying for it out of my own pocket.

Now that I was working normally, Jane and I had to justify to the Legal Aid Board why I should be granted legal aid for the case I had decided to bring against the police. After they refused to apologise about their treatment of me, I sued them for racism and negligence. At first, the answer we were given was no. So we had to go to an appeal. Jane was at her best. She had the answers to all the questions and gave me a little two-minute piece with all I needed to say. It turned out well.

We were granted legal aid, but only for the first part of the case. Then they said we should get counsel's opinion and see if the case was a goer. Even with legal aid, I was going to have to pay £108 a month: £108 a month out of my £806-a-month salary! I was also warned that if I earned more than £12,999 a year I would automatically be stripped of the legal aid.

Next day I had a meeting with John Grieve, head of the Racial and Violent Crime Taskforce, and PC Paul Charlton, my liaison officer. This was the first in a series of meetings at which the police were supposed to treat me with a bit more respect – as a victim, after Macpherson told them that I was one. Those meetings were a waste of time. They waffled on about what they were doing, and weeks, then months, down the line nothing would happen. We'd ask for information, and they'd say, sorry, they couldn't tell us because it was part of the investigation and they didn't want information to be leaked. But at the same time information was being leaked on a regular basis to the Met's two favourite newspapers: the *Daily Mail* and the *Sun*. Strangely, Mr Grieve never seemed to know where the information was coming from. It surprised me because he knew exactly who his officers were talking to and how many people were on his team, yet they could not find the person who was leaking all the information.

My car was still causing me problems in one way or another. I had had to buy four new tyres. Soon after, I went out one morning, and my two front tyres were flat. Who could have done this? Perhaps the tyres weren't put on properly? No. Somebody had let them down. Why? I don't know. Who? I don't know. But I did know that this was how you tried to break people down. It pissed me off for the day. But such is life. Obviously, whoever it was wanted me to stop what I was doing.

I was told that Paul Charlton was there to look after my needs and provide the duty of care they owed me. They thought I would believe everything he said simply because he was black. That was their mentality: well, all you blacks stick together don't you?

I told him the first time we met up, 'The only reason they've put you here is because you're black.'

'If I thought that I wouldn't have taken the job,' he said.

'Bullshit. You're in there just for the job, just for the money. So you can be one of those who say, "Yeah, I dealt with Duwayne Brooks. I was in it."' I knew I was aggressive and untrusting, obnoxious at times. But I also knew that in a weird way although the Lawrence case had damaged the Metropolitan Police, there was also some strange sort of glamour attached to being involved in it. He denied that it was an ego trip for him.

Time after time, I said to him he was a waste of time. My car was getting broken into, and he was doing nothing about it. I said it was the police. He said it couldn't be the police because the police had no business to be doing that. Well, I knew they had no business doing it, but that didn't mean it wasn't them.

Why weren't officers making house-to-house inquiries?

'If somebody had seen someone they would have told us by now,' I was told.

'Your job is to come round and make house-to-house inquiries. Not bullshit.'

'Well, have you got proof that things were stolen?'

'Why would I make it up?'

'Was the stuff marked?'

'Why would the stuff be marked in my car?'

'Did you park the car in a safe place where there were lights?'

'Of course I did. I parked my car in the car park outside the flats where everybody else parks. Nobody else's car is getting broken into, so what am I doing wrong? Am I parking it in the wrong position?'

The police were asking me all these ridiculous questions via Paul Charlton. 'Can't you tell your seniors that the questions are daft and insulting,' I said to him. 'What they should be doing is putting surveillance on my car.'

The Senior Investigating Officer Mr Jones behaved as if he didn't like me because I wasn't quiet and compliant. I didn't put up with the crap that he came out with. He thought I had an attitude problem, and I thought he had an attitude problem. Whenever I used to corner him in a meeting, Mr Grieve would come to his rescue with some bullshit statement like 'We can't comment because of this investigation.' I'd had enough. I said it was pointless having meetings if they were just going to talk rubbish to me.

In spring 1999 I was asked to identify some suspects at Southwark police station. I said to Jane I didn't want to do it because it was pointless – it was six years since Steve had been killed, and I wasn't going to remember after all this time what they looked like. I went anyway. It proved to be fruitless and nothing came of the whole process, except for one extraordinary incident.

As I walked up to the police station, Jamie Acourt was sitting outside in a car at the traffic lights, smiling. I have no idea how he found out about it.

When I told Mr Grieve at our next meeting that I'd seen Jamie Acourt, he brushed it off. 'Oh, that must have been somebody else. You've made a mistake.' Mr Jones said he didn't believe it had happened at all.

'What car does Mr Acourt drive?' I said to them.

Oh, they said, they didn't feel they were in a position to comment on that.

'Why not? Isn't he under surveillance?'

'Yes.'

'Well, he wasn't under surveillance that day,' I said.

'We can't talk about surveillance.'

'Can't talk about surveillance? OK. I'll tell you what car he drove.' So I told them and they said they'd need to investigate it, but I knew by the look on John Grieve's face that I was right.

I had a couple of meetings with Paul Charlton after that. Crude meetings. Basically, they were trying to find out what I wanted from the Met, what I wanted the police to buy me, so they could throw it back in my face. I told him I didn't need anything except protection. 'When I win my case I will demand stuff. When I'm in a position of power I'll demand stuff. Look, I demanded changes from the Inquiry and nothing has happened. When I'm in a position of power maybe the police will begin to act on what I ask for.'

The harassment intensified.

On 17 August 1999 – it was early in the evening – I was driving along when I saw that police officers had stopped two men in a car on the opposite side of the road. It turned out they were Somalians. I was worried that they were being harassed, and I knew from my own experience how important it is to have witnesses when the police get funny with you. So I stopped the car and asked the men if they were OK. They said they were fine, and I drove off.

As I pulled away one of the officers shouted that I was a 'silly cunt'. I put my hand out of the window and gave him the wanker sign. I didn't say anything.

I carried on, but as I was turning right I was flashed and beeped violently by a police van behind me. There was nowhere sensible to stop, so I had to park in the middle of the road. An officer got out of the van, came over to my door and told me to 'Get the fuck out of the car.' The officer, whose number was MM315, opened the driver's door without my permission. I slammed the door shut. He tried to grab my car keys through the window – a classic police trick. I put my hand in the way.

The officer then grabbed my collar and punched me in the face five times. A second officer then grabbed my hands and pulled them through the open car window and put a handcuff on one wrist. The officer who had punched me then elbowed me in the face twice.

By this time a crowd had gathered and was watching. The officer opened the door and dragged me out of the car and put the other handcuff on me. I was dragged to the police van by my clothes. In the van, 315 twisted the handcuffs up behind me. 'Get on the floor you fucking nigger,' he said.

'I ain't getting on no fucking floor,' I said.

I was put on a seat. 315 kept poking me in the face and twice punched me in the back of my head. Meanwhile, Officer 2 was outside the van calming down the crowd. He saw what happened in the van and rushed back in via the side door.

'Did you see that? You just saw what your fellow officer done to me,' I said. Officer 2 looked at 315, looked back at me and left the van without a word.

315 called me a stupid wanker and asked me who I thought I was. 'Where are your bruises?' he said repeatedly. He was laughing.

'I wish I was white because all the bruises would be on my face,' I said to him.

'You lot are all the same,' he said, 'racist. Don't like white people, got a problem with white people, got a chip on your shoulder.'

Officer 2 got in the driver's seat; a WPC got in the passenger's seat. I told her I'd been assaulted. She didn't say anything. I told the officers not to leave my car there because it had expensive equipment inside it. They didn't listen.

They took me to the police station and 315 told the custody sergeant that I was being racist and had bitten him on the arm. The custody record said that I had been arrested for taking a car (*my* car), for shouting 'Fucking wankers', for damaging a door lock and for biting a police officer on the arm. None of it was true.

I asked the second officer if he had seen the assault on me in the van. 'What's he saying, Sarge?' he said. 'I can't hear him. Can't understand what he's saying.' I asked him again. 'Sarge, don't know what he's talking about. I can't hear him,' he said.

'Did you see the assault?' I asked. 'Yes or no?'

He refused to answer.

'Can you please write down all he has just said,' I asked the custody sergeant. Other officers at the station were laughing and asking where my bruises were.

At 6.20 p.m., almost an hour after my arrest, the police did a vehicle check that confirmed that car was mine. I was released and bailed to return. (The bail was cancelled at a later date.) When I got back to my car it was unlocked. There was no sign that it had been broken into, but a fax machine was missing. The police never charged me over the incident and paid my employer for the cost of the machine.

But the most damaging incident of that summer happened when I was in my car in Consort Road in Peckham. I was just pulling away when a police car driving down the road tried to cross a dual carriageway and had to drive around me. As it did so, the driver shouted out, 'Stupid wanker.' I said the same back to him and drove off. He didn't have his blue light on so he shouldn't have been pulling those illegal manoeuvres in the middle of the road.

I continued down the road, and next thing I knew, there he was following me, speeding up behind me. His blue light was on now. He came up to the car.

'Get the fuck out of the car!' He pulled my door open.

I slammed the door shut. At the time I was on the phone to my cousin. 'Who's that?' she said.

'It's the police.'

'Are they speaking to you like that?' She couldn't believe it. I told her I'd call her back.

The officers searched my car and arrested me for having an offensive weapon – a metal rod – in the car and for having a stolen chequebook and a stolen debit card, both of which had the name Duwayne Brooks on them. More officers turned up, including an armed response unit and another police car. The offensive weapon was part of my tool kit: it's used to clean the inside of photocopier drums. There were other tools in my car – pliers, pincers and a screwdriver – but I wasn't arrested for them because they weren't deemed offensive.

I was taken back to the station and my detention was authorised because I had this weapon. I asked the custody officer at the station what was the reason for stopping me, and where did he see this weapon. Paul Charlton had told me about something called the GOWISE procedure – the police are supposed to explain the grounds for stopping you, that's the *G*; the object, what they're looking for, that's the *O*; then they're supposed to produce their warrant card if they are plain-clothed officers, that's the *W*; *I* is for identity, the name of the officer; *S* is for station, where they are based; and *E* is for entitlement, that is to say, the search record to which the person stopped is entitled.

I told the custody officer that the arresting officer hadn't followed GOWISE, and that I used the tool in my line of work but none of the officers had bothered to ask me what it was for at the time of the arrest.

I was put in the cell for one hour while the notes of the incident were written up. While in the cell I asked to speak to the duty inspector. They told me he was too busy. A while later, I asked for the duty inspector again, but he never came.

Five minutes later I was taken out of the cell and the inspector was sitting down in the custody suite. I asked for the search record. 'Have you not been given one yet?' he said.

'No. I would like to see what's written down, so can one be done?'

They copied it and gave it to me and I read it. 'Do you really want to pursue this?' I said to the inspector. 'I'm willing to forget about it if you just apologise now.'

No answer.

I was irate. 'Just look at what this officer's written down. Look at his reasons for stopping me. On approaching my car he noticed that this tool was behind my seat in the passenger's footwell. How could he see that from his car? And how could he see it with my suit jacket hanging up at the door. It doesn't make sense. Have you read this?'

'Come on, Mr Brooks, can you leave the station now, please. We're very busy.'

'Have you read what he's written down?'

The officers looked at each other. 'Come on now, Mr Brooks.' I was turfed out of the station.

I was told I had to attend court on Wednesday 4 August. What a waste of public money this would be. There was no way on earth I could get convicted for this.

This was the second time the police had thrown a dodgy charge at me. I had previously been arrested for driving with a Stanley knife in the compartment of my car door. I had explained to the officer from the City of London police that it was in my car because I was cutting up boxes in the workshop and had jumped in my car and thrown the knife in the door. He wasn't interested. I had to appear in court twice before the case was dropped when my employer confirmed that the knife was part of my tool kit. And now we were going to have the same waste of time and money again. This officer was clearly lying, and the sergeant said nothing.

This is one of the huge problems with the police – they stick together, support each other, even if it means lying, and the more they know they're in the wrong, the tighter they tend to close ranks.

The papers were interested to hear that I'd been charged. 'Lawrence Friend Charged with Possessing an Offensive Weapon' – everybody was keen on that headline. But no one was interested when the charge was dropped before the first hearing (as of course it was always going to be, given the absurdity of the charge). That was how ridiculous the case was, and how stupid the police were to continue with it. Then again, perhaps it was worth their while – the damage had been done, they'd blackened my name. If I had had any doubts that the police were pursuing a vendetta against me, I didn't after this latest charge.

Chapter 13

Jailed

I'd just come in from work. It was 16 September 1999, Thursday, a football-training day. We used to play down Southwark Park, Tuesdays and Thursdays. I picked up my football kit, put it in my bag and went back downstairs. It was just after 7 p.m. I got in my car, drove out of the car park and turned right onto a little road. As I drove out a Fiesta came down the road with two fat white men sitting in the front. It had to be the police.

Perhaps they needed to talk to me about my security. So I stopped. They hadn't noticed me and drove straight past. I looked in the mirror and saw they had pulled up outside the hostel. When they realised it might have been me in the car, they reversed. At the same time another car came round the corner and drove straight in front of me. Then another car came and parked right behind the first car.

The first car had Detective Inspector Sturge in it. I didn't know him from Adam, but I was to get to know him a hell of a lot better over the next few months. He came up to my window and I just cracked the window a bit. I never pull my window down when talking to the police – they have a habit of pushing their hands through the window and taking your car keys or pushing you in your face and then justifying it afterwards by saying, 'We had to do it because we thought he was going to drive off.'

DI Sturge came to my window and asked me to wind it down. I said there was no need because I could hear him. He asked me to get out of the car. I said anything he had to say to me he could say to me while I was in the car.

'Mr Brooks, a serious allegation has been made against you.'

How many times had I heard this from the police? 'Yes?' I said.

'And we need you to get out of the car.'

'Well, tell me what the allegation is.'

'A serious allegation of attempted rape has been made against you. Can you please step out of the car?'

I stepped out of the car. I noticed there was another officer videoing me.

'We are arresting you for the attempted rape and indecent assault of Miss X.' (I can't use her real name because complainants in rape cases are granted anonymity.)

They asked if I knew Miss X. I said no.

They said I was trying to deny that I knew who the complainant was. I wasn't trying to deny it. I just didn't know the girl's surname.

I had a packet of crisps and I started eating them. I knew I hadn't done anything, I knew I hadn't tried to rape or indecently assault anybody, so I was calm.

The officer pushed the camera straight in my face, trying to intimidate me. The video camera's light was glaring. They then took me from my car to their car. DI Sturge held on to me. They must have thought I was about to run. But why would I have tried to run away? I had done nothing wrong.

We got to Greenwich police station and I got out of the car. The officer still felt the need to hold on to me while we walked into the station. I was told to sit down, so I did. I waited to hear just what their story was going to be – apparently, I'd tried to rape Miss X in my room at the hostel. How were they going to deal with this situation? Attempted rape and indecent assault. Totally baffled. I was booked in, as usual, and put in a cell. Some ten minutes later I was visited by one of those volunteers who go round checking prisoners to see if they're OK in their cells, and to make sure they're not being abused. Funny that. It all seemed to be planned to go like clockwork so that I couldn't make any complaint.

Now, why would they have worried about me making a complaint from the very outset of this drama? If they knew, or even thought, they had me for something I had done, then they had nothing to worry about – I can't make a complaint about something that's true, or about being accused of having done something if I had done it.

I was in the cell for two and a half hours. They then took me out of the cell and interviewed me. They asked me all sorts of questions about Miss X. No comment, no comment, no comment. Their questions were ridiculous. If I had committed the attempted rape and indecent assault there would have been no need to ask me these questions.

Now, why do they need my side of the story if they have got evidence that I have committed attempted rape and indecent assault? My side would have been irrelevant: they could have waited till we got to court. I was sure they were after information to help their investigation because they had none.

What had happened was this. This girl, Miss X, was somebody I knew who wanted to move out from her mum's. She would sometimes come to the hostel. On 4 September I was helping out at a wedding in Bellingham when I was asked to go to Greenwich. I was in the area where Miss X lived, and I called her up and told her that I was going to Greenwich, and that if she wanted to come with me, we could talk. She asked me to pick her up from her house. I did, and then we drove to Greenwich.

At Greenwich, I went up to my room in the hostel, and Miss

X followed me. I then got a call from a friend of mine saying that I was supposed to be coming to see her. I told Miss X that she would have to go home alone because I had to go out and pick up my friend. Understandably she was annoyed with me. There was an argument and she stormed off. On the way out of the building she saw some police coming in, but she didn't say anything to them. Eventually, I left in my car and Miss X then called the police.

While I was in the cell they had taken my keys and asked me what room I was in at the hostel. 'You can't search it without me being there,' I said.

'Oh yes we can, Mr Brooks.'

'OK, go on then, search it.'

'Well, we don't know what room you're in.'

'Of course you do. If I tried to rape somebody in my room, she'll know where my room is, and she can tell you.'

'OK, Mr Brooks, we're going to put non-cooperation on your file.'

'I don't give a damn,' I said. 'It should be in that person's statement where my room is,' I said.

Obviously it wasn't. They went to the hostel and spoke to the manager who accompanied them to my room. They searched my room and took my belt – not my trousers that I was wearing on the night in question, 4 September, not my top that I was wearing, but my belt. How significant was my belt going to be?

Desperado tactics from day one. They searched my car in the station yard. According to the police, they were searching for my shirt, trousers and belt, but I was sure they were looking for stolen property. Just as they'd been looking for stolen property in my house. Anything they could find to use against me to help them in this ridiculous case.

They started their bullshit again. 'Mr Brooks, why don't you just tell us what happened? If you want we can start this interview all over again. It's not a problem for us. We've got plenty of tapes. We can do it again, and we can keep doing it till you're happy.' I didn't cooperate. They got up and left the room, tutting, saying it didn't have to be like this.

DI Sturge came back in, shrugged his shoulders and sighed. 'I'm trying to help you here, Mr Brooks, but I can only help you if you help yourself. You've got to give us something to go on, something I can give to the sergeant. I don't want you to be in there all night; I want you to be able to go home. Have a think about it.'

I was left alone in the room for a couple of minutes. I sat down and thought, Strange this, all this fuss, video cameras and all sorts, yet they don't seem to have any evidence. They didn't even have enough evidence to concoct their story. They didn't even have proof that she was at the building that night. I could have denied it, but I thought, No, I've got nothing to hide, so I'm going to say nothing. It's for them to prove the case against me, so let them prove it.

They took me to the custody suite and sat me down. 'Last chance, mate, last chance.' Their tone had changed.

'I've got nothing to say.'

'Staying silent isn't going to get you anywhere, Mr Brooks. I keep telling you that we're here to help you. You just don't seem to want to help yourself.'

I never answered. There didn't seem any point in getting into a conversation about anything. I just looked at them and smirked. They walked over to the custody sergeant at the desk.

I was charged just after midnight. 'Wipe that smile off your face, Mr Brooks, this is a serious charge against you – attempted rape. It's not something to smile about. If I was you, I'd take these proceedings very seriously indeed,' DI Sturge said. Had I really been smiling?

It came to the question of bail, and DI Sturge made representations as to why I shouldn't get bail. He alleged that I had made further threats of rape, and that ten phone calls had been made on 13 September and he had a record of these phone calls. I couldn't believe my ears. I looked at him, and he nodded his head as if to say, yes we have.

I said to the custody sergeant could he write down exactly what DI Sturge was saying because he was lying. The custody sergeant asked DI Sturge to repeat what he'd said and wrote it down. He then asked me if I had anything to say to this. I said no.

'Are you sure you haven't got anything to say to it?'

'Nope.'

'Do you not want to make representations for your bail?'

'No.'

I had to go to a room where they could take fingerprints and a DNA sample, which wasn't a problem. I just said to them I didn't want photographs taken. They told me that if they wished to take a photograph they could do.

'I'm not arguing with you, I'm telling you,' I said to DI Sturge. 'The only way to get a photograph taken is to force me and that's against the law.'

'We can do what we want when we're in here, Mr Brooks, and it's about time you realised that,' he said.

I smirked and it seemed to upset them. I knew that it was a serious allegation, but I also knew I hadn't done anything wrong, and that there would be no evidence against me, unless they fabricated it. So it felt as if I was going through the motions.

They took me to the room to do the fingerprints. 'Oh, just sit down there for a moment, Mr Brooks.'

'No thanks,' I said.

'Well, you're not going anywhere so you might as well just sit there.'

'No thanks.'

They wanted me to sit down opposite the camera. They thought that if I sat there I'd forget the camera was there and they could snap a shot of me. Even though they said they weren't trying to trick me to sit where the camera was, they'd already filled out the nameplate with 'Duwayne Brooks' and my date of birth.

They tried to get me to sit down again.

'No thanks,' I said. 'I can stand up.' They took their time rolling out the ink, but I didn't care. I wasn't in a rush. As the officer had said to me, I wouldn't be going anywhere.

Fingerprints were taken. I don't know why. The police already had my fingerprints, and fingerprints don't change. We left the room.

The two officers went back into the fingerprint room. Obviously, they were trying a different ploy. The custody sergeant then called over to me. 'Don't you want to discuss your bail then? I thought you wanted to go home for the night.'

'No, it's OK,' I said.

'Well, I can help you if you want to make representations for bail.'

'No, it's OK.'

'All right then, suit yourself. You're the one who's going to have to spend the whole night in the cell and go to court in the morning looking a mess.'

There was no point in answering him back. He was just trying to lead me into conversation, lead me into stuff they didn't know about. They wanted to get an insight into what really took place, to see if they could twist anything I said. The best thing was to say nothing.

Minutes later the officers came back out of the fingerprint room. Again, they told me that I could get my bail sorted and be home for the night.

'No, it's OK,' I said. 'You officers stick together. You heard a lie and you haven't said anything to him about it.'

'Well, Mr Brooks, he's a police officer,' the custody sergeant said. 'I'm sure if he's lying you can make a complaint about it at a later time. But as a fellow police officer I don't believe he is lying.'

'Well, there's no point in discussing it. You might as well put me in my cell so I can go to sleep.'

'OK, Mr Brooks.'

They brought me to my cell. There was no pillow, no sheets, no cover. I asked for a pillow and blanket. They brought me two covers, but there were no pillows. I was in the cell alone, laughing to myself: This is going to be a good one to win. I knew the police had gone too far this time. I knew they couldn't get away with this one.

I could tell they were going to pull out all the stops to put as much dirt against my name as possible in order to get a conviction. It was their only chance. When you're in a war you cannot think just about winning battles for the day or the next day or month; when you're in a war you have to think about the next year, the year after that. You plan for the future. You can lose little battles – things that are said about you, minor stuff you're accused of, you can let them go, but the big battles are the ones you need to win. These are the ones that show the police you're in it till the end. And whatever they were going to throw at me over the next few months I knew I was going to win this battle, and that would bolster my civil case.

Less than a month earlier, in August 1999, I had announced that I was going to sue the police for negligence and racism. That was also the month I had been charged with taking and driving away my own car – in court, my address had been read out. A couple of weeks before being charged with attempted rape, my flat had been broken into. When the police investigated, they discovered that the CCTV they had installed didn't have any tape in it.

I was convinced that this is what it was all about. I knew it. If they could get me convicted here, they could trash me in the civil case. Convicted sex offender takes on the police – who would you trust? That was what they were banking on. But this time I was proper ready because I knew it was coming.

The week before I had been in Leeds to see the play about the Inquiry. Afterwards, there was a discussion on policing. Someone in the audience asked me if I was worried about the suspects coming after me. 'No,' I said. I was worried about the fact that no one has control over those who do as they please when they please. 'Who are they?' asked another person in the audience. 'The police of course,' I said. Everybody started cheering. 'And the Police Complaints Authority are a waste of time,' I said. 'They don't investigate your complaint, they just find ways of crushing your complaint, making you look silly or worse.' I told the audience, 'I can guarantee to you that I am going to be arrested for a crime I have not committed, and you will read about it in the newspapers and see it on the news, and that will be their last effort to shut me up. Remember this.' I was telling the audience what I'd been telling myself for ages now.

And here I was, just gone midnight, Friday morning, in the police station, charged with attempted rape. I was woken at 8 a.m. and told to get ready to go to court. How was I going to get ready? I was in the same clothes I'd been in for twenty-four hours – trousers and the creased-up white shirt that I'd slept in to keep warm. There was a bit of fluff in my hair because I'd slept with one of the covers over my head. I didn't want anyone taking quick pictures of me while I was asleep. That's what they do if you refuse to have your photo taken. They wait until you're sleeping, open the hatch, and take a picture through it. I've been to identify people, and they've got pictures of them sleeping or lying down.

They asked me if I wanted to have a wash. I just brushed my teeth. I wanted everyone in the court to see the overnight sleep on my face, the tiredness on my face, the tiredness on my body. This is what the police are trying to do: drag me down, break me down, and through it all I wanted the police to notice the smile on my face. It was still there. And it would still be there for the whole of this battle.

The security van picked me up. As soon as I got in, they started giving me the look. They'd obviously been told by the officers that I was a sex offender who had just been charged with attempted rape and indecent assault.

At Greenwich Magistrates' Court I was put in another cell. I discovered I had to be in a cell by myself because I'd been arrested for a sex attack and such people are vulnerable to attacks from other people held in custody. There was a hard bench. No pillow, no cover, no nothing. I started to get cold. I asked for a cover. No covers available. I asked for a pillow. No pillows available. I had to sit on this hard bench, wrapping my arms around me, huddling up in the cell. Every five minutes I was asking for hot water.

'Don't you want any tea? Any sugar in it?'

'No thanks, just hot water.' I needed hot water to sip, to try to keep me warm and to hold on to. I tried rubbing the hot water on my chest and my hands, to warm up my body. All I had on was my shirt. Melly brought my jacket for me, but the police wouldn't let me have it – just in case there was something in there, they said.

A friend of mine called Richard used to work at the court. He was going to bring it down to me, but they wouldn't let him. Afterwards, he told me that this was the first time he'd not been allowed to take a prisoner an item of clothing. So what was the difference with me? They told him he couldn't bring the jacket down in case there were cigarettes in it. But surely if they were worried about anything in my pockets, they could always have searched them. Perhaps they were just being cruel for cruelty's sake.

The police asked if I wanted to see the duty solicitor. I said yes. A woman came in. I expected the bullshit, the attitude, the indifference, the looks, but I got quite the opposite. 'Oh, so you're the one everybody's talking about then.'

'What d'you mean?' I said.

'Don't you know?' she said.

'No.'

'You've been on the TV since six in the morning and you're in the paper.'

'What do you mean?' I said. 'I was only charged at midnight.'

'What? How long have you been here?'

I told her they'd arrested me at seven or eight in the evening the previous day and charged me at about midnight.

'Oh, of course,' she said. 'Duwayne Brooks, Stephen Lawrence. I didn't think it was true when I first heard about it and now you've told me about it I know it's not true.' She said she knew that for me to be charged at midnight and for it to be on the news the next morning, something had to be up. She said she was going to apply for bail for me.

'Is it worth it?' I said.

'Well, we can try.'

'They're not going to be interested.'

'It's best that you do apply for bail because otherwise people may think you're not applying because you are guilty.'

'Yeah,' I said. 'But what happens if we just do the opposite of what they expect us to do?'

She convinced me that it was right to go for bail. We discussed what she'd say. I told her what to say. Then she advised me on what she was actually going to say – the right way to do it.

I walked into the court and noticed that the public bench – you couldn't call it a gallery – was full of people. There were about ten or twelve people there, surprising people, people in high public positions who couldn't openly come out and support me for fear of losing their jobs, but who were showing their concern by appearing at the court. DI Sturge was in the police part. The people on the public bench made it better for me.

I turned around and looked at the magistrate. I knew he was ready for me because of the look of contempt on his face.

The prosecution started their case. They claimed that I had been harassing this girl for two years, but she'd kept saying no to me and it culminated in me trying to rape her in my room. She then ran away and dialled 999 and I was arrested at a later date. They said I'd made repeated threatening phone calls to her, just as DI Sturge had said, and that they had a record of it. They were trying to convince the judge that the parts of their puzzle fitted together – they knew they had to make it look good because they wouldn't get another chance.

The duty solicitor stood up and as soon as she opened her mouth the judge looked away. He refused to pay her any attention. I was just about to call her to tell her not to bother when the judge told her that he was not going to grant bail. I looked at her, and she looked back at the judge in silence. Remand for seven days. I'd never been in a situation where I was standing in front of a judge and I was going to be remanded – I'd seen it happen to other people, and I always wanted to know how it felt when you're there and people are watching you from behind; when all these eyes are staring at you, and then the judge turns round and says you're remanded. Other people had said to me you have to hold on tight to the rail because your legs feel as if they are going to give way, but when the judge told me I was remanded for seven days I just felt a tingling. Then I felt fear because I'd never been to jail before. I didn't know what it would be like, especially going there charged with a sex offence.

I walked back down to the cell and was searched again. I was searched going into the court, searched going back down again. Who did they think I was? What did they think I'd be able to smuggle back down, having just walked into the dock flanked by two officers and been brought back down to the cell flanked by the same officers?

I was cold again and asked for more hot water. The solicitor came down to the cell and apologised. I told her not to worry about it, that I'd never expected to get bail. That's when she started to explain to me how it must have got into the press – how the police had leaked it to the *Sun* as soon as I was charged.

'I'll call your solicitor and tell her what's happened,' she said. 'I'll pass on your papers and if you ever need me again call me.'

'OK,' I said. 'Thanks for your help.'

'Good luck,' she said, and then she was gone.

I was there for another couple of hours or so. I didn't have a watch on so I didn't know the time. More looks from the guards. It didn't matter to me. They all got smirks. I decided that was the best way to deal with those people – don't be aggressive, don't argue with them, just smile.

We were picked up and driven away from the court. The blast of heat in the van warmed me up instantly. Nobody could see me once I was inside the little one-seat cell. As soon as the door was shut, it sealed.

But I could see outside perfectly clear. As we were driving along I saw a couple of *Evening Standard* billboards. The way they were angled all I could see was 'Lawrence', I couldn't see the rest. As we got into Plumstead I saw the whole thing – 'Lawrence Friend on Attempted Rape Charge'. Fucking hell. These are the lengths the police are going to in order to rubbish me.

These *Evening Standard* billboards were all over London. It was obviously headline news. And where could the story have come from? It had to be the police. I later discovered that the *Sun* reporter was phoned minutes after midnight – in other words, as soon as I was charged. If the police want to get something into the papers the next day they have to do their own PR.

We drove into Belmarsh prison and the door shut behind us. I was looking around, trying to see what it was like from the outside. This was the first time I'd been inside a prison – I didn't have a clue what the grounds would be like.

We were taken into this congregating area. Other people were put into a room together. I was put into one by myself and told that I was a high-profile prisoner. 'Haven't you seen the papers, Mr Brooks?' I was asked.

'No. How can I see the papers?' I was shown the headline in the *Standard*.

I was checked in by a tall black officer. He made a point of talking to me. I don't know if it was because he thought I expected to get softer treatment from him or if he just wanted to impose himself on me. But I'd made a decision from the moment I was arrested that nobody was going to get through to me. I was told that because I was a high-profile prisoner, the governor needed to see me first. No problem.

I was sitting in this room for ages before someone a prisoner would never normally see so soon, who was either the governor or the assistant governor, turned up. Then I was brought out to meet him. He gave me a routine talk: 'I don't know whether you're guilty or not, but everyone in this prison claims they are innocent, nobody here admits guilt, so you're just another person. But then again you could be the only person in here who is innocent.' I started smiling.

I was told that I'd be in a cell by myself for the night and then tomorrow I'd be moved to the sex offenders' block, because it would be safe for me. They said they didn't think I'd be safe among normal prisoners who would know about me from the news.

I was left in the room for another hour or so before I was brought into the cell. The first thing I thought about when I entered was *Porridge*, the TV show set inside a prison and starring Ronnie Barker. But this cell didn't look anywhere near as cosy as his character Fletcher's. This one was horrible. The windowsill was dirty, the toilet was out in the open, the sink was dirty. The bed was on the right-hand side and further up was the cupboard. I didn't want to touch anything. I just wanted to keep my hands in the prison tracksuit that I had to put on. I still had my own shoes. I looked weird. But that's how they wanted me to look.

I put the cover on the bed, wrapped myself up in it and lay

down. I tried not to touch any other part of the cell. I lay with my head away from the toilet because I thought that otherwise I'd be suffocated by the fumes.

I was wondering what the block would be like. I remembered seeing all those pictures of cells and blocks on the news, with the pool table in the middle and the TV at one end, and the cells to both sides, and the stairs going off to the blocks. I was thinking to myself, How am I going to get on in here, what are people going to say to me, am I going to have to fight my way out of problems? Who am I going to be in a cell with? How am I going to eat the food? Everybody says prison food is horrible so how do you eat it? What if they only serve me red meat? All this was going through my mind.

Then I thought, No, only my enemies will believe that I have committed this crime – then again, even people who didn't like me would probably have more sense than to believe this. I was wondering what Jane would be thinking.

Jane knew me inside out, so she knew all she'd have to do was ask. Then I remembered that she wasn't at work, so it would be Vicky, her partner at the law firm, who'd deal with me, and Vicky didn't know me as well as Jane did. I knew it would be a big decision for the firm to make because they don't take on cases against women.

So I knew that this case, defending a man accused of attempted rape, would be a tough one for Jane and Vicky to take. But I wasn't that worried – I couldn't imagine them not defending me in this case once I had explained what had happened.

I woke up the next day and walked over to the window. I needed the toilet. I moved to the window and breathed in deeply a couple of times and then went over to the other side of the cell for a piss. I tore off some of the tissue that was there and used it to press the flusher. I went over to the window and gasped for air. It felt disgusting pissing in that toilet. I felt that if I'd breathed, I would have breathed in all the germs of all the other people who had ever pissed in that toilet. I didn't know who had pissed in that toilet before, who had slept in that room before.

They asked me what I wanted for breakfast, did I eat meat and so forth. I said no. I was brought scrambled egg and beans and had to eat it in that stinking, filthy cell. I had to eat because I was so hungry, but the thought of eating it made me feel sick afterwards. They gave me some water. I drank half of it but felt too sick to finish it.

They took me out of the cell and made a joke about me finishing so quick.

They brought me to the block. As I walked up, prisoners were out on the block and there was a group at the end who stood clapping. I couldn't believe it. Prisoners were walking up to me, 'Y'all right, mate? Y'all right?' they said. And, 'We know what's happened, mate, it's all bullshit. Don't worry, mate.' They'd heard about me on the news.

I put my stuff down in the cell and was taken out to be introduced to the 'listeners'. 'If you've got a problem, these are the people you go and talk to. If you're stressed, and you need someone to talk to, they're there for you. For instance, if you're thinking about killing yourself or you're down or your girlfriend's left you, you talk to these people. These people are experienced prisoners.' They made it sound as if it was a job. Which it was in a way. They are appointed by the officers and are introduced to us at association time when everyone's out. If you had any other problems – needed soap or towels or if you didn't have any money – you'd speak to a listener.

I was introduced to the other person in my cell – he was serving twelve years. I was told that somebody else would be joining us.

I went downstairs and other guys came up to me, giving me all sorts of advice. This tall black man told me: 'Don't tell anyone what you're in for – you don't know who's who and who will attack you. But out here, if anybody attacks you they have to go through me.' He told me who I mustn't talk to and who I could trust.

On the block they were having morning association. I never got used to that because I was only in three days: Saturday, Sunday, Monday morning. You came down, filled up your cups with hot water, collected your breakfast, talked for a bit and went back up to your cell.

When I got back to the cell, Cellmate A said he was getting ready to go to work. I didn't know what he meant. He explained that you can either go outside and do your exercise, or work. There was an area, fully fenced, that you could jog round, walk round, skip round, whatever your fancy. And there was a workroom where you would be put to doing things like assembling boxes.

He went through the regulation stuff of telling me not to tell anyone what I was here for because you couldn't trust them and so on, and then he asked my name and what I'd done. I told him. So much for not telling people what I was in for. 'Oh, most people know about you because you've been on the news. And you can read about yourself in the paper tomorrow, because we get the papers a day late here.'

He asked me if I needed anything. I told him I needed a towel, and he told me which listener to speak to when we came out for lunch. He then started rolling up a cigarette and asked if I wanted one. I said no, I didn't smoke.

'What!' he said.

'Don't smoke,' I said.

'Are you sure about that? How long are you in here for?'

'Well, I'm on remand. I hope to get bail on Monday.'

'Bo-oy!' he said. 'Bo-oy! If you're not out there by Monday you'll be smoking by Tuesday.' I said nothing would make me smoke. He gave me a doubtful look. 'You ain't got nothing to do in here really. Once you're banged up, you've got some of your books you can read and then that's it. Talking, reading or smoking while you're in your cell. See my books there – they are bibles. All different versions of the Bible.' I remember thinking to myself, Why has he got different versions of the Bible – I thought there was supposed to be only one God? I wanted to ask him, but I knew that if I did, that would be it – he'd just go on and on for hours and hours. I could feel it.

He showed me his food, and said, 'If you don't want anything, I'll have it. Get everything you can get and what you don't want, I'll have. Or we could swap it.' That's how everything works in there. You swap food for stuff. If you need something you haven't got, you just swap – cigarettes, food, toiletries.

'Are you vegetarian?' he said.

'Yes.'

'Right, you better make it known. Call one of the screws and tell them. There's a form downstairs what you need to fill out and you tick what you want for your dinner.' He showed me a canteen form that you filled out on Wednesday and took to the canteen on Thursday.

'I don't think I'll be here by then,' I said.

'Well,' he said, 'the best thing to do is get that out of your mind till Monday, because if you're thinking about that all the time and you don't get bail on Monday you're going to be devastated. It's best just to keep it out of your mind.' He gave me good advice, but he wouldn't talk about what he was in there for.

So I asked him. 'You got twelve years, mate,' I said. 'What for?'

He wouldn't touch on it. He just said, 'Oh, some bad stuff. No violence or nothing, but I'd just been set up by an organisation that I was involved with. Prostitutes from New York coming over to Knightsbridge, I was involved in all that kind of stuff. Drugs and that. And I've just been set up.' That was all he was prepared to say.

I told him some more about my case.

'Don't speak about it to anybody here. See what you just told me, don't tell nobody in here. Be careful who you talk to.'

'I don't care,' I said to him. 'I haven't done anything wrong; there's nothing they can put on me.'

'Well, just in case anyway, don't speak to nobody.'

Perhaps I was being naive. Just because I didn't commit a crime was no reason to be so sure that I wouldn't go down for it. After all there are so many people who end up serving time for crimes they haven't committed.

I made up my bed. As you entered the cell there was a bunk bed on the left-hand side. I was on the bottom bunk; the top bunk was spare. I thought I'd leave the top one for the other guy. Cellmate A was on the right-hand side. At the bottom end of his bed was a toilet in a cupboard, with a sink outside it, just to the right. At the other end of Cellmate A's bed was a window. At the end of the bunk bed there was another set of cupboards for storing snacks and clothes. This cell didn't seem too bad after the previous night's. It wasn't good by any stretch, but it was more comfortable, more lived in, because it was on the block.

The new guy was a white Rastafarian – dreadlocks, no front teeth. He was a strange sight. Then again, the whole situation, being in Belmarsh top-security prison, walking through the maze of checkpoints, talking to sex offenders, being banged up, was strange.

I think I was ultra-protected when I was in that prison. The guards and the governor knew that nothing could happen to me while I was there. Yes, the police wanted to break me down, but they didn't want me to get hurt in prison because that would backfire on them.

The white rasta wasn't on the sex offenders' block because of a crime against a woman. He had been arrested at Glastonbury and was said to have been found to have all sorts of pills on him – LSD, Es, whatever. He was allegedly part of an organisation, and it was known that he'd informed on other members of the organisation. So he'd been put in this part of the wing for his own safety.

A screw came round to check the cell. 'Brooks, are you OK?'

'Yes,' I said, 'I'm fine.'

He left.

'That's what you're going to get all the time,' Cellmate A said, 'because they can't afford for anything to happen to you. They know that I'm not a violent person, that's why they put you in this cell, but they'll be checking on you all the time. I guarantee you through the night, every hour or so, you'll hear that flap come down and they'll check that you're OK, that you're not going to try to kill yourself.'

I looked around the cell. 'What on earth could you use to kill yourself with in here?' I said. 'The only thing you could do is cut the sheets up, but there are no scissors. I suppose you could tear them up. But there's not enough height. How could you hang yourself with them?'

He wouldn't say. 'I don't want to tell you, mate, I don't want to tell you, mate,' he kept saying. 'I don't want to wake up in the morning and see you hanging.'

'Come on, man!'

'No. I'm not going to tell you.'

I left it there.

'When I get to know you a bit better, and I know I won't wake up and see you dead in my cell, I'll tell you.'

Through that night the three of us talked. The white rasta, Cellmate B, gave us the rundown of the gangs that controlled him and his friends and how they sent them out to sell drugs. He expanded on why he was in this block. He told us that word had gone round that he'd informed on one of the top men in the drugs gang who had then put the word out for him to get done in while he was in jail, so the best place for him was in the sex offenders' wing – that was where you were most protected from other prisoners. I noticed how protected I was when I was moved to different parts of the wing – you couldn't move anywhere, not even thirty yards down one corridor, without the security getting the go-ahead over the radio.

Both guys smoked throughout the night. It was terrible. I had to put up with the smoking because there was no one on the wing who didn't smoke whose cell I could have moved into. Even if there had been another cell to move into, I don't think I would have because I felt comfortable in this cell. I didn't know what the black guy was in there for, not in detail anyway, but I felt he would look after me, protect me, if anyone tried anything.

The first dinner I got was vegetable pie with a couple of roast potatoes and a cup of hot water. I came back upstairs and sat there looking at it. For some reason, you couldn't get cold water; you had to get your water from a hot urn and if you wanted it cold you had to leave it to cool down. Dinner time in prison. I couldn't believe it. What was I doing here?

For Cellmate A it was a routine because he'd been in so long. He laid out his knife and fork, poured juice into his cup, poured water on top. He looked as if he was sitting in style at his dining table as he tucked in. I couldn't see Cellmate B because he was sitting on his bunk, but I could hear him eating away. And then there was me, staring at the food, thinking, Where do I start, how do I tackle it? I pushed the fork into the pie and water squished out from everywhere. Slop. I turned the pie over and there were a few chunky bits. The rest was just pastry.

I tried the chunky bits which were supposed to be Quorn. It melted away in my mouth to pure water. I tried the pastry: it was revolting. I swallowed some, and my stomach cramped up instantly. I looked over and Cellmate A was just chomping away. It could have been a feast. Obviously, he'd got used to the food. If you're serving such a long stretch you have no choice: you have to get used to the food. I ate the roast potatoes and they were OK. I gave the rest to Cellmate B. Cellmate A had already added boiled eggs to his dinner, so he'd had a right munch. But Cellmate B was starving, so he had my food. All I was left with then was an orange and apple. I washed the apple and ate it, and saved the orange for later.

I began to think about the toilet. What happens if you need a shit? How are we supposed to breathe in this cell if one of us shits and it really stinks? How embarrassing is it to shit in there?

One of the screws came to the cell to collect the trays. We had to leave the trays outside the cell for the trolley. We were allowed one more cup of water and then that was it, lights out. Lights out didn't really mean lights out. Saturday and Sunday night the lights were on till 2 a.m. I put the cover over my head and fell asleep. That was the only way for me to pass the time – to sleep it away. I fell asleep early and woke up around two, and the light was still on and they were talking. I was listening for a bit, and Cellmate A said, 'Well, Duwayne mate, the best thing for you to do now is sleep. You need to get used to it, and the only way to get used to it is to sleep and gradually get used to the fact that you are in jail. Don't forget you're in jail when you're sleeping, because if you believe it's a dream, when you wake up you're going to be in shock.' He was right.

While I was sleeping I tried not to forget I was in jail. But all through my sleep I kept telling myself that this had to be a dream. And as I was sleeping I was building up hope inside me, telling myself, I know I've got to wake up soon, it's got to come round to morning soon and then I'll wake up and find it's not true. Idiot.

I woke up Sunday morning devastated. But why was I kidding myself? Cellmate A had already told me how I was going to feel. I was in jail and I was going to be here till Monday at least. I still hadn't got a towel. All I had was a toothbrush. I got up and brushed my teeth, then we all went down for breakfast. I got my water and walked round picking up the food. I thought I knew somebody behind the counter – the people serving us the food were prisoners from other parts of the building. I was looking at him, and he looked at me with disgust.

'Don't I know you from somewhere?' I said.

'You don't fucking know me,' he said. 'Who the fuck do you

think you're talking to, pervert?' He slammed my food down on the plate.

'What's your problem?' I said.

'Don't fucking talk to me.'

'Brooks, just move along,' an officer said.

I came to the person who put the bread on my plate. When he came to put it on my plate I moved it out of the way and it dropped on the side.

'You want some? You want some?' he said. I just looked at him.

'Brooks, you're causing trouble, Brooks, just move along,' the screw said.

'They've got a problem,' I said. 'They need to have some manners and serve the food properly.'

As far as they were concerned we were all sex offenders. And those serving us weren't sex offenders, so they felt superior. The food was slammed down for everyone on our wing. They looked at us all with disgust. It was horrible. In the end, one of the screws got my breakfast for me and brought it over.

I walked back, ticked the food for the evening and went straight back to the cell. I was sure I knew the man who had slammed the food down at me. How can he talk to me like that? He's going to have to apologise, I thought to myself. If he didn't remember me he should have just said he didn't remember me, but he didn't need to start swearing and ranting and raving. Remember you're getting locked up at night-time just like me, I thought.

Back in my cell, Cellmate A gave me a talking to. He told me not to get involved. 'You're only going to be here till Monday, so don't cause problems for yourself. There's no point in not getting on with those guys, because they're the ones who always dole out the food. Just try to get on with everybody here.'

I ate some of the breakfast because I was starving. But the more I ate, the more sick I felt. I kept thinking about the toilet.

How do I go on it? Should I wait till everybody has gone? Gone where? Or should I just go in there. My question was answered for me.

Cellmate A went to the toilet and was there half an hour. After five minutes I could smell it. I put my food down. I couldn't eat. I felt sick. I got back into bed and covered my head with the pillow. How can you eat when your cellmate is stinking out the cell with his shit? His toilet habits weren't the worst thing. He'd be talking away from his bunk and you'd see his hand casually moving up and down, then faster, more urgent, and his voice would briefly take a turn for the funny. He could have been a bit more discreet.

I fell asleep. One of the screws woke me up. 'Brooks, exercise time.' We were taken down and out into the yard.

'Start walking, Brooks, you can't stand here. You've got to walk around.' I started walking. Somebody noticed me.

'Duwayne!' I looked up. 'Duwayne, it's me!' I didn't quite catch his name. 'Duwayne, are you all right?'

'Yeah, I'm OK.' I looked up to find his window. I wasn't sure who it was, but I had an idea. 'What are you in here for?' I asked. It just came out of my mouth without thinking. I remembered what Cellmate A and everybody else had told me – don't ask people what they're in for and don't tell people what you're in for.

Before I could say anything else to him, he shouted: 'Rape, blood, rape.'

'Rape?'

'Yeah, I raped my baby's mother and she got me done. I could be in here for life. Life, blood. Don't matter, though. It's only life, blood.'

'Brooks, move on. Don't let me have to tell you again otherwise your exercise will be cancelled.'

I started walking. I didn't give a damn about exercise. Walking around the yard wasn't exercising me. And I wouldn't be here after Monday.

But the voice was ringing in my head. 'Life, blood. It's only life, blood.' I'd been here for forty-eight hours, and it was terrible – disgusting, degrading, mentally disturbing – and this young man had just told me that he could be in here for life and he was laughing about it. I couldn't understand him. Of course, once you've been sentenced you've got to serve your time, but if he was who I thought he was, he'd been in prison before, and once you'd been in here you wouldn't want to come back again if you had any sense. No sane person would want to go back to prison having been in here regardless of how hard life is on the outside.

It's hard to explain just what prison does to your brain. I remember when Terry Waite was captured in Lebanon, and I always used to hear about it on the news. I used to think, He's only in jail and he's got his friends with him. Well, Terry Waite's experiences must have been a million times worse than mine, sitting in a room blindfolded as days turned into weeks and weeks turned into months and months turned into years, not knowing where he was, stuck inside the four walls. And here I was free to talk to people, not constantly locked up, but still I felt my brain shutting down. My brain was clamped; I couldn't think properly. My speech started to get funny, slurred. That's what prison does to your brain, within days, and this guy, this merry rapist, was jumping around happy, like he was glad to be here, as if it was his true home.

I walked around the yard another four or five times, just looking around the grounds, at how the fences were put together to stop people jumping over; looking at where you could run to if you did jump over. You'd need serious assistance. The only way out of there would be by helicopter. You couldn't bust out, and you couldn't drive out because there were two massive entrance/exit gates.

We were called back in and went straight back to our cells. Ten minutes later Cellmate A returned. He had been to work, building boxes. He said he had to keep his mind occupied because he was getting bored, so he went to work on the boxes.

I asked him how long we'd be in here for now.

'Oh about half an hour, and then we'll go out on association, play some dominoes, play some pool, watch some TV.'

Cellmate B had arrived in the cell on Saturday morning. He had been chain-smoking ever since, and sharing his roll-ups with Cellmate A. Every few minutes he'd roll one for himself and one for Cellmate A. Eventually, he ran out. What happened next left me shocked. I thought we were all friends in that cell. And I thought Cellmate A and Cellmate B were much closer friends because of the way they shared the roll-ups and stayed up late talking to each other, while I cut myself off from them and tried to sleep.

Cellmate B had finished all his tobacco and was gasping. He looked in the ashtray, and around the cell, for any bits of tobacco he could put together and smoke. Cellmate A then got up calmly, went into his cupboard and pulled out one fat bag of tobacco. He had a packet of red Rizlas and a packet of green Rizlas. 'Mmmmm,' he said, trying to decide which to go for, and then pulled out the red Rizlas. Cellmate A then built up one big tobacco roll-up, lit it, took in a deep breath full and blew out, saying, 'Yeaaah!' It was so deliberate, so cruel. He then went and leaned by the window, put the radio on classical music and continued smoking. I couldn't believe it. Cellmate B had shared all his tobacco with Cellmate A, and now Cellmate A was smoking his, relishing Cellmate B's pain.

I felt funny. I knew Cellmate B wanted to ask for a roll-up, but he was too scared. Cellmate A and Cellmate B were sitting there having a conversation about drugs, yet Cellmate B refused to ask Cellmate A for a roll-up, and Cellmate A refused to offer.

The screws came and we were let out. I went downstairs and was told I could use somebody's phonecard to make a call. 'Be careful, though, Brooks. Don't let the screws see you because we're not allowed to use other people's phonecards.' That policy had been introduced to stop bullying.

I realised I was being watched. Not by the screws but by this mentally disturbed guy. I stopped at the top of the stairs to confront him. 'Why d'you keep watching me?' I said. 'And why d'you keep following me around whenever I'm out on association?'

'Ah no, no, Duwayne. You know what? I've got pictures of you and Stephen at home. I've collected all the articles. I know you're innocent. I know you're innocent, but I don't know why they are doing this to you.'

'OK,' I said. 'But can you stop following me because I don't like it.'

'Oh, Duwayne, I'm all right, mate. I'm all right. I'm all right.'

But he wasn't. His cellmates wanted him out of his cell. Whenever we were out of the cells, they were complaining to the screws, asking them to do something about him.

Saturday night he got his dinner, blew his nose into the food, mixed the snot in and ate it. His cellmates complained that they couldn't take it any more, they couldn't eat, they didn't feel well when he was around. Just looking at this guy made me feel sick. I told him to back off and not come near me. 'Don't speak to me and don't let me see you looking at me,' I said. I walked off back down the stairs to my friends and started playing dominoes. Halfway through the game one of the guys came to me with his Jesus shit. 'I knew you were coming, Duwayne. Jesus told me you was coming and he told me to tell you not to worry. You be strong and you'll be out of here. Don't worry, nothing can happen to you in here. Be strong.'

'Thanks,' I said. 'I will be strong and I hope nothing does happen to me here. But thanks.'

He wasn't the only one talking about Jesus, but it was strange. Why were they talking about Jesus now? Before they committed the crimes they were allegedly in here for (most of the prisoners claimed to be innocent), why didn't they think of Jesus then?

This guy had his own cell so he must have been there a long time. I didn't ask him because by now I'd remembered the rule – don't ask anyone why they are here; if they want to tell you, they'll tell you, but don't ask.

We continued playing dominoes. He kept tapping me on the shoulder and saying, 'Don't worry, don't worry, you'll be OK. Don't matter how long you're in here, you'll be OK because Jesus knows you're innocent.'

Most of the black guys were playing dominoes, and most of the white guys were playing pool or watching TV. So there was a group of black people who stuck together and a group of white people who stuck together. It reminded me of when I used to play football – the black boys would warm up with the black boys, the white boys would warm up with the white boys, and then you'd just get a few black and white kids warming up together. It wasn't a hostile thing, and it wasn't that they didn't like each other; it was just that they had different ways of doing things.

There was a wide range of ages among the black men playing dominoes. I looked around and was shocked. Why was there a woman officer here without a uniform on? I never said anything. I just kept it to myself and looked and listened. Gradually it dawned on me that there was something unusual about her, but I couldn't work out what. I had never seen anyone like this before.

Association time was over and we had to go back up to our cells. As soon as we got back, I asked Cellmate A, 'Why have we got a woman on our block?'

'Woman? Where did you see a woman? I've been here for quite a while and I ain't seen no woman around here.'

'That woman who was downstairs,' I said.

Cellmate B started laughing. 'That's not a woman, that's a man-woman.'

'But he sounds just like a woman,' I said. 'Her voice.'

'That's a man-woman!'

'So what is he or she doing here then? I don't understand – what sexual offence has this person committed?'

Cellmate A said, 'Well, I haven't asked, and I don't advise you to go up and ask. Just keep it to yourself.' So I did.

When we came down for dinner, I didn't say anything to the people who were serving our food this time. I was watched by two screws, so I just collected the food – roast chicken, peas, potatoes and fruit. The fruit was the only thing I ate. I was trying my best not to eat anything hard that would make me shit. Pissing was easy. I could hold that till I left the cell and then I'd quickly run in the toilet and piss. But a number two was a different matter – I just didn't want to do it.

When you're outside you don't think of those things – going to the toilet in private, and what food you can eat so you don't have to shit. When I was younger people would say, 'Don't do that because you could go to jail,' and you'd think, Yep, I could go to jail, I could cope. Now I know I am so fussy about things there is no way I could manage in jail. I couldn't last more than a week. I'd only been in Belmarsh two days and I already felt that half my body had shut down. I was imploding. There was no pain, but I was imploding mentally.

I gave my food to Cellmate B and just ate the fruit and drank the water. When our plates were collected I got a cup of water, poured it into a different cup and then got another cup. As soon as that one cooled down I drank it. I needed to get some liquid inside me.

It felt as if I'd lost weight. I was looking really skinny now, and it was only two days I'd been in here. I wondered what I'd weigh when I came out. When you're booked into prison you're weighed so they can find out if and why you are losing weight in prison.

On Sunday I slept as much as I could. I got into my bed, pillow over my head as usual to block out all noise and light and prison and thought. Block out everything. I wanted to be in a void.

'Well, Duwayne mate,' Cellmate A said, 'I hope it all goes well for you tomorrow, but if I was you I wouldn't think about it today. Just wait till you get the call. Don't sit down and worry about it. I see you're trying to sleep your way through it – that's the best way.' Again, he told me that I'd gradually get used to it, I'd start reading and I'd be all right. He was simply preparing me for not being released, because he didn't believe I would be. I didn't want to hear it now. I just wanted to sleep my way to freedom – blink my eyes and then it would be Monday.

I had the sheet over my head and was just blocking out the world. I wanted to think about nothing, but pictures of Steve and me kept coming into my mind – sitting on the wall waiting for a bus, down at the kebab shop, watching kung fu movies, running back trying to beat his mum's curfew, the attack, his blood bubbling up in his jacket. I felt sick. It was seven years since Steve had been killed, and here I was in prison charged with a sex offence. Somehow, I knew it was all connected, but I found it hard to work out exactly how. I'd been attacked, my best mate had been murdered in the attack, and for some reason the police resented me so much, perhaps resented the fact that I had lived to tell the tale of their racism and their incompetence, that they wanted to stitch me up bad. And I suppose having me banged up in jail accused of a sexual assault had to be regarded as a success by their standards.

But I had faith in Jane, my solicitor. I knew she wouldn't let me down. She wouldn't allow me to stay in here. She knew what it would do to me, and she was going to fight for me. I thought about all the people she could call on for help to get me out of here. Perhaps the police hoped to keep me here as long as possible to see what damage they could inflict on me mentally. Maybe if they broke me down completely, they would have turned round and said I was mentally unfit to be tried while telling everyone that I was guilty. That would have suited them perfectly, because they knew they didn't have a case to make.

Chapter 14

I'm Free

I woke up Monday morning bright and early again. I was told I had a visitor. It couldn't be Jane because she was on maternity leave. One of the officers told me that someone had phoned up over the weekend to say they would visit today.

I went through the usual rigmarole – breakfast, back up to the cell, sitting around. Then I was called.

'Are you dressed, Brooks? Are you ready?' Dressed? I'd been wearing the same clothes for three days – tracksuit bottoms and sweatshirt (prison clothes) and my work shoes. I looked a mess, but it didn't matter – I was only in prison, I wasn't going anywhere, nobody could see me on the streets, and we were all in the same boat. Wearing the same clothes didn't mean anything to me.

They took me over to the visiting rooms. On the way over I met another acquaintance of mine – I don't know what he was in there for, but it wasn't the first time he'd been in jail. I don't know what it is with these guys – going to jail, being released, committing crimes, going back to jail. I suppose it's hard when you see your friends have got stuff through crime and you think, Well, if they can get away with it, I can get away with it – and then you do it and get caught and end up jailed.

I went into the interview room, and it was Jo, who worked at Jane's office. She had come to ask me what had happened. I told her I didn't want to say too much because the room was probably bugged and I hadn't given the police any information about what had happened. They were desperate for any information they could get to build a case against me. But I gave her a rundown of what took place and how I had completely forgotten about the incident on 4 September, because in my mind there wasn't an incident to remember.

I told her that while I was in jail I kept asking myself what really did take place, did I do something I shouldn't have, did I go into a trance, because the way I'd been treated it was as if I must have done something seriously wrong. But I didn't know what.

I said to Jo that nothing took place on 4 September, nothing that warranted my being charged with attempted rape and indecent assault, nothing that warranted my being charged with anything. If there was a charge for dumping someone, maybe they could have charged me with that – but nothing else.

Jo told me that they were going to court today to get me out and she didn't see any reason why I shouldn't be released, although the police still hadn't given them the papers – so I'd been charged on the Thursday, been in court on Friday and now it was Monday, and the police still hadn't given my lawyers any papers whatsoever. They could tell the world that I'd been charged with a disgusting crime, but they didn't provide my lawyer with any documents that explained why.

I went back to the cell. It was a lonely walk. I'd been happy to see Jo and hear that Jane's office was working to get me out, but the walk back was so desperate, so silent. I felt I was fading away, melting away, erasing myself. It didn't take long to reduce someone to nothing in prison.

Whatever Cellmate A had told me, I had to keep telling myself, I will be out today, I will be out today. A couple of hours after I got back to my cell I was told I had another visitor. I made the same journey over to the visiting rooms. It was Alex and Tony from Movement for Justice who had come to see me. They were the first people to book a visit.

I told them how awful it was in here, but that Jane's office was going to court to get me out today. They asked me if I felt confident.

'Yes,' I said. 'If there was going to be a problem I think I would have known about it. But there isn't going to be a problem because there's nothing to keep me in here. I'm totally innocent. There's not even a speck of dirt on my shoes that they could use against me. That's how clean I am.' Alex kept asking me if I was sure. 'Alex, you know me by now. If there was anything to worry about I would have told you a long time ago. '

About ten minutes later a screw came up to me and tapped me on the shoulder. 'You're out,' he said.

'Yes!' I jumped up. 'Yessss! Fucking yes! I'm out of this place.' Pure elation. Like I'd come on in the last ten minutes of an FA Cup Final and scored the winner. It was so sweet, so good. For a moment, my body felt so alive. I didn't know what to do – whether to sit down, stand up, walk, run. I said to Alex, 'D'you mind if I go now? I want to get all my stuff and get out of here.'

'Yeah, yeah, yeah. Go on. We'll wait for you!'

But little did we know how long it would take me to get out of that hell-hole.

I went back into the room and was strip-searched. They asked how was I feeling? I said I was OK because I was leaving now.

'Oh, are you?'

'Yeah.'

'You've got bail?'

'Yeah.'

'Oh, you should have said. We wouldn't have strip-searched you.'

'Oh well, it doesn't matter,' I said. 'You got your pleasure.'

'Now, now, Mr Brooks. Now, now. We have to do our job.'

'Yeah,' I said. 'But why am I opening my arse to you? You know I don't smoke.' They were looking for drugs.

'It's normally the non-smokers who take in the stuff for the smokers.'

'Well, I'm out of here now so I don't need to go through this humiliating act any more.'

I walked back to my cell. I was happy, but my mind was still imploding. This place was designed to break you down, to sap you of strength. I asked myself how the other guys could ever be happy here. Fuck it man, I said to myself, why am I thinking like this, it's nothing to do with me, I'm getting out of here.

I got back to my cell. Everybody on the block already knew and they were congratulating me. 'Well, Duwayne, it was nice knowing you. Don't expect to see you here again, though,' the listener said. 'You don't seem like the kind of person who's going to go out there and commit a crime and get yourself back in here. I can see that in you.'

I felt bad that I was so happy to be leaving, because these people had been so good to me, but I had to get out. I couldn't have survived another week. It was one of the hardest things I've done in my life. I'd done more dangerous things, but they were easier to cope with.

I was brought down into a room and told to wait there; that it wouldn't take long. I was in that room for four hours. Four solid hours! What was the point of taking me off the block to put me in solitary confinement for four hours? Was this their last way of punishing me, or is this what they do to everybody? I didn't know.

I was distraught sitting in this one room until, finally, they came to get me. I thought something had happened: that maybe they had changed their mind because it was late and that I wouldn't be released till the next day. But no. The same black guy who booked me in was booking me out. He gave me my bail sheet and asked me to sign it.

I looked at the bail sheet. Although I'd been given bail, the conditions were strict. I had to stay in Birmingham; I wasn't allowed in London. I had to observe a curfew between 11 p.m. and 7 a.m. I had to sign on at a designated police station Monday, Wednesday, Friday. I looked at the bail officer. He told me to sign it: 'You don't want to be in here, you don't need to be in here, and you shouldn't be in here. Sign it. Make sure I don't see you back here again.'

I signed it, they gave me my stuff and I walked off. Something told me to look back round again. He was looking at me, and he said it again: 'I don't want to see you back here.'

I didn't need to be told twice. I knew what he meant.

'I can tell you for free, you're never going to see me back in this place.'

Me and two other guys were released at the same time. We were walking back to the gate. Because I had only been in there three days, I hadn't paid attention to my prison number. Before they release you they always ask for your name, date of birth and prison number. I gave them my name and date of birth but I couldn't remember my prison number. They said they couldn't let me out unless I gave them it.

'OK,' I said, 'let me look in my bag.' I was searching my bag, but then a lady said, 'Don't worry, Duwayne, we know who you are. Just go through.'

The gates started opening. The feeling was indescribable. The outside world was coming back to me. I was free.

Strictly speaking, I wasn't free. I was under those fierce conditions. But I didn't care. The conditions were nothing compared to prison. Melly and my guardian Mr McBean were waiting for me outside. I met Mr McBean when I told Noel Penstone that I wanted to play football, and he said he knew someone who ran a team. It was Mr McBean, and he had later suggested that he become my guardian. They told me what had happened at the court. It was just a fiasco. The judge hadn't wanted to let me out.

An ex-girlfriend of mine, Sophie, who lived in Birmingham, had read about the case in the *Sun* on Saturday. She rang my phone and Melly had answered it, and told her what had happened. Her mum, Joyce, was a care worker who lived in Birmingham but often travelled the country taking on special cases for short periods. She was working in Croydon at the time, and Sophie told her all about it, and Joyce said she wanted to be at court for me. So they organised it with Jane's office.

When they got to court they found out that the police had accused me of something else. This time I was supposed to have been harassing the victim. They still hadn't presented one shred of evidence even at this stage.

The court had to be held up till Joyce arrived. When she got there she made a character statement for me. The judge had made it clear that she didn't think I should be free to roam the streets of London, that I was a very dangerous person, especially to women. She was only prepared to grant bail with ridiculous conditions.

Joyce said that she had grandchildren and her daughters, and that they would be around if I was to stay with them in Birmingham. The judge didn't like the idea of me being there. She tried to put Joyce off, and told her that I may be on bail a long time. Joyce said she didn't care, she wanted me at her house so that she could look after me, because she knew what they were saying was all untrue.

After all the wrangling, they eventually agreed to give me bail. They asked for more than £20,000 bail money as security, assuming I wouldn't have access to such a fortune and that I would have to remain banged up. Of course, I didn't have that kind of money, but fortunately Nick Kent of the Tricycle Theatre stood bail for me to the tune of £19,500 – delivered to the court in premium bonds. I found it ironic that a white man who barely knew me was turning out to be my saviour. Mr McBean, also the head of Knights, the charity I do some voluntary work for, stood £1000 surety.

I had to go back to the hostel to get my stuff and I had to be in Birmingham at 9 p.m. latest to sign on at the police station, otherwise I would have broken the first bail condition. I picked up my car, phoned Greenwich police station and asked them for my diary. My diary had never made it to the prison. All my other stuff had, but not my diary. Actually, when I was first brought to the police station and they showed me my possessions, I couldn't see my diary. When I was in the custody suite, I'd not seen the diary either. But when I read the custody notes, it was apparent that they'd taken my diary out long before then. So what were they doing with it?

They said they didn't know where it was. OK, no problem, I'll get it next time I'm in London. I got in the car and headed straight for Birmingham. I didn't get very far before the car broke down. I called the AA and was picked up some forty-five minutes later. They couldn't fix it so they called one of their trucks in. I told the AA man all about my case, and how I needed to go to Birmingham because I wasn't allowed in London. 'OK,' he said. 'Do you need to arrange a hotel?' The terms of the AA cover are that you get one night's stay in a hotel and you get taken any-where in Britain you need to go.

I wanted them to take me to the local garage in Birmingham, but the garage was shut, so they took me to my bail address, which was in Winson Green. That first night I couldn't sleep. I was speaking to Joyce, and she was crying. She was one of the people trying to convince me to settle with the police, and to drop the civil case. 'You can't win against the police because there's just one of you against all of them,' she said.

I just listened. What was the point of giving up? Especially now they'd taken it this far. There was no way I was going to give up. They could have done me for something else, speeding or not wearing a seat belt, but attempted rape and indecent assault . . . no way. How could I give up after this deliberate attempt to damage my character beyond repair?

The first few days and nights I sat on my own and thought about what tactics we should use to beat the police in this case. The police had made a smart move by keeping all the documents. They hadn't given us anything, so we didn't know what the case against me would be. Then again, they didn't know what my argument would be.

Jane was on leave and had passed my case on to Darren White. I think she felt easier, less compromised, with a male lawyer looking after me in a sex case against a woman. She knew that the police could easily concoct evidence. I knew that, too. But I was convinced that this time they couldn't concoct any convincing evidence – no forensics, no witnesses, nothing.

Joyce would come home in the evening from work if she'd done a day shift, and she'd come in in the morning if she'd done the night shift, and the first thing she would put down were two nourishment drinks. She said I needed to get my strength back and build my body up because I looked weak, as if I'd lost a lot of weight.

It was strange. I'd been in custody from Friday up till Monday. When I went into Belmarsh I weighed 10 stone, and when I left I weighed 10 stone, but I looked about 8 stone. Even though I'd not actually lost weight, my body was worn down because I'd not been able to eat the food.

Joyce made me a big breakfast every day – eggs, beans, plantain, bread. If she was working nights, she'd make it first thing when she arrived in the morning. If she was doing the days, she'd make it at night and put it to the side. So when I woke up in the morning while she was still sleeping, my breakfast would be ready for me and I'd just heat it up.

Joyce did everything for me. She looked after me like her son: she always said I was like one of her sons. It was some years back that I had been seeing her daughter. She believed I really liked her daughter because I used to come all the way from London to Birmingham to see her. And I did like her. But it didn't lead to anything permanent and eventually we split up. Now I was back in Birmingham she was seeing someone else. It didn't really matter to me because I wasn't there to see her. I was there by force. I had no choice.

I went to start my car, and it started first time. But I knew there was a problem. Sometimes it started, sometimes it didn't. There had to be a problem with one of the spark plug leads. I called in the AA again. The guy was on the car for two minutes before he pulled off the king lead. 'There's your problem, mate, the king lead is broken. Go and get a new one and the car will be fine.'

I got a new king lead, plugged it in and the car was fine for a week. Next Friday, one of my tyres was flat – I discovered knife marks.

I called Paul Charlton, one of my liaison officers. I had two liaison officers now, Mr Charlton and a man called Barry McDowell, because a liaison officer was not allowed to see you alone while you were on bail. I told Mr Charlton what had happened and he said I should report it. 'What's the point?' I said. 'I'm sure police officers are supposed to make checks on me to make sure I'm observing the curfew, so if there were any tiny discrepancies – say, I was back home five minutes after eleven – I'd be straight back into jail. So I bet they already know about the car.'

Having said that, I would sit in my car and watch to see if I was being observed, and I never spotted a police car observing me in the whole six weeks I was in Birmingham.

I spent £30 on a new tyre. Two days later, the clutch cable broke. I had to get the AA to tow my car to the garage. It was disastrous – I had to get a taxi to sign on at the police station. The cab fare to the police station was £4, so for a whole week I was paying £8 just getting to and from the police station.

I went down the job centre to apply for benefit. I explained what had happened, and they said to me they would find out if I could get my money backdated. I was broke and looking for a job. I applied for job-seeker's allowance, but the Department of Employment wrote back to me saying that my circumstances did not warrant me getting the job-seeker's allowance, but I could appeal. I was sure the appeal would be pointless, but I was desperate.

I was spending my time in the library, reading up on all the things that were said in 1997 and 1998 about the discussions leading up to the public inquiry. The more I read the more new things I found out. I also read up about the so-called steering group that was set up after the Inquiry, which involved the Lawrences and a number of other people but not me. I phoned Darren, my lawyer, and said I wanted to be involved. Darren said that now was not the time to be worrying about my involvement with a steering group, I should be thinking about my case.

'What is there for me to think about? There is nothing I can do until we go back to court. I want to be on this steering group and I want you to get my bail conditions changed for me.'

Earlier, Jane had written to the Home Secretary, Jack Straw. She received a reply saying these people were hand-picked and I was not one of the chosen few. Basically, the letter said why would they need or want me on the committee when they already had the Lawrences. Great! So I was the main person in the whole case who had witnessed what had happened, and I wasn't allowed to be on the steering group created to make sure all the recommendations Macpherson made were implemented. Such is life.

My committal hearing was coming up at Greenwich court. Movement for Justice had arranged a rally. They wanted to bring together as many people as possible to show I was well supported. I told Alex that was fine, but that he needed to be careful. I didn't want anything to happen to him in the meantime while he was here supporting me. I told him the police knew they were not going to get a conviction, and that there was bound to be a backlash, and I didn't want him caught up in that.

'No,' he said. 'I don't care. I'm out to get you free, and that's what I'm going to do.'

Darren wanted to build up an abuse of process argument. He went to a hearing to try to get my bail conditions changed so I could return to London. The application failed. While I was in Birmingham I couldn't do any work – another way of breaking me down. At the hearing, the police suggested that someone from Birmingham had called the alleged victim and threatened her. Now this was strange. Nobody was supposed to know I was in Birmingham, and especially nobody who knew the alleged victim.

A few weeks later, I was back in London for the committal. I pulled up outside the hostel in Greenwich and met Mr McBean. Since I'd met him he had changed me so much, turned me into the person I am today. Without him the police would have had an easier ride, but he had shown me how to be strong, where to be strong, what to say, how to say it. He had made me a thorn in their side.

He said to me when I went into the committal I must go round the court and shake hands with everybody who had come to support me, even if I didn't know who they were. 'Be very thankful to everybody,' he said.

I walked around, and everybody came to greet me. The television cameras were there and I just felt so important. I felt that people out there did believe me. I felt I wasn't alone. In the police station, in prison, in Birmingham, despite all the help I had had, I still felt alone, but here I felt good. When everyone hugged me I felt their warmth.

There was an old lady there. She was about eighty and needed two people to help her up the stairs. I asked her why she had come, and she said, 'I know what the police are doing is wrong. I know you're innocent, Duwayne. I'm here to support you.' I could have cried.

She put so many people to shame. This eighty-year-old lady who could barely walk had come down to the court on a bus.

There were many people in south-east London who knew the case was going on but they couldn't make it – what upset me most was that the same thing was happening to the children of these people. Their children were also being victimised by the police, and I felt that I was fighting for them as much as for me. I might have felt let down by them, but this woman made up for it. It was so touching.

I walked inside the court and the waiting area was packed with family and friends. It made me feel that I didn't need to worry. I said to myself that there was nothing the police could do to me – if there are all these people supporting me here, there must be so many more who aren't here.

Darren had met the guy from the CPS. He asked me to come into a room for a chat. Darren told me that the guy handed him a bundle of papers and it was only when he started reading them that he realised they had dropped the attempted rape. The CPS guy hadn't even bothered to tell him. Darren said he wanted to see why they had dropped the attempted rape, so he carried on reading through the stuff. He couldn't believe it. There was nothing in the file that could warrant a charge of attempted rape. Indecent assault at a stretch, but nothing of attempted rape. And even here we are only talking about what their files said, not what actually happened.

'We won that part then,' I said.

Darren asked why they had charged me with it in the first place if they knew they had nothing.

'Come on, Darren, you know as well as I do that a charge of indecent assault wouldn't have created nearly as much publicity as attempted rape.' Rape is a disgusting crime. An attempt to rape is just as bad. They knew that to associate me with rape was as damaging as it could get. That's their game, I thought. 'Darren mate,' I said, 'luckily I like playing games, because nobody can beat a natural. You can have all the practice in the world but you cannot beat a natural, and I am a natural.' I didn't believe it, but I was feeling cocky.

'Steady on, Duwayne,' he said. 'We don't know what else is going to come. There's no forensics here, nothing.'

'Darren, there ain't going to be no forensics because I never touched her.'

'Yeah, well, but . . . let's wait and see,' he said.

Darren's attitude was always to wait and see. I got it in my head that he didn't really believe me. I knew Jane and her partner Vicky did – if they'd had any doubts they wouldn't have let Darren take the case.

Although the police had dropped the charge, they still felt they had enough to warrant an indecent-assault charge. This is, of course, a much less serious offence.

I came back out of the room and reported back to Mr McBean. 'Waste of time. They've dropped the attempted rape. There is nothing in that file. Nothing.'

'OK, that's what I want to hear,' he said.

I started greeting more people. 'We're here to support you, Duwayne. We know what's going on.'

Everyone wanted to know who the girl was. I said I couldn't tell them; I'd leave it to her. If she wanted people to know, she'd tell them, but I didn't want to give out her name. I couldn't give out her name because I wasn't allowed to.

I spoke to Richard, my security guard mate at the court. 'Everything all right?' I said.

'Yeah,' he said. But he didn't sound all right. 'Well, we were told not to walk by the front of the court. We've been told we have to go out at the back because it's too dangerous to go out at the front.'

'Too dangerous?' I said. 'Richard, let me tell you something. There is nobody here who is going to be violent. There is nothing to be violent about. Just me being here with this crowd has created the publicity. There is no need for any violence.'

I couldn't believe it. After all, this wasn't the first time they'd had publicity at Greenwich Magistrates' Court. There was certainly plenty of publicity when the Lawrence suspects were there. But today staff had been told not to go through the front, only the back. Was this another form of institutional racism? Had they taken special measures because I was black and many of my supporters were black?

We were called into court. DI Sturge made a point of coming to say hello to me. 'Are you all right, Duwayne?'

'Yes, Mr Sturge. I am fine.'

I sat down behind the dock. A boy had just been remanded in custody for murder. And in the blink of an eye a girl had run into the court to attack this boy. I've never seen a magistrate move so quickly in my life. The girl burst through the door. And one step, two steps, three steps and the magistrate was up and out the back. But nobody else seemed to move. Nobody except the girl who had burst into the court and the boy who was held in custody. He saw her coming and he ran for the door. The security then stopped him, at the same time helping her to catch him. She unloaded kicks and punches, kicks and punches, kicks and punches, and then security realised what had happened.

DI Sturge came over to me as if he was trying to rescue me. 'Oh, Duwayne, you better come this way, quick.' I looked at him, and he read my mind: Fuck off from me.

I wasn't involved in this, I wasn't worried about anything, I didn't know this girl, this girl didn't know me, and there was no reason for her to attack me. Why should I run away? Security were trying to grab hold of her, and half the court was running out.

They caught the girl, and court staff came to ask me if I was OK. I asked myself why was I getting all this attention, why should there be anything wrong with me? The girl ran right past me to attack somebody else. Did they expect her to attack me, I began to wonder.

I was next up and the magistrate came back in. He was worried. 'If anything like that happens again, I'm emptying the court. We'll have no one in the public gallery and I will order a closed court.'

The hearing took place, and I was committed to crown court. Another date was set, and the bail conditions were kept unchanged. The CPS were obviously still worried about me interfering with the 'victim'. The CPS loved to talk about the victim. I made the point to Darren that she was an *alleged* victim, that she couldn't be a victim of a crime that hadn't been proven.

It was 5 November, two months since the assault allegedly took place. I was arrested on 16 September, and this was the first time we'd seen any documents.

Court was over, and I had to be back in Birmingham by 11 p.m. I went back to Joyce's. The drive back to Birmingham was great. To beat an opponent you have to think of every possibility, every intricacy, every way you could lose. You can't expect to beat an opponent just because you are better or more skilful or intelligent. You have to be good at everything, and then you have to have luck on your side to finish off the game.

Actually, in this case, I didn't think I did need luck. I went through it all in my head. They could only go by what the girl had said if there were no forensics, which there wouldn't be, and it would be my word against hers. I didn't know if the police knew that she had been to the hostel a number of times before, and even been in my bed on one occasion. I'd been downstairs and when I returned she was in my bed, saying she was cold. I'd made it clear to her that there was nothing going on between me and her and there never would be. But she still came to see me. I'd also made it clear that once I'd finished work I wasn't driving through the traffic to meet her. If she ever wanted to see me she had to come to Greenwich. Which is what she did.

Now, I didn't know if the police knew all this. If we were in court, my barrister would obviously ask her why, if I had been harassing her for sex as she said, was she visiting me at my hostel in Greenwich and why had she even got into my bed on one occasion.

I started reeling off questions in my head for the barrister to ask. I arrived at Joyce's house. I looked at the clock. Two hours had passed. Bloody hell, that went quick. I was well happy. I couldn't wait for the next hearing. In fact, I couldn't wait for the trial.

Next day, I asked Darren if we couldn't skip all these waste-of-time court appearances and go straight to trial. I had nothing to hide.

'We haven't got all the papers,' he said.

'Not having all the papers doesn't disadvantage us,' I said.

'We really need to know what they're saying,' he said, time and again.

I was just eager to get it all out in the open. I knew the police were in for a hiding even without seeing the rest of the documents.

My excitement started to grow. The disclosure trickle started. We were getting more and more documents: part of a notebook here, part of a notebook there; this statement here, this statement there. Darren began to realise that the CPS weren't going to get anywhere. He asked me why they were continuing with the prosecution.

I said to him, 'Darren, this is all about me, it's nothing to do with anything or anyone else.' I knew that whatever happened they would prosecute the case, and try their best to get me convicted. They couldn't withdraw now having gone so far. Imagine the negative publicity – 'Duwayne Brooks, the man who was racially stereotyped by the police, has had all charges against him dropped.' It would have been another blow to the Met's reputation. While they continued fighting there was still a chance of securing a conviction.

Finally we got the statement that the complainant allegedly made about me harrassing her. She had been told by the police that I had to stay in Birmingham. While I was in Birmingham she got a phone call from someone with a Birmingham accent. It was obvious: the police were using her. And perhaps she was using the police in some way. The more documents that were disclosed, the more Darren realised that I hadn't done anything.

The Monday, Wednesday, Friday signing-on was still there. I'd arrived late for some of the signings-on, and when I got to the police station I was given stress. 'We can lock you up, Mr Brooks. The reason you're under these bail conditions is to make sure you don't run away. If you turn up even five minutes late we can suspect you of having run away and issue a warrant for your arrest.' If I was going to run away I would have done so a long time ago. And if the police and CPS really thought I was going to run away, they would have taken my passport. I said to the officer that the bail conditions were nothing to do with me running away, that they were all about inconveniencing me and causing me 100 per cent stress. They must have done a profile of me, I told him, and decided that this was the best way to break me down.

'Now, what's so special about you, Duwayne Brooks?' said the officer. 'Sign the documents. And leave please.' I did as I was told.

Living in Birmingham had its problems. How would I pay rent for my property in Peckham? I had made it clear to Hyde Housing and the police that I wasn't paying any rent. From the day my address was released in court in August I had told Paul Charlton that I wasn't staying at that property any more and they needed to find me somewhere else to live. The police had agreed, especially after the August break-in, that it was unsafe for me to stay there.

Hyde Housing told me to fill out a form for housing benefit and they would do the rest. I told them I'd been working in London. 'It doesn't matter,' they said. 'Exceptional circumstances. Housing benefit should pay the rent.' OK. The ball was rolling on a variety of fronts – housing benefit, job-seeker's allowance, job hunting and information gathering. I was job hunting just in case I'd be up here till the trial began in January or February. As for the information gathering, I was reading about other indecent-assault trials and stocking up some more knowledge on the Lawrence case.

We won the next bail hearing in November 1999. After two months. I was allowed back in London. But guess what? I was not allowed into south London. I was not allowed over the Thames. I had to stay at my friend's house. Francoise lived in east London. Again, this was supposed to be a safe-house. New video equipment was installed outside. But my car was soon broken into, and nothing was recorded on video. Two days later it happened again, and then Francoise's car was broken into twice. Nothing recorded. Some safe-house.

Because I wasn't allowed in south London I only worked in the West End. Luckily, my boss had kept my job open for me while I was away. Well, I say luckily, but I suppose he kept it open because I was good at it.

The CPS sent me a letter to confirm the new bail conditions. It felt as if they were rubbing it in. I was getting all worked up, and then I remembered it was a game. You've got to take a step back from what is happening to remember it's a game. That's the key. If you're in the game, and you lose your mind, you lose the game.

I told my friends in Birmingham that I was allowed back in London. Joyce was happy for me. She wanted me to go back up to Birmingham at weekends when I had finished work so I'd be safe. I told her that I couldn't. I was going to stay in London and just work and stay home. I felt that if I travelled anywhere, the police might bring more spurious charges against me. Go to work, stay in, go to work, stay in – that's how it was.

Forest Gate police station was my signing-on station. My bail signing-on time before was 8 to 9 p.m., but I changed it to between 5 and 8 p.m. to give me more flexibility. If I finished work I could go straight there earlier. This was when all the stress started back in London. I had been told by Mr Charlton that Francoise's house was supposed to be a safe house. He said that nobody knew I was staying there except those in the Met who needed to know.

'Does Mr Sturge know?' I said.

'Well, he would do.'

'Well, he doesn't need to.'

'He does because he's the officer in charge of the case and he needs to know where you are at all times.'

'But if he knows then others may know,' I said.

'There's nothing you can do about that,' said Mr Charlton.

'It can't be a safe-house then, can it?' I said. I told Mr Charlton I wanted hourly patrols. I didn't feel safe. Back in London, I was easy pickings. Easy pickings for car break-ins, easy pickings for hate mail.

'Let's wait and see,' said Mr Charlton.

My first day signing on at Forest Gate police station was a joke. Nobody knew I was supposed to sign. Mr Charlton had said that if there were any problems I should call him, so I did. He called the station and they still didn't know anything about me. He told me to get them to do me a card and sign it just in case.

The next signing day was Wednesday. Still nobody knew that I was supposed to sign on at the station. But I signed on the same card that I started off, just in case. Friday, they finally knew and they were waiting for me, and I signed. The following Monday I signed without a problem.

Then it started on the Wednesday. Normally when I went to sign there was an officer looking out for people going in to sign. But this time there was only one officer on duty, and there were three people ahead of me. Those three people took three hours. So even though I had arrived on time I ended up signing late. That was a regular problem at Forest Gate. Sometimes I would get there for 5 p.m. and not sign until nine.

When I had been kept waiting hours to sign I would put the time down that I had arrived, and on a few occasions when I put the time in they would cross it out and put the later time in. I would then refuse to sign it.

'If you don't sign, I'll arrest you.'

'Well, arrest me then. I've been here since six.'

'How do I know you've been here since six?'

'Look on the cameras,' I said.

'Those cameras don't work.'

'Well, what's the point in having cameras in a police station if they don't work?'

'Well, nobody's going to come in a police station and commit a crime are they?'

'So why have you got cameras then?'

'Look, Mr Brooks, if I was you, I'd just sign and leave.'

'I'm not signing. I'm not signing 9 p.m. I've been here since six. If I sign it, I go down as an hour late and it goes on my record and it goes to the court. So I'm not signing.'

I was asked to wait outside. You went into a little room to sign, and the door shut behind you and you were locked in. In theory, it was false imprisonment, because you couldn't leave without them pressing a buzzer. I said that to them. 'Tough,' they said.

'But you're falsely imprisoning people. I can't leave when I want to leave, so it's false imprisonment.'

'Whatever you want to say, Mr Brooks, whatever.'

I made a complaint to the inspector. Everybody knew when I was due to sign, and I wasn't the only one signing. Why couldn't there be an officer there just to sign people on?

'Why should you have preferential treatment, Mr Brooks?' he said.

'I'm not asking for preferential treatment. I'm just asking to be signed on in my time. If I turn up at five or six I don't expect to sign on at nine.'

'Well, Mr Brooks, you should turn up when the station is empty.'

'I don't know when the station is empty.'

I received a letter from an inspector at Forest Gate station agreeing that there were problems with signing-on. They were short-staffed, they said, and sometimes it was hard to get two people on the front desk. Right. It was so hard that sometimes they'd have an officer sitting down, just watching. Maybe that officer was being trained. Whatever, it shouldn't take more than ten minutes to sign.

I was told that when I came in I should knock on the glass and make the officer aware that I was there. The first time I did it, I was told never to do it again. The officer made it clear to me that when she was busy, she was busy, and she didn't have time to be noticing people coming in to sign. I told her about the letter. She didn't believe me, and she said she wanted to see it. Next time I went in I showed it her, and she was surprised that I'd received such a letter. 'Nobody else gets this treatment,' she said.

'Well, do the others make a complaint? They may get stroppy with you, but do they take it further?'

'Probably not,' she said.

'I took it further because I thought you were involved in the piss-taking.'

'Nothing to do with me,' she said. 'I'm just an overworked front-desk worker.' She finally agreed that it was crazy I'd been kept waiting so long.

The trial date was set for January. The more Darren and me talked the more useless the case against me seemed to be. After the alleged incident in my room, the girl had left and walked down the stairs. Some minutes beforehand somebody had phoned 999 from the front office of the building and put the phone down. The operator had contacted the police and sent them round to the hostel. The police happened to be in the building at the same time the alleged victim had walked down the stairs. She had walked straight past the two officers and out of the building. She had claimed she was distressed and crying after she had left my room. But if she had walked past the officers distressed and crying, surely one of those officers would have stopped her and asked her if she was OK. Any normal person would have done that.

According to the statement she had been waiting outside for the police. The police then turned up and asked her what was wrong. 'Nothing,' she said. 'I just want a lift home'! They asked her what had happened. 'Nothing,' she said. 'I dialled 999 to get a lift home. I know I shouldn't have, but I'm stranded here and I need to get home.' Somehow, this request for a lift home grew into an allegation of attempted rape – I am not allowed to say how here because I have been told it would be contempt of court, a criminal offence.

The police still hadn't passed over all the documents. One of the documents they hadn't handed over would turn out to be about a woman they had brought in to help the alleged victim. The girl's mother and family had made it clear that they didn't believe her. They had told her that the police were out to get me and that they were using her. She didn't want to hear that, and the police didn't want her to hear it.

So they brought in a mediator to help her. The mediator was a Macpherson recommendation, and this was the first time one had been used – in a case against me! The mediator was there to help witnesses from ethnic minorities who distrusted the police. The woman they chose was a close friend of a police officer at Greenwich police station, Sergeant Solley, who had worked on the Lawrence case. At the Macpherson Inquiry it was alleged that they had been having an affair. It had been denied. But, Sergeant Solley and Augusta Gibril did knew each other well, as she later accused him of rape. There was no way that both of them should have been involved in this case. There was an obvious conflict of interests.

When the police discovered what was being said to the alleged victim at home, they contacted Sergeant Solley and asked him to see if Augusta Gibril would work with the girl. Augusta ended up making a statement, which was unsigned and incomplete, to WPC Chapman. The statement claimed that Augusta believed the alleged victim was not telling the truth – and the CPS suppressed it for three months.

The trial was due to start but the girl's mother was not in the country. I had been told that she'd left the country because she did not want to get involved as she did not believe I had assaulted her daughter. It wasn't the first time her daughter had been involved in such wrangling. There was an incident when she was allegedly interfered with by a member of her church – it had destroyed the man's marriage, but no one found out what really happened. And there were other incidents that could not be proved either way.

The days leading to the trial went by, and still we had not received all the documents we had asked for. We wanted all the contemporaneous notes that were made at meetings, and all the statements made by officers and witnesses. Darren had to go to court yet again to demand that the documents were disclosed to us before the trial.

The trial date came and went. It was adjourned to February. We still hadn't had the documents, and the complainant's mum still hadn't returned. I had been told that when her family heard that she had made this complaint against me, they all gathered at her house and pleaded with her to drop the case. The police worried that she would succumb to the pressure of her family, so they brought in Augusta Gibril to give her support.

Augusta was there to instruct her how to give evidence and to ease any doubts she had. The police put the complainant in a hotel. They had promised her all sorts of security – a flat with furnishings, and financial assistance if she continued with the case.

She started to waver. Half the time she was staying with her boyfriend rather than at the hotel. From the notes I got the feeling that the police had pressured her: if she didn't go ahead they would tell her mother that she was at another man's house. By now the complainant had made it clear to friends that she didn't want to continue but was being forced to.

A letter arrived for the officer in charge of the case. The complainant had been to see solicitors and had instructed them to tell the police to drop the case. This was a week before it was due to go to court in March 2000. Normal police practice is to act on the complainant's wishes in these matters. In the notes we were given by the police we discovered there was another girl who had complained that she had been raped, and the same officer, WPC Chapman, was involved. This girl had complained she'd been raped, so all her clothes had been taken from her and were being forensically tested. This girl, according to Chapman's notes, did not want to continue with her case. So Chapman then brought all her clothes and all her belongings back to her, and that was the end of it.

In my case, the complainant had also said that she didn't want to continue, but the police couldn't have taken a more different approach. Instead of doing what she wanted them to do, the police pressured her. It would turn out that on the day before the case finally went to court, a Sunday, the police went round to see her and pressed her to come to court on the Monday.

Why were they so desperate for her to go ahead? If she had said she didn't want to go to court, why should she? She had already made a statement saying she wanted to speak to the judge before the case started to tell him that I hadn't attempted to rape her and that all I'd done was sit down on the bed – my bed. So why were the police so anxious to get her to court?

Although my legal team had decided to argue abuse of process, I wanted to go ahead with the case, and prove my innocence, rather than get the case thrown out on a technicality. I was so confident I couldn't lose. But Darren kept reminding me that even though I was telling the truth, the way I tell the truth may not be to the jury's liking: they may not like my style, my body language, and they could convict me on that.

Another game. This time it's not against the police, it's against the judge and jury and prosecution barristers. The other team might be telling 100 per cent lies, but whichever team performs best is likely to win. I wanted the case to go ahead because I wanted all the officers to give evidence. OK, they'd managed to work out their stories between them for court, but I didn't believe they could keep up their lies under the pressure of my barrister Julia Krish's questioning.

At 2 p.m. on 20 March, the court started with the formalities. After they were done with, the judge told me I could sit down. To my left were the press. In front of me to the right were the CPS. It seemed that the high-ranking people at the CPS were at this case. It was a bit strange, this just being an indecent-assault case, yet we have all these high-flyers sitting in the courtroom giving me daggers. To the left were Julia and Darren. To the right and up was the public gallery. I could see Melly and a few other friends.

We started our abuse of process argument. My legal team gave the skeleton argument to the judge. After a few minutes, the judge decided he needed a two-minute break. He made an excuse and left. I beckoned down to my legal team. 'I told you,' I said. 'He has gone to make a phone call and let them know that there is no case against me.'

After ten minutes he returned, and the case started. But I felt sure he had made it known that Humpty Dumpty couldn't be put back together again.

From the start the judge seemed hostile to Julia. Everybody noticed it. I looked up to Melly and everyone else in the public gallery. They were worried: you could see it on their faces. But I reckoned that the judge knew the case was over, and so he was going to give my barrister a hard time just for the fun of it.

Julia began to feel the pressure. The courtroom was getting

tense. I could feel it. Julia began to stutter a lot, and the more she stuttered the more the judge interrupted. He was doing it on purpose to undermine her, and it was working.

Meanwhile, we were still waiting for the police notebooks that reported the Sunday-afternoon meeting. The prosecution barrister hadn't received them either. The police said they had forgotten to bring them to court. They knew the case was starting today. How on earth could they forget to bring the notes? The prosecution barrister said he didn't know. I could see he was a battler. He didn't want to lose his case. He wanted to be the one who sent me to jail. I felt he was taking it personally. Everybody seemed to be taking it personally. I thought, Can this be the effect my name has on people?

Jane was working in the background now. She had written to Mr Calvert-Smith, the head of the CPS, to inform him that there was nothing in this case to proceed with. The CPS is supposed to proceed with a case only if there is a reasonable chance of winning. We had been told earlier that he hadn't seen the letter. But here the prosecution said that the CPS had seen the letter and decided that there was no need to refer it to the top man, the director of public prosecutions. The next minute they seemed to be saying that he had seen the letter and that because he hadn't said anything he obviously wanted the case to go ahead. They seemed to be saying whatever suited them at any particular moment.

Julia played on the fact that the police had been round to the complainant's house the day before but had failed to bring their notebooks to court. It emerged that none of the police officers, except Chapman, had made any relevant contemporaneous notes of any of their meetings. Unbelievable! Police officers had met up in a highly irregular way with the complainant and not made any contemporaneous notes. Yet these same officers were able to make statements dated 20 and 21 January about incidents that were alleged to have happened in October, November and

December.

The judge was disturbed. Julia then went on to talk about how the complainant had not wished to attend court. Again, Julia pointed out the irregularities and asked why the police hadn't respected the complainant's wish to drop the case. When a complainant changes his or her mind usually the police just accept it. They don't normally harass the complainant as they had done here.

We wondered how the prosecution would present their non-case. There was no evidence whatsoever to back up the complainant's allegation: no witnesses, no forensics. My word against hers. Or it could quite easily be my word supported by hers, from what I had heard.

The first people we wanted to question were the officers who saw her leave the building, but we could never find out their names. She had said she walked past two officers after she had left my room, and that she was stressed and crying. Now, the reason the officers were at the hostel in the first place was because someone had made a 999 call, hadn't said anything and had put the phone down, and they were sent to investigate.

If they had seen this girl crying and distressed, surely the first thing they would have done was stop her and ask her what was wrong. But no, they just ignored her. This was the prosecution's first blunder.

The day was over. I got up and stretched and was getting ready to leave the dock when the prosecution barrister asked the judge if he could remand me till tomorrow. He obviously feared that I wouldn't turn up. The judge looked at him, and then looked at me, and then looked at him. He didn't even turn to my barrister. 'I don't think Mr Brooks will not turn up. Isn't that so, Mr Brooks? You'll be here for ten o'clock tomorrow morning, won't you?'

'Yes, sir.'

'Well then. There you go.'

The prosecution barrister looked at the clerk, the clerk turned to the judge, but the judge wasn't interested. Why did they want me to stay the night? What did they have in store for me in the cells? We didn't win that day, but I felt good.

I walked out and had a little meeting with Darren and Julia. I said to Julia straight that she had to stop stuttering. 'If you keep stuttering it's going to upset your flow and it's going to seem as if you're making it up as you're going along. We need to be flowing. We don't want to give the prosecution no chance to come in, and we don't want to give the judge no chance to come in.'

Darren thought I was out of order. But in my situation I had to tell the truth. If you let things slide and don't say anything about it, you'll come to a bad end, and I didn't want that to happen to me.

I called Jane and told her what had happened. She spoke to Julia and told me that Julia was upset about her performance and things would go better tomorrow. I said to Jane all she had to do was not stutter and we'd be fine. Jane said that even good barristers stutter occasionally.

'Yes, they do, everyone stutters sometimes, but Julia was stuttering because she had been knocked out of her stride,' I said.

I went back to Francoise's and looked at the whole case again. I was checking to see if there were any holes that we might have missed over the six months. The police still hadn't given us any telephone records showing I'd made ten phone calls with further threats of rape. The police hadn't provided us with any evidence of these calls. I looked at it and thought, This is great – I want to hear what Sturge has to say about this.

I went to sleep early because I wanted to have a clear head for the next day. This was the day that the case was either going to be thrown out or started.

I still wasn't worried because I knew we had devastating questions to ask the prosecution – questions that would expose their lies for what they were. The CPS had nothing to ask because anything they asked could be switched back on to them and used against them.

The way the justice system works in a criminal trial in Britain is that the prosecution has to prove beyond reasonable doubt that I committed the crime. I did not have to prove my innocence. But here, I could prove that I hadn't done anything.

The next morning I got to court and met up with Julia and Darren. Julia looked different. She was glowing. It seemed as if she had decided to just go for it.

I wasn't worried about losing. I knew that if the trial went ahead, it would be worse for the police. All their lies would be exposed in court. It would have been nice to see them humiliated. The judge would have probably stopped it at half-time anyway, saying I had no case to answer after the complainant had given evidence.

But now the target was simply to get the case stopped. We continued the abuse of process argument and Julia was a different person altogether. She was flowing. It was good to watch. The judge kept interrupting, like yesterday, but Julia just waited for him to finish, totally unflustered, and then continued with her argument. She knew the case inside out and was inspired and confident.

I looked up at Melly. She was nodding her head approvingly. Those who had been here yesterday could see the difference. Julia was on fire.

The prosecution stood up to talk. The argument was about who would call Augusta Gibril. It was still up to the prosecution. If she was not a witness of truth, who could rely on her? The arguments went on till lunchtime.

The police barrister started to get personal. He felt the judge was on his side so he could go a bit further than normal. He tried to make me look stupid, suggesting that just because I was part of the Lawrence case I felt I was above prosecution. He said the fact that this was a 'high-profile case [was] utterly irrelevant', and that our letter to the DPP 'goes too far'.

Why was the barrister getting personal? When you're confident you get cocky, not aggressive and personal. It was obvious he had no confidence when it came to calling Augusta Gibril, who was supposed to be a witness for the prosecution. He didn't want to call her because he knew she was a liability. She had made that statement way back in the early days around November and in it she had said she didn't believe the complainant, even if she hadn't signed it.

Apparently, what happened was that WPC Chapman took a statement and Augusta Gibril had to leave before it was finished. She was never asked to come back and complete her statement. Why not? Perhaps because it was not in the police's interest to have her complete it. We only got the statement in January, although it had been written in November. The CPS barrister felt she was less of a menace if we called her as our witness, because then we would not be able to cross-examine her. The idea that the defence should call someone brought into the case by the prosecution was crazy.

We had got a witness summons against her. She had spoken to Darren but wouldn't sign a statement for 'us'. She had fought to try to stop us getting the summons. She was stuck, damned whatever she did – she was involved with and had a responsibility to the police, but she also had to be loyal to her community. How would it affect her work and life if the police blamed her for the failure of this case? But on the other hand, how would it affect her work and life if the black community knew that she had helped to get me convicted?

We refused to call her, saying why should we when she was the prosecution's witness. They knew they couldn't call her because they didn't have a clue what she would say. If she stuck to her statement she would have rubbished the complainant and damaged the police beyond repair.

I knew in my heart that, despite all the bravado of the prosecution's barrister, he wasn't going to call Augusta – that we'd won. Darren wasn't so confident.

'Anything can happen in court,' he said.

The judge came back and made himself comfortable. He nodded to us all, each in turn. He looked at me to see the expression on my face. It was straight. But I was excited. My hands started sweating. I was twitching. I had a feeling that the judge was going to blast the prosecution and that would be the end of it. He asked the prosecution if they were going to call Augusta. They started dithering with excuses and he interrupted them.

'I just want a straight answer,' the judge said.

'No, your honour, we are not going to call Miss Gibril.'

And that was it. The judge looked at Julia. Julia didn't have anything to say. She didn't need to say anything.

The judge ripped into the prosecution. He said the use of Augusta Gibril as a mediator had been disastrous: that the police failed to brief her role to her properly, and then when she did make her statement they waited six weeks before asking her to sign it. 'This delay is even more baffling . . . or worrying,' he said. He ruled that the prosecution's 'series of errors and inconsistencies' had fouled up proceedings. 'Bearing in mind the conflicts and inconsistencies, it would be unfair to try Mr Brooks. Therefore I will stay the proceedings,' he said.

I wanted to laugh. The judge said I was free to go. I nodded my head, said thank you, and left. Outside the courtroom I stood and looked at a plaque on a wall in the Old Bailey. It commemorated the extension of the Central Criminal Court and it had been laid on my birthday, 27 September.

I looked over to my left, and Sturge was sitting down with WPC Chapman. This was the first time I'd really seen Chapman. There the two of them were: Chapman with long straggly brown hair and balding Sturge. I walked over to him and smiled. He knew what he had tried to do, but this time I was the only one smiling. I started laughing at him. Then I walked off. The judge had given Sturge a grilling in his summing-up, but he still got off lightly.

I walked into a room to have a conference with Julia and Darren about what we were going to say to the press. Darren said I should apologise to Julia for what I had said to her about the stuttering. I apologised, but commented on the fact that she was totally different today. None of that mattered now. Julia had won the abuse of process argument.

We wrote out a statement, and I decided I would deliver it outside the court. Once I walked out of the Old Bailey's doors, I felt so happy. I gave my statement to the BBC news and just walked off. The police had tried to ruin me, and had failed again. I've had many battles with the police, but this had been the key battle in the war. My victory enabled me to go on with my civil case against the police. If I had lost this case, the police would have used it to destroy me – if they could have told the world I was a convicted sex offender, everybody would have lost respect for me. And lost respect for others. I knew there were many people in powerful positions fighting for me behind closed doors. If I had been found guilty, I would have damaged their careers as well.

Jane told me that because the case had been stayed the CPS could try to get me back in court if 'new' evidence turned up, but I didn't give a damn. I knew I was innocent.

I walked away from the court and headed off for south London. The relief of being able to go there was as great as the relief of winning the case.

My not being allowed in south London had been such a ridiculous condition. There was no way I was going to attack or harass the complainant, and I had also made it clear that I didn't want anybody to contact her. I felt sorry for her in a way; felt that she was just as much a victim of police corruption as I was.

As I got to Blackfriars Bridge my body filled with tension again. I had to remind myself that I wasn't under curfew any more. I was free.

I walked across the bridge, and it felt wonderful. It felt as if my world had opened up again. The bail conditions had taken the world I knew away from me and crushed my mind. I had not visited any friends in south London while I had been curfewed. Tonight I would be free to go wherever I fancied and nobody would be able to say a word to me.

All those months under the ridiculous bail conditions had been tough. But now I was free.

That night I didn't stay at Francoise's, I stayed at another friend's. It was the first time I could go out properly. I wish I hadn't though. The same night Francoise's car got petrol-bombed.

This was a house with security surveillance, supposedly, twenty-four hours a day. I'd asked Paul Charlton, my liaison officer, to make sure there were hourly patrols of this cul-de-sac.

No one but the police knew where I was living. Amazingly (well, not so amazing to me), there was no video footage of the petrol-bombing. Even though I'd been told by Paul Charlton where to park my car – under the street lamp, where Francoise also parked her car – there was no video footage. They even had the cheek to ask if somebody in the family had been playing around with matches near it, because they found a box of them near the car. Meanwhile, they didn't even do door-to-door inquiries to ask if anybody had seen anything.

It was a sharp, nasty reminder of where I stood with the police. I might have won that particular court battle, but the war raged on. The same morning the London *Evening Standard* knocked on Francoise's door. They had been told that a car had been petrol-bombed and it had been linked to me. Francoise hadn't called the *Standard*, the neighbours hadn't called the *Standard*, so who else could it have been? It had to be the police. Someone in the police must have made it known that the car had been petrol-bombed? Why? What was their objective? Again, nothing was recorded, and no one was caught. Some protection!

It didn't really frighten me, but it upset Francoise hugely. I said to her that this was the kind of thing that was going to happen. She said she knew and that she was still prepared to support me.

The police said the car had been petrol-bombed at 4 a.m. On the same day, hourly patrols began outside Francoise's house. I asked Mr Charlton why we had hourly patrols now? 'Because you asked for them,' he said.

'I asked for hourly patrols four weeks ago. After all the break-ins and now the petrol bomb, we get hourly patrols. What is the point of having hourly patrols now? It's too late.' It was a joke. In public, they said I was a protected witness, but in reality they didn't do anything about it until the damage had been done.

Two days after the petrol-bombing, I pulled in to the cul-de-sac, and a police car was there. The police officer was too busy looking around to see where she was going. She almost drove into me. Then she had the cheek to sit in the road. I needed to turn left, but she was blocking the road, so I had to turn right.

As I turned right, the police car followed me. I drove to the end of the cul-de-sac to turn round and they drove up right behind me and blocked the road. The driver got out of the car and walked up to me. She said they were doing patrols in the area because there had been a number of break-ins and they wanted to know who I was and why I was there.

These patrols were here to protect me and Francoise's property! Yet I was being questioned as to why I was here. I couldn't believe it. The officers were here to protect me, and they didn't even know what I looked like.

I told them who I was, and they were shocked. They apologised, but said I shouldn't have been on my phone. So I made the point that I had been stationary while I was on the phone, but they should have been looking where they were going while they were driving. They left.

An hour later I got a call from Mr Charlton, my useless liaison officer. Whether he was useless because he was useless or because he was powerless to help me, I will never know. What I do know is that we are very different people. Before I am a photocopying engineer, I am a black person. My job doesn't come before my friends, my relationships, the community. Paul Charlton is a police officer before he is black. Now, I know many people will say that that is good and proper, but he was brought in to look after me because he was black and he was supposed to know what a black person's needs were, but he was always a copper first and foremost. A white officer would have been just as capable of doing the job that he did, but to protect themselves the police brought in a black officer hoping the relationship would be different. It was tokenism.

Mr Charlton had told me that the police at Greenwich had been upset that I got bail. They thought my getting bail was something to do with CO24, the Racial and Violent Crime Taskforce that John Grieve headed. Why didn't the police at Greenwich want me to get bail? What difference did it make to them whether I was in jail or not?

We reported the attempted-rape/indecent-assault case to the Police Complaints Authority. How on earth would the police and the CPS and ultimately the PCA be able to justify or defend DI Sturge's comments in the custody suite? How would they manage to work together to fix this one up? Almost three years after the case ended, the complaint still hadn't been dealt with.

I finally moved all my stuff out of Francoise's house. When I was moving, I felt I was taking the war with me away from that little cul-de-sac. Amazingly, before I moved there, there had been no break-ins to anybody's car, and once I moved in my car and Francoise's car were continually broken into and damaged. The police said it was a coincidence. Since I moved, there haven't been any break-ins or damage to anybody's car in the cul-de-sac. So what does that say? If the police were not involved, who could it have been?

Chapter 15

A Cop-Out

The Police Complaints Authority was set up in 1985 as an independent body to investigate the police after incidents in which members of the public alleged that the police had behaved improperly or corruptly. Its so-called independence was a joke. Even those who worked at the PCA would admit, in confidence, that it was a joke. They didn't investigate the complaints themselves. They merely appointed a police force to investigate the complaint, and then the police force would report their results back to the PCA. In 97 per cent of complaints against the police, the officers were found not guilty. And even the 3 per cent of officers who had a complaint against them upheld were not necessarily disciplined.

Jane gave me a rundown of the PCA – what they are supposed to do and what they don't do. She told me not to expect any results from our complaints. On the rare occasions that officers were disciplined, they tended to get a smack on the hand and told not to do it again.

My first complaint was against Detective Sergeant Dougal. Dougal was the officer who arrested me in 1993 for criminal damage after the race riots at Welling, and I made the complaint at the time. I had never experienced such behaviour from a police officer. This was the first time I'd been arrested for an offence. However suspicious I was of the police, I never thought a police officer could behave in such a manner. He was arrogant, rude and abusive, and showed an incredible lack of respect for me and, most of all, my solicitor – the way he spoke to Jane at the police station in front of other officers, the way he spoke about her in the car, the way he behaved at my mum's house was shocking. He wasn't interested in anybody except me. All he wanted to do was get me. Even though I'd never met the man before, it was like he had a personal vendetta against me. He had tunnel vision, and all he could see at the end of the tunnel was me.

Jane advised me to make a complaint about him. To me, it seemed like a waste of time, because he was a police officer with a number of years' experience and I was just a black kid. Who was going to be believed? Even so, we made the complaint. I had to give a statement to Jane. It was embarrassing because I had to tell her what he had said in the car about her not having had sex for ages, and who would want to have sex with her anyway – but if we were going to make a statement we had to tell 100 per cent truth. I made a reference in my statement to the things the officers had said about young women walking up the street. They seemed more interested in them than anything else while we were driving.

The PCA state that they turn complaints around in 120 days. Total bullshit. Maybe they turn round complaints in 120 days if the complaint is rubbish, but when the police have to cover something up it takes a hell of a lot longer than 120 days to get the results. The officers being questioned delay, the police force investigating delays, and the PCA delays.

We got the confirmation back from the PCA that they had received our complaint. 'Let's see what happens here,' said Jane.

I was excited because by now I was expecting a result; I was expecting DS Dougal to get in trouble for what he had said. Even though Jane had told me nothing ever gets done, it felt more positive.

A couple of months down the line we received the interim statement. No decision can be made unless the interim statement has been issued by the PCA. But the interim statement we received was rubbish – it simply stated that the complaint had been investigated to an acceptable standard and they were completely satisfied.

After the interim statement, the investigation is officially handed back to the police, who then decide whether or not to take disciplinary action. The PCA are supposed to recommend disciplinary procedures against an officer where the complaint has been upheld, but they cannot enforce it. The decision lies with the police.

In the case of DS Dougal, the PCA didn't feel there was any evidence against him. It was basically my word against his, and predictably his buddies in the car and back at the station backed him. That's how it usually works. The complaint was dismissed.

'It's as we expected,' said Jane.

'Is this organisation here to investigate police crime or cover up police crime?' I asked her. She didn't answer.

The PCA is supposed to be there for us: for ordinary people, poor people, vulnerable people, people who live on run-down estates, people who don't have the cash or influence to make sure they don't get shafted by the police, people who don't have a say in society. But it isn't.

Over the years, I have made a number of complaints against the Met. I could have made twice as many as I did, but I limited them to the strongest cases: the ones where the officers had blatantly convicted themselves out of their own mouths, or by their own actions.

There were so many times I had been harassed by police officers on the street since Steve's death. Don't get me wrong – we used to get stopped and searched plenty when he was alive, but

I'd lost count of the number of times it had happened in recent years. One of the reasons for the increase was the fact that I was driving my own car, and, as records show, the police are very keen on stopping young black men impudent enough to drive, or even own, a car.

I was once arrested in Lewisham outside MFI. About six riot vans turned up, plus normal police cars and police vans – just to arrest me, because I had refused to be searched by an officer who didn't have a reason for searching me.

I was taken to Lewisham police station, and when I got there I was told I had been arrested for TDA: taking and driving away. I'd been at Lewisham police station so often that the custody sergeant knew me.

'Brooks! What the fuck are you doing here again?'

'Ask your officer,' I replied. 'He knows why he's brought me here.'

'He's been arrested for TDA, sir.'

The sergeant asked the officer where I'd been arrested.

'Lewisham Way, sir.'

'What car was he driving?' said the custody sergeant. 'A white Fiat Uno?'

'Yes, sir.'

'Take the handcuffs off him and get him out of here.'

I started laughing. I'd been arrested so many times for TDA that the sergeant knew my car, my details, my address, everything.

The sergeant took the officer to one side, behind the desk, and spoke to him. I don't know what he said, but within minutes I was walking out of the station. I'd been arrested in Lewisham (where a crowd had formed and watched everything that took place), brought to the police station three or four minutes' drive away, and I was out long before anyone had caught the bus up to demand my release.

I thought those kind of incidents were not worth making a

complaint about – all the PCA would have said is that as soon as the mistake was realised, I was released.

The biggest complaint we took to the PCA was the Lawrence complaint. It was based largely on all the information we had gathered from the Macpherson Inquiry. We would have made a complaint earlier, but we didn't have enough facts at our disposal – because the Lawrences had brought the private prosecution they had all the documents, and they were unwilling to share much information. We didn't have any, except for titbits from Jane's own investigations involving private investigators or hearsay.

I made my complaint to the PCA and prepared myself for their cover-up. But it would be a tough one for them. All the stuff we complained about – how I had been racially stereotyped from the night of Steve's death onwards, how I wouldn't have been treated as I was if I hadn't been a black boy – had already been proved in the Macpherson Report. In fact, it had pretty much provided the basis for his conclusion that the police were institutionally racist. So it would be interesting to see how the PCA could wangle their way out of damning the officers in this case.

The complaint was made in February 1999, just after the Report was released, and was instantly dismissed by the Met. They refused to accept it, saying that the Lawrences had already made a complaint so there was no need for me to make one.

It didn't make any sense. It wasn't as if me and the Lawrences were part of the same team. It wasn't as if we had experienced the same treatment by the police. And it wasn't as if we were fighting together for justice. We were on two separate paths. The police knew that because they helped to create the two separate paths.

The police were happy to work alongside the Lawrences because they regarded them as 'respectable'. After all, they hadn't experienced first-hand the police racism at its worst. I was a young black man who had seen too much and wouldn't be quiet about it. After Macpherson, I became an even bigger figure of hate for the police – I was the living symbol of everything they had been accused of. There was no point in resenting Steve – he was dead. But I was still alive, and I seemed to bear the brunt of their anger.

A number of letters were sent back and forth between Jane, saying why my case should be investigated separately from the Lawrences', and the Met, saying why it shouldn't. It all became a bit surreal. In the end, we decided to make a complaint against the officer who was refusing to accept my complaint. Because he couldn't make the decision about whether or not we could complain about him, the complaint had to go somewhere else. After that, we received a letter saying that they had now decided that the complaint was actually worthy of investigation.

The officer who had refused to process my complaint about the Lawrence case was Detective Chief Superintendent Russell. We had made it in February and he refused to process it in March. On 11 March 1999 we made another complaint – against Russell – for refusing to investigate my complaint. Both complaints were to be investigated by the Kent police, who would then report back to the PCA. We later found out that Russell, like a number of officers in the Lawrence case, was due to retire in July 2000.

It should have been such a simple investigation, a five-minute complaint that should have easily been completed within the PCA's 120-day target. But the investigation into why Russell didn't want to accept my complaint took an astonishing six months. Now, the police and the PCA both knew he was due to retire in July. Was the delay so that Russell could get off scot-free and retire happily with his pension intact?

In September, we received the interim report, saying the investigation had been completed to the satisfaction of the PCA. So now it had to go back to the Met, and we expected a decision and report by February 2000 at the latest – five months for the commissioner to finalise the report on disciplinary proceedings. February came and went, and we had heard nothing.

March, April, May, June, still nothing. We could see July loom-ing, and still nothing. We kept writing to the PCA to ask what was happening, and the only response we got was 'Sorry for the delay.' They didn't answer any questions: what was happening to Mr Russell, what was the decision? We phoned up regularly, but nobody was available to speak to us.

My Lawrence complaint was treated completely differently. The Met kept writing and asking if they could speak to me. 'Can we have a meeting with Mr Brooks so we can see if he can repeat his complaint to us without referring to a document?' It was an unusual request to say the least.

In order to take my complaint further, they claimed that they had to speak to me to make sure that it was really me who had instigated this complaint. The Met were suggesting that Jane was forcing me to complain. It was so insulting – the suggestion seemed to be that I was too thick to make a complaint off my own back, and that Jane was manipulating me every which way for her own ends.

Whenever they wrote requesting a meeting, we told them to put down their questions in letter form, and we would answer them in writing. As far as Jane and me were concerned, that was the best way, because in meetings where notes were taken so often the notes were inaccurate, or people seemed to forget what they had said and later retracted it. Once they were written down in letter form, no one could change their answers.

Again the Met wrote back and said they thought it would be much simpler to speak to me and ascertain what I wanted to happen in this investigation and why, and what my complaint was based on. It made no sense. They had received a detailed letter explaining exactly what the complaint was about and pointing out all the parts of the Inquiry relevant to the com-plaint.

Even though we had sent them all this, they still had the cheek to send back passages from the Report asking us whether we were referring to this part in relation to this officer, and that part in relation to that officer. It was absurd because we had already sent them everything they needed.

The PCA and Kent police wanted to meet me, and later that year we decided to have a meeting. Jane's partner Vicky had taken over my complaints about the Met.

The PCA representative and officers came in all prepared with their little speeches. But they didn't know how I would take it – would I be a gullible sucker and take it all in, or ask awkward questions? They stuck up a chart describing all the issues and the problems they expected to encounter in this investigation. Even though Macpherson had already thoroughly documented what the officers had done wrong, they said that they expected to face problems in their investigation. Typical, I thought.

They explained in detail how the PCA worked, and how the Kent officers would do their investigation. I already knew the structure because Jane had explained before, but I listened politely to make things go as smoothly as possible.

'As you can see,' the PCA guy said, 'because of the amount of tasks we have to complete it will take much longer than the 120 days it normally takes us to turn around a complaint.' They said they saw it lasting at least six or seven months, even though they couldn't put a time limit on it. 'But throughout we will be working at full capacity to resolve the complaint because we know, Duwayne, what happened to you and we wouldn't like it to happen to any members of our family or our friends.' Here we go. Time to be patronised. Establishment people always used to say that: 'Oh, it was so terrible what happened to you. We wouldn't want it to happen to anybody else. How did you cope?'

The officer from the Kent police told me where they were setting the investigation team up and said that any time I felt like coming down to see what was happening, I'd be welcome.

He said that it was unusual for the Kent police to be doing

things like they were in this case. 'We don't normally have big meetings with complainants. But because this is a special case things are going to work differently,' he said. He was doing his best to make me feel important.

I was watching his body language. While he was talking, his hands were constantly shaking. He rarely made eye contact with me. Whenever he started to stress a point he would briefly look at me and then his eyes would turn to his colleagues. They would nod their heads to him, and he would nod his head to them. It was as if the others were there to bolster his confidence. As long as his colleagues were nodding to him, and agreeing with what he was saying, he felt he was doing a good job.

He started talking about the individual officers. 'This is where we're going to have the most problems,' he said. 'Finding the time to interview each and every officer, them being available for us, and not giving us the runaround. It's going to be hard, Duwayne. Officers go on sick leave sometimes, they take holidays, and we have to wait for them. We can give them appointments, but ultimately we need to wait for them to make themselves available.' It was as if they were preparing me for their failure.

'Hold on,' Vicky said. 'A number of these officers are due to retire. Is this going to be over before their retirement?'

'Well, we are going to try our best to interview each and every officer as quickly as we can.'

'So are you going to interview the officers who are coming up for retirement first?' Vicky asked.

'Well, we don't have a schedule for interviewing yet. All that has to be decided according to the availability of the officers.'

What a cop-out. What he was basically saying was that he didn't have a clue who they were going to be interviewing, and they didn't really believe they would interview any of them because the officers would just make themselves unavailable, especially those who were due to retire. There was no way they would get to interview those who were just about to complete their thirty years and walk off with their handsome pensions. The investigation was stuffed from the start.

But he refused to admit it. 'Nothing can stop the investigation,' he said. 'Eventually these officers will have to speak.' But it was all bluster. He'd already admitted they didn't have to.

It was right at the end of the meeting that they hit us with the sucker punch. 'After the Kent police finish the investigation, the PCA can only recommend that officers be disciplined. Ultimately, it's up to the Met.'

'What's the point in wasting all this time and money when you have no power to discipline?' I said.

'That's how it's always been with the PCA, Duwayne. We oversee the investigation, and if we believe discipline is appropriate then we will recommend it.'

'What happens if, at the end of the investigation, you decide officers should be disciplined, but the Met disagree?' I asked.

'Well, it's very unlikely that will happen. When we recommend an officer be disciplined, the Met usually agree. And in this case, we believe that if we recommend disciplining any of the officers you have complained about, our recommendation will be followed.'

The meeting was over. I shook everybody's hands. 'Nice to meet you, Duwayne. I've been wanting to meet you just to see what type of person you are.'

'Well, thank you.'

'Keep the fight up. Keep fighting.'

'I will do. Don't you worry.'

One hundred and thirty-two days passed, and the investigation seemed to have made little progress. In fact, none of the officers had been interviewed. What had they been doing over the past four months? Sitting on their arses, wasting time, wasting taxpayers' money?

*

I asked Jane what we could do to speed up the Russell complaint. It seemed that even if any disciplinary procedures were instigated against him, he'd be on the Costa del Sol lapping up the sun long before then.

'We can seek a judicial review into the delay and force the PCA to come out with a decision,' she said. We wrote a letter to the PCA threatening a judicial review. We eventually got the decision on Russell. He was going to get the equivalent of a slap on the wrist with a ruler. This was decided four weeks before he was due to retire, and I didn't believe there was going to be a hearing within that time – it takes around six months for there to be a hearing.

The problem was that the PCA was so toothless. (They realised that themselves, and would later be reformed.) Because they didn't have the clout to demand that officers were present for interviews, the police could do as they liked. Officers could stick two fingers up at the Police Complaints Authority from their sickbed or their sunlounger.

The complaint against Russell was a waste of everybody's time and money. Why hadn't they simply told us the truth and said he was going to retire, so there was no point in complaining about him? At least we would have known where we stood. I would have then withdrawn the complaint and we would have concentrated on other issues.

The report into the Lawrence complaint was finally finished by October 2000. It had taken eighteen months to work through. We had complained about ten officers. If they had interviewed only one officer a week that would add up to ten weeks, plus four weeks to write up a report. If we were being generous we could have given them six months to complete the report. Eighteen months was inexcusable. Although they had promised us all the information we wanted, they refused to update us or explain the delay.

But we still had to wait to be shown this report into my

complaint about how I had been treated by the police after Steve was killed. The months went by, and every time we asked where it was we were just told, 'You'll have it soon, you'll have it soon.' I asked a few newspaper reporters to ring the PCA and find out the reason for the delay. 'Mr Brooks will be getting the report in the next few weeks,' they were told.

We finally got the report in autumn 2001. The PCA had warned us it would take a little longer than 120 days, but we had waited around nine hundred days from start to finish. Nine hundred days! And for what?

Of all ten officers we complained about, two were given the primary-school treatment: the slap on the wrist, the written warning. Of the others, the PCA said that during their interviews the officers had refused to cooperate.

How can the police be allowed to refuse to answer questions to an authority investigating a complaint against them? The police are members of the public who have been given the authority to uphold the law and apply the law in their day-to-day dealings with the public, yet somehow they are unaccountable. These are the very same officers who complain when suspects refuse to answer questions in an interview because it gives them time to build a story. A few years earlier I had refused to make a statement about the riots, and the police were furious about it. Back then I felt what I was doing was unfair, but I was within my rights because my silence could be, and was, taken into consideration.

What was most astonishing was the overall conclusion. The PCA found that none of the officers who had refused to answer questions in interviews could be found to be racist or to have racially stereotyped me because they had not told their side of the story. Amazing! The police were evading the long arm of the law – and they were being helped by the very complaints authority set up to investigate their wrongdoings.

The logic was staggering. This would be like a suspect who refused to make a statement to the police automatically being acquitted because his side of the story had not been heard. The PCA ruled that they could not make a clear judgement. They could not believe my complaint that the police had been negligent and had racially stereotyped me because they had only been given my side of the story. It wasn't even true. The PCA had all the evidence that Macpherson had gathered at his Inquiry in front of them. And he had been happy enough to declare which officers had been guilty of racist behaviour. But the PCA decided to revise history.

I might have been sceptical about the PCA, but I never imagined that they would be crazy or cowardly enough to go into denial about Macpherson's findings. And it wasn't as if Macpherson had been some revolutionary lefty whose findings could be discounted as politically biased.

The officers had behaved just like the suspects had when they refused to answer questions about what happened on the night of Steve's murder. The Met closed in – officers of all ranks refused to answer questions. At times, it looked like a set-up to make sure that just as no one was going to be found guilty of Steve's murder, no officer would be found guilty of negligence in the subsequent investigations.

We heard about the one officer the Lawrences had complained about who was due to face disciplinary proceedings. Detective Inspector Ben Bullock, the deputy senior investigating officer in the initial investigation into Steve's murder, was the only officer not already retired whom the PCA had recommended should face disciplinary action. But it emerged that even he was going to retire in the spring, and would also get off scot-free, pension intact. In public, the Police Federation, his trade union, simply blamed the PCA for having taken so long with its investigation, and said that it had never been a secret that Bullock was due to retire after thirty years' service. They had a point, though in private they must have been thanking the PCA and the Kent police for dragging it out for so long.

So what did Mr Bullock do? He simply handed in his notice. He must have thought that it was unfair for him to take the blame for the attitudes and behaviour of the whole force, and he was right to. But he never said it publicly.

The most disturbing part of the investigation, for me, involved Detective Sergeant Coles, who was known to associate with Clifford Norris, David Norris's criminal father, and had been spotted on a number of occasions with him. For some reason, throughout the Inquiry Coles was granted the privilege of anonymity, and was referred to as Sergeant XX. But I have always wanted to know how come, of all the thousands of officers in the Metropolitan Police, he was one of the handful chosen to 'protect' me at the private prosecution when I was being kept in a hotel at night?

It was never chased down at the Inquiry. Macpherson decided there was nothing in it because nothing had happened to me. Obviously, I would have to have been killed before they would have investigated it, and then I wouldn't have been in any state to vouch for the police corruption.

I complained to the PCA about Coles 'looking after me', but they didn't even attempt to interview him.

To end it all, the PCA concluded that they would have recommended more disciplinary procedures if only the officers had not retired. What a joke! Everybody knew the officers were retiring all along, yet rather than speeding up the investigation the PCA had delayed it. And why did they delay it? Because of my civil case against the Metropolitan Police.

The police knew that if they were damned by the PCA report, I would use it in my civil case against them, and no matter how many brilliant barristers they employed their position would be impossible to defend. And this was something the police obviously couldn't face. So, unbelievably, rather than face up to the truth, which everybody now knew because the finding of institutional racism had been so widely reported, they simply decided to revise history, to wipe the slate clean. Although the Inquiry had ruled that the officers had been both racist and negligent, the PCA told us with a straight face that they could not prove that the officers had acted in a racist manner – this was despite the fact that Macpherson's findings had been largely accepted by the then Commissioner Sir Paul Condon. It was as if the public inquiry had never happened.

Chapter 16

Reclaiming my Life

Steve died in 1993, in a way it could be yesterday. In another way it feels like a lifetime ago. It is a lifetime ago – Steve's lifetime.

People ask me if I think it could happen again. I'm never quite sure what they mean. It's such a complicated question. Superficially, there has been great change, great progress. Most people in Britain have heard of Stephen Lawrence. Most people know that the police were found to be institutionally racist in a huge, damning public inquiry. And undoubtedly, the police are trying to change. They have to if they are going to be treated with any respect or trusted by the public.

But how much have things really changed below the surface? Could Steve be killed in the same way today? Yes, of course he could. Could the Metropolitan Police investigate the case so hopelessly again? Yes, of course they could. Could the Met victimise a black person as they victimised me for exposing their incompetence and bad habits? Yes, of course they could.

I'd love to say Steve's case and everything that happened afterwards was a one-off. But it wasn't. It just happened to be the flagship case. For a variety of reasons – the campaigning of his

Chapter 16

Reclaiming my Life

Steve died in 1993. In a way it could be yesterday. In another way it feels like a lifetime ago. It is a lifetime ago – Steve's lifetime.

People ask me if I think it could happen again. I'm never quite sure what they mean. It's such a complicated question. Superficially, there has been great change, great progress. Most people in Britain have heard of Stephen Lawrence. Most people know that the police were found to be institutionally racist in a huge, damning public inquiry. And undoubtedly, the police are trying to change. They have to if they are going to be treated with any respect or trusted by the public.

But how much have things really changed below the surface? Could Steve be killed in the same way today? Yes, of course he could. Could the Metropolitan Police investigate the case so hopelessly again? Yes, of course they could. Could the Met victimise a black person as they victimised me for exposing their incompetence and bad habits? Yes, of course they could.

I'd love to say Steve's case and everything that happened afterwards was a one-off. But it wasn't. It just happened to be the flagship case. For a variety of reasons – the campaigning of his parents, my campaigning, the knowledge that the chief suspects were known immediately and ignored, the Met's unwillingness to accept the attack as racist in the face of all the evidence – it became the case that symbolised everything that was wrong with the police in Britain.

But you don't have to look far to find equally shocking cases. In December 1994, Shiji Lapite was stopped by two police officers in north London for 'acting suspiciously'. Half an hour later he was dead. The cause of death was given as 'asphyxia from compression of the neck consistent with the application of a neckhold'. He had suffered thirty-six to forty-five separate injuries, his larynx and neck were bruised, and a cartilage in his voice box was fractured. At the inquest one of the officers described him as 'the biggest, strongest, most violent black man' he'd ever seen. In fact, he was five feet ten. PC McCullum admitted kicking him twice in the head as hard as he could, and said he was using reasonable force to subdue a violent prisoner, and PC Wright admitted applying the fatal neckhold and biting him on the chest. The coroner told the jury they could only deliver a verdict of unlawful killing if they were satisfied that manslaughter had been committed. The unanimous verdict was unlawful killing, which is so rare in death-in-custody cases. Yet, astonishingly, the Crown Prosecution Service ruled that there was insufficient evidence to charge the officers.

A few months after Shiji Lapite's death, on 3 May 1995, thirty-three-year-old music promoter Brian Douglas was driving home when he was stopped by two police officers, PC Mark Tuffy and PC Paul Harrison. The officers ordered Brian and his friend Stafford out of the car, and hit Brian on the head with a new American-style long-handled baton. Brian Douglas died from his brainstem injury, having been taken to hospital twelve hours after the injuries were inflicted. At the inquest PC Tuffy claimed that he hit Brian on the upper arm and the baton slid up to hit his neck. Several witnesses said they saw PC Tuffy raise his arm and bring the baton down on the back of Douglas's head. His brain ricocheted against his skull. Medical experts said that the impact was the equivalent of him falling from eleven times his own height onto his head. Unbelievably, the inquest jury delivered a verdict of death by misadventure.

In March 1996, Gambian asylum seeker Ibrahima Sey was forced to the ground in the rear yard of Ilford police station, sprayed repeatedly with CS gas, and, once inside the station, held face down for fifteen minutes. Only when he went limp and stopped breathing was an ambulance called, and he was still handcuffed when it arrived. He was dead by the time the ambulance reached the hospital. It emerged at the inquest that two officers had stood on his legs while he was held inside the station. The verdict was unlawful killing. Yet again the Crown Prosecution Service ignored the inquest verdict and decided there was insufficient evidence to prosecute the police. All these cases were brilliantly explored in a film about deaths in custody called *Injustice*. Not surprisingly, the police threatened to sue the film-makers and tried to have the film banned.

Since 1969, more than a thousand people have died in police custody. Many were suicides or accidents, but many also followed incidents in which the victims were restrained or beaten by police. Only one of these deaths – that of David Oluwale, the first black man to die in custody, in 1969 – has resulted in an officer being convicted of a crime.

Even now, despite the frenzy surrounding Steve's murder and the Macpherson Report, we see police unwilling to treat the murders of black people as racially motivated. And the CPS often unwilling to prosecute. A classic case is that of the former pop star Michael Menson, who died of his injuries in February 1997, two weeks after he was found, his clothes in flames, on the North Circular Road in north London. Menson had been in a band called Double Trouble and in the eighties had had five hits, but he had a history of mental breakdown, so the police decided that, although there was no evidence, he must have set fire to himself. It was thanks only to the persistence of family and friends that the police were forced to reinvestigate. Eventually, almost three years later, one man was found guilty of murder and another of manslaughter.

At the top levels of the Metropolitan Police, they are undoubtedly keen to rid the force of racism – not necessarily because they think it is a terrible evil, but because they have to if they want to be seen to be doing their jobs decently. At lower levels, I don't think it is so positive. Many police officers are still irate at Macpherson, fuming that they have been labelled institutionally racist. Rather than learn their lesson, and try to improve themselves, many officers feel wronged and look for revenge.

And revenge, as far as they were concerned with me, was proving that I was a bad 'un all along, and trying to get me banged up as a sex offender. I hope that the police will never come after me again, but I am not confident. Again, I'm hardly the only black man to be persecuted by the police over a period of years.

Look at the case of the Lindo family and Haringey police, a branch of the Metropolitan Police, in north London. Delroy Lindo was Winston Silcott's best friend. Silcott was convicted of the murder of PC Keith Blakelock at the Broadwater Farm riots in 1985. Although the conviction was overturned in 1991, Silcott remained the great satan for the police. Delroy Lindo's friendship with Winston Silcott seems to have been enough for the police to victimise him. In recent years, he has been charged more than twenty times by the police for trivial offences – the most laughable of which was sucking his teeth in the presence of police officers.

Delroy's complaint about victimisation finally resulted in a landmark report by the Metropolitan Police Authority. It found that he and his family had been racially stereotyped and harassed by the police. So did the police learn their lesson? Did they apologise to the Lindos for having ruined their lives? No, they simply claimed the report was unfair, and bizarrely threatened to sue their employers. A short while after the report was published, Delroy's son Tyrone was knocked off his bike by an unmarked police car containing officers who were among the forty who had threatened to sue the Met.

Most disturbing of all, just after the report was published in 2000, Tyrone Lindo was charged with murder of a young Somali boy in a case where the police had no evidence – in fact, they had plenty of evidence that he had not been at the scene of the killing. When the case finally came to court, almost a year after Tyrone was first charged, the prosecution said they would drop the murder charge if he and a co-defendant pleaded guilty to the less serious offence of violent disorder. They convinced him that if he didn't accept this plea he could well go down for murder. In the end, Tyrone pleaded guilty to violent disorder because he was so terrified of being found guilty of murder. But he told the judge that he had only done this because he would rather serve a short sentence for a crime he hadn't committed than risk serving life for a crime he was no more guilty of. In the summing-up, the prosecution barrister admitted to the judge that they had had to change the charge to violent disorder because there had never been any evidence that Tyrone had murdered or even attacked the Somali boy.

When we monitor the progress in tackling police racism, we also have to look at what's happened within the police. After all, one of the reasons that the Met was so racist was that there were so few black officers.

But what has actually happened to those black officers within the Metropolitan Police? Again, you don't need to be a genius to see a disturbing pattern. Many of those who have challenged racism, or simply had the cheek to be black, have found themselves the subjects of disciplinary investigations or strong criticism. Tarique Ghaffur is known as the top non-white police officer in the

Met. He wrote the Lindo report, and was given a terrible time over it by rank-and-file officers who implied that he had found in favour of the Lindos only because he wasn't white.

Then there was the terrifying case of the police officer Gurpal Virdi. Virdi, having served in the Met for decades with an unblemished record, complained that he had been sent racist hate mail. An investigation concluded that Virdi had sent himself the racist hate mail, and sent out the racist hate mail to other officers. What a load of rubbish! What kind of sick mind do you need to dream up a scheme like that? And why? Presumably to prove that racism is a figment of the black imagination. Virdi was sacked from the Met and had to fight for years to clear his name. And sure enough he did. He won a huge payout from the police. Amazingly, Virdi decided that once his name was cleared he would rejoin the police and fight racism from within. He is now working with Tarique Ghaffur.

In 2002, another shocking case against a black officer was concluded. Leroy Logan was one of the most senior and most outspoken black officers in the Metropolitan Police. Not only was he a chief inspector, he was also the chairman of the Metropolitan Black Police Association. In 2001, Logan was accused of fiddling expenses back in 1999. He had claimed £80 for a hotel room booked and paid for by the Black Police Association. As soon as the mistake was pointed out, he repaid the money. But that wasn't good enough for the Met. They wasted £1 million investigating his alleged corruption, and in the end the inquiry simply cleared him. Logan said that he would never have been investigated in such a manner if he had been white.

The police must have spent well over £1 million trying to stop me suing them. At the Macpherson Inquiry my legal team said it was crazy that the commissioner of the Metropolitan Police was somehow above the Race Relations Act, and we proposed that he should be brought within it. When Macpherson accepted our recommendation, we decided to sue the commissioner of the Met for racism and negligence.

The police have spent the past four years fighting us in the courts. Not fighting the actual case, but fighting over whether or not we had the right to sue. In March 2002, we thought we had finally won when there was a landmark ruling in the Court of Appeal allowing us to sue the commissioner and senior officers. It was headline news. Jane was so happy. She told the newspapers, 'Because of Duwayne's persistence, for the first time police officers can be held to account for the way they treat victims and witnesses of crime.'

But did the police accept defeat graciously? No way. They simply took it to the House of Lords. The Met are desperate for my case not to go ahead, not only because they know they haven't got a leg to stand on, but more importantly because it will set a precedent. If I successfully sue the police for negligence and racial stereotyping, it will open the floodgates. That is why they were so happy to pay Mr and Mrs Lawrence £320,000 in an out-of-court settlement.

Ten years on, nobody has been convicted for Steve's murder, and I'll be surprised if anybody ever is. Every few months (usually when an anniversary is on the way) we hear that the police are about to make or have just made new arrests, but up to now it's just been PR. We regularly hear they have new evidence, but I don't think they have any more evidence than they had forty-eight hours after Steve was killed – and there is no way they are suddenly going to deliver forensics ten years after the event.

In July 2002, Neil Acourt and David Norris were jailed after racially abusing an off-duty police officer (although they were released early because of overcrowding in prison). So many people celebrated, and said at last justice had been seen to be done, but to me this seemed every bit as unjust as the fact that Steve's killers weren't apprehended in the first place. The only concrete evidence was that Norris had thrown a paper cup out of the car. One or both of them had allegedly shouted 'nigger' at the off-duty officer. When they were convicted, Acourt left the court shouting that it was a fit-up. Hate them as I do, I couldn't help but agree. If Norris and Acourt had not been who they are, there is no way they would have been charged, let alone convicted.

There has been talk of prosecuting the suspects for the attack on me. But how would that be justice for the murder of Steve? Anyway, I've had it with giving evidence in court. I've been humiliated enough times in the witness box, and have no intention of going through that again.

After ten years I want to try to put it all behind me. I've lived this Lawrence life long enough. I need to get on with my life, move away from the police and the courts and the press. For ten years I have toiled against the police, and that is too long for anybody. If they apologised to me tomorrow, I would be prepared to settle with them. For some reason, they were happy to apologise to Mr and Mrs Lawrence, but could never quite bring themselves to say sorry to me.

It's been a terrible, painful experience, but it has also taught me a lot and, I think, helped me to help other people. I go to meetings about various forms of injustice, talk to people, and try to show them that it is good to be strong, and even when you are weak it is best to create the impression that you are strong. But I believe I've done all I can do to help victims of crime who have been mistreated by the police, and don't feel it's healthy for me to continue with this Lawrence life.

It's been a long, hard battle for black people in this country. And for virtually every black person, on an individual level, it's been a struggle.

I remember the very first march I went on, way back in 1981. The march was about the Deptford fire – thirteen children died after the house was set alight, supposedly by racists. No one has ever been charged for it. I got lost on the march and found myself sitting in the back of a police carrier with a number of other lost kids, watching the crowd go by. Whenever one of us saw our parents, we had to point them out. I pointed out my mum, and they went and grabbed her, and we were reunited. At that age, I didn't really know what the march was about.

Although my story is not a typical one, I feel that in many ways my life has been the typical life of a black kid who grows into a young man and discovers that racism is everywhere: on the streets, in the work place, in politics, in the media and in the justice system. But we also have to face up to problems in the black community. Look at mugging. In Lambeth, it is the black youngsters who are responsible for a fair part of the street crime and burglary, yet we as a black community are denying that, and are getting upset that it's always in the press. The first step in solving a problem is admitting that it exists, but we won't admit to failure in our community.

For me, one problem with black boys is the breakdown in discipline. There has been a huge change in the relationship between parents and children over the years. In Jamaica, where my parents were born, the discipline is much tougher. When black kids started growing up in Britain, they, like the Indians and Pakistanis, rarely got into trouble. But because the discipline collapsed, so did their respect.

As well as respecting others, we must start to respect ourselves, to take pride in our achievements. Black people have made such a positive contribution to Britain, and it is a contribution that is often ignored or shunned. We have helped to strengthen and modernise this country. We might historically have done the rubbish jobs that white people felt were beneath them, and to a great extent we may still do them, but without black people the NHS wouldn't run, the transport system wouldn't run, nothing would run.

Yet, with a few exceptions, we are still treated like second-class citizens. Many white people still believe that we shouldn't be in this country, but they would never question their right to be in Africa. I was once told that white people have a gene that makes them racist. I don't really agree with that – I've got too many non-racist white friends – but sometimes you look at white people as a mass and it's a tempting theory. London still has plenty of problems, but it is a relatively mixed, multiracial society these days. Go out of London though, into the home counties or into the country where you can go days without coming across a black face, and you experience the full brunt of British racism.

There has never been true, simple justice for black people in Britain. Steve's murder, and the Macpherson Inquiry that followed, promised for a while to transform Britain. The death of Steve, terrible though it was, could have heralded a revolution in the Establishment's attitude towards black people and racism. But it didn't.

I will never be able to explain how that night, 22 April 1993, changed my life. You never plan for a death like Steve's, you never expect to be attacked on the street. You may be wary of certain areas, you may think you might get into rows at a pub or a club, but you never expect to be attacked while you're minding your own business. The attack did things to my mind and body that I didn't know were possible. It gave me a dose of paranoia that I would never wish anybody to have. No amount of counselling or protection could get rid of it, because once you have been subjected to an attack like Steve and me were you can never feel truly safe again.

It has changed me as a person in complicated ways. I have no time for people who have hardly anything in the world to worry about but haven't got the drive to make a life for themselves. I suppose I want people to get off their arses – if I could do it while all this was going on around me, so can those without a care in the world. But I have also become much more left-wing: much more aware of miscarriages of justice, and of how people without money and contacts in high places (in other words, most black people) are powerless.

*

What's happened to the other people in the story? Mr and Mrs Lawrence divorced after the Inquiry concluded. Mrs Lawrence emphasised that the divorce was nothing to do with the stress of Steve's murder. 'For many years I have felt alone and unsupported,' she told the press in yet another thinly veiled attack – this time on Mr Lawrence. Meanwhile, Imran Khan ended up paying me a total £5000 for negligence. At the same time, he became known as Britain's great civil-rights/anti-racism lawyer. Michael Mansfield cemented his reputation as the great left-wing-cause barrister. In 2000, the drama *The Murder of Stephen Lawrence*, executive produced by Yvette Vanson, the wife of Michael Mansfield, won a BAFTA award. All the officers Macpherson criticised have retired. Ros Howells received an OBE for her work fighting racism. Paul Boateng, who had been so vocal about the need to sack Condon till he changed his mind, became Britain's first black Cabinet Minister. Commissioner Sir Paul Condon was not sacked but left on his own terms soon after the Macpherson Report was published. Alex Owolade, a truly good man who has consistently supported me through the years, was fired from his job at Lambeth Council after trying to help employees who told him they had been racially victimised by a member of staff.

When people ask me how racism has changed in Britain, I tell them I can't speak authoritatively for anywhere but London. I live in London, drive round London, observe it on a daily basis. I see all kinds of attitudes in London. I go to repair photocopiers in companies where they watch me like a hawk – whether this is because I'm black or they don't think I can do the job, I wouldn't know. I've been to places where they want to check with the firm first to see whether I'm legit. I know white people don't get that kind of treatment at my firm, but for some reason I sometimes get it. And that's London where there's a multiracial society.

As for the rest of the country, I see there has been less change in attitudes because there has been no pressure to change – this country changes only when it is forced to. Ten years ago, if you had said Eltham was a racist area, few people would have believed you. Now Eltham is well known as the racist capital of London. Even so the area is not as stringently policed as Brixton. The police have named Lambeth as the number-one borough for mugging, but although Greenwich is the number-one borough for racist attacks, even now the police don't seem that interested in addressing this.

They still seem to treat mugging as a more serious crime than a racist attack. True, mugging is a disgusting crime. But mugging is nothing to do with colour – it's to do with poverty, addicts needing their drugs, hunger. It's a fact that most of the muggings in Eltham are committed by white people and little is said about it; whereas in Brixton, where much of the street crime is the work of black people, the police cannot stop talking about it. And they use black street crime to justify their stopping more black people than white people.

The first excuse the police used was that there were more black people on the streets because there were more black people without jobs. But why? Then how do you account for more black people being stopped in cars than white people? There are certainly not more black people on the streets driving than there are white people. Do they suspect all black people of carrying drugs? Do they think that because many black people are unemployed there must be something funny going on if they are driving a car? Four years after the public inquiry, there is an even higher percentage of black people being stopped than white people.

There are still many racist incidents happening in south-east London, and most of them go unreported in the papers. The situation between the police and public is just as inflammatory as it was when Steve was killed. All it may take is one more case to fire up the public and there could be anarchy: no-go areas for the police. What will happen when the black community starts taking vengeance for the crimes committed against us? I hope

I'm wrong, but I can see a future where people will call out the police to the estates just to have a go at them.

Four years on from Macpherson, the Met have still not shown us that they want to punish racist officers. Look at the case of PC Steve Hutt. He called someone he was arresting a 'black bastard' in February 1999. His job was taken away from him, and then, unbelievably, two years later he was reinstated. I wrote to the Home Secretary to ask him why, and he said that prominent black people in the community and the boy's mother did not want him sacked and didn't believe he was racist, so his job was given back to him. What kind of nonsense is that? Meanwhile, I read about a police officer who lost his job for being cruel to a dog. For me, that just about sums it all up.

A police officer loses his job after brutalising a dog, and another is disciplined for covering it up, but none of the officers involved in the Lawrence case or any of the subsequent attempts to slur my name have been sacked. So what has changed? It would be comforting to think that Steve had not died for nothing, but I'm not sure it's true. Even in 2003, it's easier for a dead dog to receive justice than it is for a dead black man.

Index